A
Chicken
in Every Pot

Also by Kate Heyhoe

Cooking with Kids for Dummies

Harvesting the Dream:
The Rags-to-Riches Tale of the Sutter Home Winery

Coming in 2004:
Macho Nachos

Kate Heyhoe is also co-founder and Executive Editor
of Global Gourmet® (globalgourmet.com),
the Web's first food and cooking ezine,
founded in 1994.

A Chicken in Every Pot

Global Recipes for the World's Most Popular Bird

Kate Heyhoe

Executive Editor of *Global Gourmet*®
www.globalgourmet.com

Photography by
Thomas Way and Kate Heyhoe

CAPITAL
BOOKS, INC.
Sterling, Virginia

Capital Books, Inc.

P.O. Box 605

Herndon, Virginia 20172-0605

ISBN 1–931868–32–8   (alk.paper)

Heyhoe, Kate.
   A chicken in every pot : global recipes for the world's most popular bird / Kate Heyhoe.— 1st ed.
      p. cm.
Includes index.
   ISBN 1–931868–32–8 (alk. paper)
   1. Cookery (Chicken)   I. Title.
   TX750.5.C45H48 2003
   641.6'65—dc21   2003000007

Printed in the United States of America on acid-free paper that meets the American National Standards Institute Z39-48 Standard.

First Edition

10 9 8 7 6 5 4 3 2 1

To Thomas Way,
Who feeds my spirit and soul daily.
Life with you is good!

Acknowledgments

Besides dedicating this book to Thomas Way, I have to thank him first and foremost for his tasting, editorial, and technical skills. He made the recipes better to eat and to read. I'm also grateful to Richard Lobb of the National Chicken Council and U.S. Poultry & Egg Association (EatPoultry.com) for providing accurate and up-to-date information on chicken. My thanks to Kathleen Hughes and Capital Books for recognizing that there's always room for more chicken, and to Lisa Ekus for her talent and encouragement as my agent. To my readers at *Global Gourmet*® (globalgourmet.com), I appreciate your readership, support, and feedback on these and all my other recipes at the site.

And finally, my thanks to the Whisker-Licking Gang (Pookie, Zombie, Wolfie and Tamale), who all agree: Chicken is good!

Contents

LIST OF RECIPES   XI

CHAPTER 1

The World's Most Popular Bird   1

The Author's Confession   1

Birds on a Budget   2

FlavorPrints: Blueprints for World Cuisines   3

CHAPTER 2

A Brief History of the Chicken   5

Chickens by Land and Sea   5

From Free-Range Rocky to Red Jungle Fowl   7

CHAPTER 3

Bird Basics—A Chicken for Every Pot, Pan, Grill, or Wok   9

Thrifty Chickens, Bargain Buys, and Conveniences   9

Serving Sizes: How Much to Buy   10

Chickens Little and Big   10

Safe Handling and Storage of Chicken   13

Do-It-Yourself: Jointing Chickens and Boning Breasts   16

Brining for Flavor, Tenderness, and Texture   22

Meal-Morphing   25

CHAPTER 4

Whole Birds   27

There's nothing simpler than cooking a whole chicken, although a chicken split into two halves comes pretty close. These one-bird recipes, roasted or cooked on the stovetop, are designed for simple satisfaction, with flavors that travel from China to Spain.

CHAPTER 5

Chicken Packages Piece by Piece   41

Try these quantity recipes for thrifty chicken buys—great for those jumbo packs! These recipes cook from four to six pounds of chicken pieces. Serve as many as eight persons, or feed just a few mouths and save some pieces for encore performances.

CHAPTER 6

Chicken Plus Six Ingredients (or Less!)   49

From pantry to table, these meals feature chicken and just a few select ingredients. Salt, pepper, and chicken aren't counted in the "six" components, but the few ingredients that join them are tossed together effortlessly to make meals that are exotic and worldly, without being complicated or time-consuming.

CHAPTER 7

Thirty-Minutes-or-Less Chicken Meals   69

Beat the midweek madness—make these meals in almost no time (most can be prepared in only twenty minutes). They're quick to fix, but they certainly don't skimp on flavor. You just get to enjoy 'em sooner.

CHAPTER 8

Chicken in a Bowl: Soups, Stocks, and Stews   81

Everyone knows chicken soup is good for what ails you. Serve it Asian-style with ginger and wontons. Sup on comforting winter warmers like chowder, gumbo, stews, and even the folk cure for the common cold: Jewish chicken soup with pleasantly plump matzo balls.

CHAPTER 9

Broiled and Grilled Chicken   105

Outdoor grills and indoor broilers cook chicken quickly, with savory recipes for Chicken Churrasco with Chimichurri Sauce, Cuban Sour Orange Chicken, Tandoori Chicken, and Portuguese Grilled Chicken Oporto, and stops at a few other countries along the way. Need to perfect your grilling and broiling skills? The first two recipes in this chapter provide the basics of grilling and broiling chicken.

CHAPTER 10

Savory Stovetop Chicken   129

In many parts of the world, ovens are a luxury; most foods are cooked in pans directly over the flame, including these skillet dishes, stir-fries, and sautés. Take a tour de France with chicken in wine, mustard, or tarragon. Spice up your voyage with Moroccan and Indian chickens, and sweeten your day with coconut curries from the Caribbean to Malaysia.

CHAPTER 11

Chicken Bakes, Casseroles, and Braises   181

The world knows that casseroles, baked chicken, and long-cooked braises make cozy meals for everyday dining and casual entertaining. Warm up with a Spanish paella, a Greek pot pie, or California-style chicken pieces roasted with goat cheese and fresh cherry tomatoes.

CHAPTER 12

Salads, Sauces, and Little Bits   191

Cool, crunchy, and crisp—these salads feature chicken as the key ingredient. Got odds 'n' ends of cooked chicken meat from previous recipes? Toss them into salads or mix them with sauces and spices. Ground chicken plumps and crumbles in wontons or salads. Livers get lively in pâtés and bacon-wrapped cocktail nibbles, and crunchy fried chicken bites are luscious enough to make a meal in themselves.

INDEX   225

Recipes by Chapter

CHAPTER 4

Whole Birds

Barcelona Brown-Bag Chicken and Vegetables   27

Char Shu Cornish Hens   29

Char Shu Marinade   29

Citrus-Brined Chicken, Roasted with Near East Rub   30

Citrus Brine   31

Ginger-Poached Chicken and Broth   33

Lemon-Rubbed Roaster with Six Garlic Heads   35

Lemongrass Roast Chicken   36

Southwest Skinny Chicken (Pressure Cooker Recipe)   37

Whole Chinese Red-Cooked Chicken   39

CHAPTER 5

Chicken Packages Piece by Piece

Bangladesh Drums   42

Boneless Breasts for a Crowd   43

Buckets of Oven-Fried Chicken   44

Roasted Chicken Breasts for Sandwiches and Salads   45

Sesame-Seeded Teriyaki Wings   46

Teriyaki Sauce   46

CHAPTER 6

Chicken Plus Six Ingredients (or Less!)

Chicken in Saffron Cream Sauce   50

Crispy Comino Chicken Wings   50

Fingerling and Rosemary-Smoked Chicken Hash   53

Miso-Chicken Yakitori   54

Moo-shu Chicken Wraps   55

Nutty Pounded Paillards   56

CHAPTER 6 *(continued)*
One-Pot Chicken, Mushrooms, and Saffron Rice   57
Pollo alla Diavola ("Devil-Style Chicken")   59
Roasted Thighs with Apples, Normandy-Style   61
Rosemary-Smoked Chicken Halves   62
Saffron Poached Chicken   64
Ukrainian Portobellos and Garlic-Laced Livers   65

CHAPTER 7

Thirty-Minutes-or-Less Chicken Meals
Chicken in 5-Minutes' "Thyme,"   70
Chicken, Scampi-Style   70
Herbed Bistro Chicken Breasts   72
Parmesan-Crusted Chicken   73
Pollo Rojo (Pressure Cooker Recipe)   74
Spicy Eggplant and Chicken with Sesame   74
Summer Chicken and Eggplant Parmigiana   76
Tipsy Chicken Paillards   78

CHAPTER 8

Chicken in a Bowl: Soups, Stocks and Stews
African Chicken and Peanut Stew   81
Basic Chicken Stock   83
Belgian Chicken Braised in Beer   84
Chilled Fire-Roasted Tomatillo and Grilled Chicken Soup   86
Chunky Chicken, Corn, and Potato Chowder   88
Cock-A-Leekie   90
Ginger-Wonton Soup with Spring Onion Oil   91
Gumbo Ya-Ya   92
Hungarian Chicken Paprikás   94
Jewish Matzo Ball Soup   95
Lemony Garlic Chicken and Broth   96
Mexican Poached Chicken   97

Rustic Tortilla Soup   99

Thai Hot 'n' Sour Chicken Soup ("Tom Yam Kai")   100

Vietnamese Glass Noodles Soup with Lemongrass Roast Chicken ("Mien Ga")   102

CHAPTER 9

Broiled and Grilled Chicken

Basic Grilling: Cooking Chicken on an Outdoor Grill   105

Method: Indirect Grilling, or Grill-Roasting   107

Method: Direct Grilling, Covered and Open   107

Basic Broiling: Cooking Chicken in a Broiler   108

Aromatic Anise Chicken: Roasted, Grilled, or Spatchcocked   109

Anise Rub   109

Anise Baste   109

Barbecued Korean Drums   110

Chicken Churrasco with Chimichurri Sauce   111

Chimichurri Sauce   112

Chicken of the Moors   112

Moorish Marinade   113

Cuban Sour Orange Chicken   114

Cuban Sour Orange Marinade   114

Filipino Coconut Barbecued Chicken   116

Filipino Coconut Marinade   116

Grilled Chicken Fajitas   117

Grilled Chicken in Minty Chutney   118

Grilled Lemon-Dill Chicken   120

Ground Chicken Kebabs   121

Jamaican Jerk Chicken   122

Jerk Marinade   122

Juicy Grilled Grapefruit Chicken   123

Grapefruit Marinade   123

La Tunisia Chicken and Grilled Onions   124

La Tunisia Marinade   124

Portuguese Grilled Chicken Oporto   126

CHAPTER 9 *(continued)*
Tandoori Chicken   127
Texas Barbecue Dry-Rub Chicken   128
Texas Dry-Rub   128

CHAPTER 10

Savory Stovetop Chicken
Aussie Alfredo with Warrigal Greens   129
Cooked Warrigal Greens   131
Basic Breaded Chicken Cutlets, or Scallopine   131
Japanese "Chiken" Katsu   132
Tonkatsu Sosu   132
Chicken Piccata   133
Pollo alla Milanese   133
Chicken Parmigiana   134
Caribbean Chicken in Coconut Curry   134
Chicken Adobo   135
Chicken and Pork Pad Thai   136
Chicken Calabrese   138
Chicken in Wine with Balsamic-Herb Gravy   139
Chicken Schnitzel with Lemon-Mushroom Sauce   141
Chicken Vindaloo   142
Chinese Honey-Lemon Chicken   144
Honey-Lemon Sauce   145
Coq au Vermouth   146
Corinthian Chicken and Olives   148
Creole Mustard Chicken Breasts   149
Greco-Roman Chicken Rolls   150
Green Chile Chicken Breasts   152
Indonesian Chicken with Green Beans   153
Irish Hen with Bacon and Cabbage   154
Israeli Couscous with Chicken and Olives   155
Middle Eastern Spice Rub   156
Maille Mustard Chicken and Pasta   157

Malaysian Coconut-Chicken Curry   159
Moroccan Chicken in Spiced Tomato Sauce   161
Moroccan Spice Mixture   161
Pasta with Roasted Garlic, Chicken, and Vodka Sauce   162
Pollo con Pipian Verde   163
Sesame Pipian Verde   164
Porcini and Prosciutto Fricassée   165
Quick Chicken, Artichokes, and Feta   167
Quick Vietnamese Chicken with Crisp-Cooked Snow Peas   168
Crisp-Cooked Snow Peas   170
Quinoa con Pollo   170
Shredded Pueblo Chicken   173
Spiced Chicken, Fennel, Raisins and Rice   174
Sweet 'n' Sour Kumquat-Kiwi Chicken   176
Sweet 'n' Sour Sauce   176
Tarragon Chicken and Artichoke Hearts   177
Three Pepper Chicken Stir-Fry   179

CHAPTER 11

Chicken Bakes, Casseroles and Braises

Bangkok Chicken   182
Greek Pot Pie   184
Paella de la Casa   186
Roasted Fesenjan Hens   187
Fesenjan Sauce   188
Roasted Chicken Pieces with Cherry Tomatoes, Goat Cheese, and Basil   190

CHAPTER 12

Salads, Sauces and Little Bits

APPETIZERS AND LITTLE BITS

Chicken Liver and Shiitake Powder Pâté   193
Chicken Liver and Truffle Oil Pâté   195
Chicken Wontons   196
Fried Chicken Drummettes with Hot Pomegranate Honey   197

CHAPTER 12 *(continued)*
Hot Pomegranate Honey   198
Golden Chicken Mandu (Korean Dumplings)   199
Chicken Mandu Filling   201
Chojang Dipping Sauce   201
Mozzarella Chicken "Bruschetta,"   202
Rumaki   204

SALADS AND SALAD DRESSINGS
Chicken "Salad" in Rice Paper Rolls   205
Lemon-Caper Mayonnaise   205
Chicken Salad Siam   206
Siam Dressing   207
Chicken Salad on Soba   208
Dilled Cucumber-Chicken Pasta Salad   209
Napa-Hazelnut Chicken Salad   210
Ras el Hanouth Chicken on Spinach, Kumquat, and Fig Salad   211
Ras el Hanouth Spice Blend   212
Sour Cream, Dill, and Cucumber Dressing   213
Southeast Asian Chicken Salad with Spring Onion Oil   214
Southeast Asian Dressing   214
Thai Minced Chicken Salad (Larb)   215
Warm Chicken-Mushroom Medley on Mixed Greens   216

SPICES, SEASONINGS AND SAUCES
Concentrated Red Chile Sauce (Pressure Cooker Recipe)   217
Global Gourmet Herb Seasoning   218
Homemade Garam Masala   219
The Global Gourmet's Garam Masala   220
Near Eastern "Sesame and Sumac" Rub   220
Pico de Gallo   221
Pudine Ki Chutney   222
Spring Onion Oil   222
Summer Fresh Tomato Sauce   223
Toasted Sesame Seeds   224

CHAPTER 1

The World's Most Popular Bird

In 1928, Herbert Hoover promised Americans a chicken in every pot—and a car in every garage. But it's the image of a simmering plucked chicken that we remember most from his speech, not a shiny hunk of mobile metal. When the stock market crashed the following year, that chicken became more than just a symbol of prosperity; it came to represent comfort, family gatherings, and good times as well.

No wonder Hoover reached out to Americans with a chicken. This same humble bird has raised spirits and nurtured families in almost every culture worldwide for centuries. As a food source, the chicken is healthful, economical, prolific, easy to transport, simple to prepare, and pleasing to eat—all properties that have contributed to the chicken's indisputable stature as the world's most popular bird.

The Author's Confession

Having now duly (and sincerely) praised the chicken for all its wonderful attributes, I have a slight confession to make . . .

I wrote this book not because I'm obsessed with chicken—but because I'm obsessed with flavor.

But chicken is so bland, you're probably thinking. *It can be mild to the point of being boring.*

Herbert Hoover's Chickens

Herbert Hoover's famous I.O.U. to Americans, promising them a chicken in every pot, wasn't totally original. Either Hoover or a speechwriter borrowed the phrase from Henry IV of France, who said in his coronation speech, "If God grants me the usual length of life, I hope to make France so prosperous that every peasant will have a chicken in his pot on Sunday." At some point, the Republican National Committee's paid ads expanded Hoover's promise to "two chickens in every pot," along with not one but two cars in every garage. Today, the lure of a weekly chicken isn't likely to get a politician elected, but not until after World War II and the introduction of modern production methods could the common folk afford a weekly chicken.

And that's precisely why I love it. I have a passion for experimenting with flavors. Chicken is the ideal conduit for tantalizing my tastebuds with a creative array of spices, herbs, and exotic seasonings. With chicken, I can savor the world's great cuisines any night of the week and never have to leave home. Instead of planes, trains, or automobiles, chickens are my magic carpet to the far corners of every continent. And I don't have to pack my bags.

I enjoy lamb, beef, pork, and seafood, but none of them is as versatile in the kitchen as the humble chicken. I'm not saying I need a spiced-up, revved-up meal every night. At times I yearn for the benign flavor of chicken enhanced simply by salt and pepper. Sometimes you need plain foods for balance. What would meatloaf be without mashed potatoes, or sweet 'n' sour pork without steamed rice? Depending on how it's seasoned, chicken can be either the star of the meal or the support player.

Birds on a Budget

Chicken is also as easy on the budget as it is on the palate, though many shoppers miss out on great bargains.

After years of buying boneless, skinless breasts, many of today's home cooks are clueless when it comes to preparing a whole bird, the thriftiest chicken deal of all.

Whole birds are suitable for more than just roasting. In this book, whole chickens appear in roasting pans as well as steamers, grills, big pots, and woks, with seasonings ranging from Kashmir curry to West Texas barbecue. You can also separate a whole bird quickly into two, four, six, or eight parts, with just a few nimble knife strokes—adapting the bird to endless recipes and saving a few cents at the same time.

When it comes to boneless, skinless chicken breasts, convenience costs. For those tightening their budget belts, I'll show you how to skin and bone chicken breasts at home in just a few minutes. Though with so many versatile recipes for bone-in breasts, such as Moroccan Chicken in Spiced Tomato Sauce (chapter 10) and Cuban Sour Orange Chicken (chapter 9), you may be tempted to skip the boning process altogether.

Jumbo packs are my favorite time and budget savers. At home I usually cook for only my husband and myself, but I'm always glad to pick up a family-size four- to six-pound package of chicken parts. I usually divide the package in half. I'll cook one half that day and marinate the other half for the next night's meal or precook the meat for salads and sandwiches. Any leftovers can be "meal morphed" into entirely new dishes, as I explain in chapter 3.

FlavorPrints: Blueprints for World Cuisines

If you want to enhance your knack for creating chicken recipes on the fly, explore the world of "FlavorPrints." A FlavorPrint is an array of seasonings that characterize a particular cuisine. It's what makes Thai food taste "Thai." It puts the "olé" in chicken to make it suitable for Mexican tortillas, rather than Italian lasagna, for instance.

In my house, when the age-old question "What's for dinner?" surfaces, the next question I ask goes something like "What are you in the mood for—Chinese, Indian, Middle Eastern or Southwestern?" The answer steers my course in the kitchen and helps inspire me to whip up something creative and satisfying, rather than boring and routine.

You already know that chicken is endlessly versatile as a conduit of flavor. The recipes in this book are selected to represent the wide world of chicken, and, I hope, the FlavorPrints scattered throughout these pages will inspire you to devise your own original recipes to suit your mood and the ingredients at hand.

I encourage you to travel with your chicken. Go beyond your neighborhood supermarket. Visit local ethnic markets. Take a culinary shopping trip to Chinatown, Little Saigon, or Bombay Boulevard. Order exotic spices and ingredients online or by mail-order catalog. Even if you've never used some of these ingredients before, the recipes in this book will introduce you to their inherent tastes and cooking characteristics. If you're totally clueless about a spice, heat it in a bit of butter or oil and taste it on a piece of bread to get an idea of how it might be used. Raw spices taste . . . well, raw. Cooking them releases their flavors.

Throughout this book you'll find FlavorPrints for a full range of distinctive national or regional cuisines—use them to map your chicken's world tour. But keep in mind that, ultimately, all cooking is local, so cooks along a coast will use different ingredients from those in the mountains, even if they're only a few miles apart.

CHAPTER 2

A Brief History of the Chicken

Long before the birth of Christ, a bird, never seen before in the valley of the Blue Nile, reached the court of the pharaohs. Neither the architectural grandeur of the court nor the "gold-draped" Pharaohs could silhouette its beauty. A bright red comb rested regally on its head and shiny green and red feathers clothed its body, finally ending in an eclipse plume. The Egyptians had never seen a bird that laid so many eggs. When it crowed, they listened with rapt attention. When it walked around the court, everyone made way. It became a showpiece in the Pharaoh's court. Fascinated, they adopted the bird. Everybody used to be shown the chicken, and training camps were set up on how to get this wild red jungle fowl to lay eggs.

—Daniel Madhav Fitzpatrick and Kazimuddin Ahmed
"Red Roving Fowl," *Down to Earth Magazine*, December 15, 2000

Ancient Egyptians were among the first to rear domesticated chickens on a large scale by using incubators. But even before the bird established itself on the African continent, chickens and their eggs had long been feeding villagers and royalty alike in regions stretching as far away as Thailand and Indonesia.

Chickens by Land and Sea

The fluffy white bird with scarlet comb we eat today is believed to have originated in the Indus valley—or the jungles of Malaysia, depending on whom you consult—as an ancient relative of the Red Jungle Fowl, a breed that still roams wild.

But over the years the chicken as we know it has undergone more makeovers than Michael Jackson. Chickens breed rapidly. A singular genetic trait can become a full breed characteristic within just a few successive generations of hatchlings, so domestication evolved quickly.

Some say the Red Jungle Fowl was first domesticated for its fighting abilities. Others believe that the eggs and their value came first. Men would sneak up to the nest to grab the eggs for food. At some point they realized it was easier just to grab the bird and have the eggs delivered to them. The fowl grew comfortable, too, in this relationship: It had a safe place to live, with warm surroundings with plenty of food. So the birds adapted, lost their interest in flying, and became domesticated. Now that they were settled down, the birds readily began laying eggs. Because the species bred so quickly, it was easy to develop desirable strains and crossbreeds in a short period, resulting in the eventual move from the bright Red Jungle Fowl to the white domesticated chicken, or *Gallus domesticus*.

By the thirteenth century B.C., the domesticated fowl had spread to China, India, and the Near East by way of trade routes. The chicken arrived more recently in the Mediterranean. We don't know exactly when it first appeared there, but evidence suggests the Greeks and Romans honored the chicken as early as the sixth century B.C. The bird is not mentioned in the Old Testament, though it does appear in the New Testament. Aristotle and the ancient Greeks praised chickens, and in Athens, it was noted that a chicken delivered an egg a day. The Romans deemed the chicken sacred to their god of war, Mars, and Plato describes public cockfights as a diversion from laboring.

How chickens settled in the vast continent of Africa is not well documented, but researchers believe they arrived in three different ways. North Africans probably met the fowl through Roman and Muslim conquests. The sub-Saharan peoples were introduced to the bird via trade routes of the Red Sea and Indian Ocean, and Portuguese explorers no doubt brought chickens with them to Africa's western coast.

Medieval Europeans commonly raised chickens, again mainly for their eggs. Later, chickens were introduced to the New World by Columbus, other explorers, and colonists. Wherever these travelers went, by land or sea, they brought chickens with them, packing them up in crates, stowing them as cargo or strapping them to beasts of burden.

In one sense, the birds became almost as good as gold—settlers and explorers found they could trade their birds with the local peoples. Latin Americans and Native Americans immediately recognized the virtues of this domesticated foreign fowl. After all, they were already familiar with their own indigenous birds, especially turkey, and the Aztecs regularly trapped geese and ducks. So in both the Old World and the New, people welcomed the chicken as a valuable bird, just as they do today.

From Free-Range Rocky to Red Jungle Fowl

Today's domesticated food chickens are a far cry from the stringy, scrawny birds once destined only for stew pots—chickens that gave rise to the term "a tough old bird."

Not until the early twentieth century did we dedicate flocks for their meat. Before this, the hens were important mainly as egg-layers. As such, only certain birds were eaten for their flesh. Hens that lived past their egg-laying prime were not worth their feed, so they became dinner. But as egg producers these birds were never fattened. The very little flesh they yielded was tough and stringy, which is why so many early chicken recipes call for simmering the birds slowly in lots of water to tenderize them. Into a stew or stockpot these tough old birds went.

The other typical dinner bird was the male. Chicken eggs are produced like eggs in human females—automatically. Because hens don't need to be fertilized by a male just to lay eggs, the males become dispensable. Yet unlike the ropy old hens, spare male birds weren't just cooked and eaten—they were savored. Cockerels, or roosters, can be dangerously fierce and aggressive, but when castrated they become docile and are known as capons. At the same time, their flesh becomes quite tender and meaty, and they grow even larger—weighing in at a whopping eight to ten pounds. Compared to the tough old females, capons were much preferred for eating, and recipes for capons commonly appear in Old World and New World cookbooks.

After thousands of years in existence, the handsome Red Jungle Fowl (*Gallus gallus*), believed to be the genetic mother of all modern domesticated chickens, still runs wild—but perhaps not for long. Described in India as "critically endangered," existing strains of Red Jungle Fowl have been so genetically contaminated by other wild fowl, and ironically by its own generations of domesticated offspring, that less than 1 percent of Red Jungle Fowl stock may be pure. Some birds' plumage may look like that of the original wild fowl, but their DNA reflects traits that cause many environmentalists to call these birds a "chicken in jungle fowl clothing." As a result, captive-breeding and other wildlife preservation programs scattered about the globe are working to save the original species from extinction.

Back to the fowl's gift of the domesticated chicken. In today's markets, plump, white-skinned chickens rule the roost, so to speak. In early days, no one cared what the chicken's skin looked like. Under their colored plumage, chicken skins, like those of dogs and cats, can be mottled, black, brown, or red—not the uniform yellow or creamy white of the white-feathered birds raised for today's aesthetically conscious consumer. Yet the color of the skin has no effect on the flavor of the bird.

Decades of poultry mixing eventually crossed two domesticated breeds, the White Rock and the Cornish, to produce today's commercial eating chicken. Foster Farms, Zacky, and Perdue are among the North American brands most commonly sold in supermarkets, and their heavy-breasted birds are anything but scrawny or stringy. Upscale and health food markets sell specialty free-range chickens such as Rocky the Range Chicken, a brand valued for extra-tender, flavorful meat resulting from chickens that, to some degree, are free to roam. (For details on chicken types and buying tips, see chapter 3.)

Regardless of the brand bought or the plumage plucked, the whole world appears to love chickens now more than ever. Vegetarians and a few religious sects avoid chicken, but overall a whopping 43,241,000 metric tons of chicken were consumed worldwide in 2000. In 2003, Americans alone are expected to consume more than eighty-one pounds of chicken per person (about eighteen pounds more than of beef), up from a mere forty-eight pounds per person in 1980. And the trend for greater consumption of chickens continues to grow.

CHAPTER 3

Bird Basics—
A Chicken for Every Pot,
Pan, Grill, or Wok

Thrifty Chickens, Bargain Buys, and Conveniences

Many cooks today have no idea how to cook a whole chicken, let alone cut one up. Yet whole chickens are some of the thriftiest protein-packs in the market, often selling for as little as fifty-nine cents per pound. At that price, a family of four to six can dine for under $2.50, about the cost of a six-pack of Cokes. On the other end of the scale, feeding the same family a main course of boneless, skinless chicken breasts—at up to $7 per pound—can cost as much as $21. For that price, you may as well eat out.

I admit that boneless, skinless breasts are quick, easy, and ultra-convenient. But with just a little practice, you can bone a package of breasts, joint your own chicken, or just split a chicken in less time than ordering at a KFC drive-thru. Save the bones for stock, and you've made an even smarter financial move.

Here's another money-saving tip: One by-product of the demand for boneless, skinless breasts is dark meat pieces. Processors have been left with a glut of thighs (boned and boneless) and legs, which they often sell at amazingly low prices. Jumbo packs, as much as five pounds or more of chicken parts, also save money. If you don't want to cook the whole package at once, you can divide it up into two recipes, or freeze half the contents.

This book shows you how to cut up whole birds and how to bone and skin chicken breasts. It offers recipes for cooking jumbo packs of chicken parts, including dark meat pieces. But it also reaches out to today's palate-savvy diners with recipes that take chicken around the world, recipes that are simple to make yet exotic in flavor. Rest assured that whatever chicken you buy, you'll find a recipe here that makes it taste like a million bucks—franks, pesos, yen, or euros. As our Global Gourmet (globalgourmet.com) motto says, "We bring you the world on a plate"—and in this case it's the wonderful world of chicken.

Serving Sizes: How Much to Buy

Generally, allow about 3/4 pound (twelve ounces) of chicken per serving when using whole birds and parts on bone, but for hearty eaters, plan on closer to one pound (sixteen ounces) per serving. When cooking boneless, skinless pieces, plan on four to six ounces per serving. For parts on bone but with the skin removed, eight ounces should feed one person.

Of course, the amounts vary from person to person and by the dish itself. Sometimes with really hungry guests or really tasty chicken, I've seen two servings scarfed up by each person, so plan accordingly. Side dishes also figure into serving portions; pastas fill you up more than light summer salads. And a chowder of potatoes, corn, and cream will require less chicken per person than a meal of grilled chicken, green beans, and cornbread.

Chickens Little and Big

Chickens are classified by their size, weight, and age when processed.

Poussins—A French favorite, poussins are chicks around three weeks old. They weigh about one pound and feed one person.

Cornish Hens or Rock Cornish Hens—Though they carry a fancy name, these birds are just young chickens—about thirty days old. They weigh one and one-half to two pounds each and feed two people.

Broilers or Fryers—Most weigh between three and one-half and four pounds, though five-pounders are not uncommon in today's supermarkets. An average-size broiler

Pop Quiz: What Is a Paillard?

Is it . . .

A) a type of pot pie?

B) a French restaurateur?

C) a thin, flattened cut of meat?

In the late nineteenth century, a very savvy Monsieur Paillard (PI-yahrd) hosted some of France's most fashionable guests, including the most elite patrons of the day and the chic, chichi theater crowd, at his two Paris restaurants. Besides creating such elaborate dishes as Pommes Georgettes (potatoes cooked whole, hollowed out, and filled with a creamy crawfish sauce), he served a specialty of veal sliced thin, pounded even thinner, and grilled or lightly braised. This scallop of veal came to be known as a paillard, and today it refers to any thinly pounded slice of beef, fish, veal, or even chicken. So if you answered B and C in the pop quiz, you're on your way to the CIA (Culinary Institute of America)!

Because paillards are so thin, beware of tearing the meat when pounding and of overcooking them. A few seconds too long, and your tender morsel will taste like an old worn shoe. Remember that after foods are removed from the flame, they continue to cook because of residual heat, even very thin foods. So remove the chicken while it's just a tad pink in the center to keep it moist when served.

To make chicken paillards, use boneless, skinless chicken breast halves. You can flatten them on a cutting board, naked or between sheets of plastic wrap. Use the smooth side of a meat pounder, not the dimpled one. If you don't have a meat pounder, flatten the meat with a rolling pin or smooth-bottomed jar. Pound from the inside and thickest portion out to the edges. Don't overdo things: You want the meat of fairly uniform thickness, but if it's too thin, it will tear. A thickness of one-third to one-fourth inch is fine. If cooking many paillards at the same time, tent them with foil or keep them warm in a low oven, just as you would flapjacks.

or fryer feeds four people. A "fast-food"-size bird, served at restaurants, weighs only about two and one-half pounds.

Roasters—These mature, meaty birds weigh from five to six pounds and are plump enough to feed six to eight persons.

Capons—Fat and juicy, these castrated males are fattened up for extra flavor and weigh from four to seven pounds.

Stewing Hens—When a hen's egg-laying productivity ceases at between twelve and twenty-four months, into the pot she goes. Her tough, stringy, but flavorful, meat is best suited for broths and long-simmered dishes like stews. Good luck finding stewing hens at today's supermarkets. Country farmers are a more likely source.

Organic and Free-Range Chickens—These definitions are as clear as mud, or as grainy as chicken feed. U.S. Department of Agriculture (USDA) standards require that free-range chickens have access to the outdoors for at least part of the day. When they get adequate exercise, these birds tend to be more flavorful, with flesh that is firm but not tough. But free-range hens that merely visit a small pen for a short time taste no better than standard processed chickens. Free-range birds cost more

The Battle of the Breast . . . or Breasts

I've never understood why people have two breasts and chickens have only one. Anatomically speaking, a chicken is said to have only one large breast, which consists of two "breast halves"—the pieces most commonly packaged for sale—separated by the breastbone. Call me crazy, but this sounds like two breasts to me. Cookbook authors have always been instructed to refer to these two pieces as breast halves or split breasts, and when sold joined together, as a "whole breast." But in common usage today, most home cooks consider a chicken breast to be a single piece of white meat with only one set of ribs attached, or in the case of boneless pieces, the white meat that was once attached to only one set of ribs. I considered using the popular terminology in this book, but was afraid things would just get too confusing. So I'm chicken-ing out: I reluctantly relent and adhere to the standard terms (cockeyed as they are) of olden days: a whole breast consists of two uncut halves, and a split breast or breast half is the piece of meat on either side of the breastbone.

Scoring Chicken

Scoring boneless, skinless chicken breasts or thighs allows marinades to penetrate more quickly and deeply, and the pieces cook in about two-thirds the time of nonscored meat. Gently slide the blade of your knife (such as a chef's knife) across the meat surface, cutting about one-eighth- to one-fourth-inch deep in parallel gashes about one inch apart. Rotate the piece about 90 degrees and do the same thing, creating a diamond pattern. Flip the meat over and score it in two directions on the other side as well. If your cuts are slightly deeper in the thickest part of the meat, the breast will cook more evenly. Just be careful not to cut all the way through, or you'll end up with two chunky pieces instead of one.

than standard hens, but the tender, flavorful meat of true free-rangers justifies their higher price. According to USDA standards, "organic" birds must be certified as having been fed only organic feed (which is grown without toxic and persistent chemical fertilizers, pesticides, or herbicides) and raised without antibiotics or hormones.

Kosher and Halal Chickens—Kosher chickens are brined briefly in saltwater before being slaughtered according to Jewish laws. The water removes impurities and, at the same time, seasons the bird. Halal chickens are slaughtered according to Islamic law but are not brined. Supermarkets and butchers in Muslim communities sell halal chickens, and even McDonald's serves halal Chicken McNuggets in some Detroit and California franchises.

Safe Handling and Storage of Chicken

Poultry labeling terms have changed over the past few years. Today, "fresh" means poultry has been stored at 26 degrees and above. Chickens stored between 0 and 26 degrees cannot be labeled fresh or frozen, so the term "hard chilled" is often used. And "frozen" means poultry stored below 0 degrees.

Like all fresh meats poultry is perishable and must be handled properly to prevent the risk of bacterial infection. Salmonella is the main culprit—a bacterial strain that's hard to detect because it doesn't give off foul odors (no pun intended) and doesn't produce discoloration.

The rule of thumb is never, ever to let raw poultry or its juices come in contact with foods you plan to eat raw (such as lettuce) and always to cook chicken thoroughly, which kills the bacteria.

This means that for safe chicken handling, you should:

- Make sure chicken packages don't leak raw juices. For added safety, never store raw poultry, even when wrapped, above or next to foods you plan to eat raw.
- Wash all surfaces that come in contact with raw poultry well, using hot, sudsy water, before letting them come in contact with other foods. These include knives, utensils, cutting boards, countertops, sponges, dish towels, and your hands.
- Prevent salmonella from developing by storing fresh poultry properly: Refrigerate in the coldest part of the fridge for two days, or freeze raw poultry for six to nine months. Cooked poultry will last three to four days in the fridge, or up to four months in the freezer.

The National Chicken Council recommends the following tips for safe handling, storing, and cooking of chicken.

Before You Cook:

- Refrigerate raw chicken promptly; never leave it on the countertop at room temperature.
- Packaged fresh chicken may be refrigerated in its original wrappings in the coldest part of the refrigerator.
- Freeze uncooked chicken if it is not to be used within two days.
- If properly packaged, frozen chicken will maintain top quality in a home freezer for up to one year.
- Thaw chicken in the refrigerator or in cold water—not on the countertop. It takes about twenty-four hours to thaw a four-pound chicken in the refrigerator. Cut-up parts, three to nine hours.
- Chicken may be thawed safely in cold water. Place chicken, in its original wrap or a watertight plastic bag, into cold water. Change water often. It takes about two hours to thaw a whole chicken.

- For quick thawing of raw or cooked chicken use the microwave. Thawing time will vary.
- Always wash with soapy water hands, countertops, cutting boards, knives, and other utensils used in preparing raw chicken before they come in contact with other raw or cooked foods.
- When shopping, buy groceries last. Never leave chicken in a hot car, and refrigerate it immediately on reaching home.

While You're Cooking:

- If chicken is stuffed, remove stuffing to a separate container before refrigerating.
- When barbecuing chicken outdoors, keep it refrigerated until ready to cook. Do not place cooked chicken on the same plate used to transport raw chicken to grill.
- Never leave cooked chicken at room temperature for more than two hours. If not eaten immediately, cooked chicken should be either kept hot or refrigerated.
- The marinade in which raw chicken has been soaking should never be used on cooked chicken. (However, rapid boiling for three minutes will kill any bacteria, so boiled marinade can be used as a sauce with or to baste cooked chicken.)

To Check for Doneness:

- Always cook chicken well-done, not medium or rare. If using a meat thermometer, the internal temperature should reach 180 degrees for whole chicken, 170 degrees for bone-in parts, and 160 degrees for boneless parts.
- To check visually for doneness, pierce chicken with a fork; juices should run clear—not pink—when a fork is inserted with ease.

After You Cook:

- Cooked, cut-up chicken is at its best refrigerated for no longer than two days— whole cooked chicken, an additional day.
- If leftovers are to be reheated, cover to retain moisture and ensure that chicken is heated all the way through. Bring gravies to a rolling boil before serving.
- If you're transporting cooked chicken, put it in an insulated container or ice chest until ready to eat. Keep below 40 degrees or above 140 degrees.

Do-It-Yourself: Jointing Chickens and Boning Breasts

Cutting a whole chicken into pieces saves money, and it takes just a few minutes to do.

With a little practice, you can joint a chicken in less than three minutes, or bone and skin four chicken breasts in less time. All you need is a sharp, heavy knife, such as a chef's knife, and a cutting board. Other tools, such as poultry shears and boning knives, are handy but not necessary.

Tip: A paper towel will give you a better grip on poultry. Use it to hold the bird if it slips while cutting, or to hold the skin as you pull it off.

WHOLE BIRDS, FAT AND ALL

To prepare a whole chicken for roasting or cutting into pieces, first remove and discard any lumps of fat from the cavity. Pull out the giblets if included. If you don't plan to use the giblets right away, freeze them. (I keep a giblets container in my freezer, dropping in new additions until I'm ready to turn them into a pâté, rumaki, cornbread stuffing, or giblet gravy.) Rinse the chicken inside and out under cool running water, and pat the chicken dry with paper towels. Then proceed with the recipe. Be careful to avoid contamination by cleaning the area with hot, sudsy water.

How to Cut Up a Chicken

CUT THE BIRD INTO FOUR PIECES

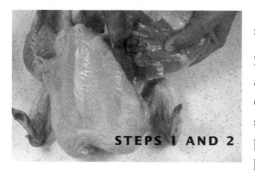

STEPS 1 AND 2

1. Place the chicken on a cutting board, breast side up.

2. Grasp a leg and thigh portion in one hand and pull it away from the breast. With the chef's knife in the other hand, cut through the skin and flesh between the thigh and breast, placing the knife more closely to the thigh to prevent cutting through breast meat. When you get to the bone, bend the leg back, twisting it to break the joint, which makes a cracking noise when it snaps. Cut straight through the tendon in the middle of the joint. Set the leg and thigh piece aside. Repeat with the other leg.

3. Place the bird breast side down on the cutting board with the tail end farthest away from you. Hold the tail securely with one hand. Using a sharp knife or poultry shears, cut along the spine next to the backbone from the neck to the tail. Flatten the bird on the cutting board with your hands and cut along the other side of the backbone, removing it from the ribs.

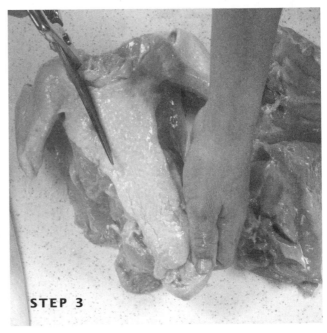

STEP 3

Tip: Two delicious meaty nuggets—known as the oysters—lie on either side of the backbone just behind the thigh joint. To remove them before splitting the bird, use a paring or other small knife to cut through the skin, then work the knife under the oysters to release them.

4. Place the knife on one side of the breastbone and cut through, dividing the breast into two halves. You now have a chicken cut into four pieces.

STEP 4

CUT THE BIRD INTO SIX OR EIGHT PIECES

5. To separate the leg from the thigh, hold the drumstick with one hand, so the joint forms a V shape. Cut through the joint where the line of white fat appears. Repeat with the other leg-thigh section.

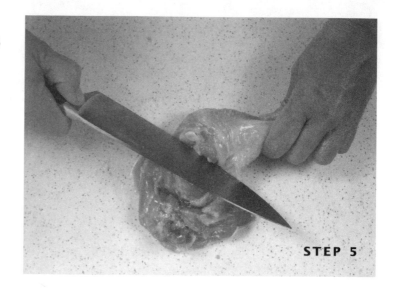

STEP 5

6. To remove the wing, pull the wing away from the breast and cut through the joint. Or, to keep a portion of the breast with the wing, slice through the breast half on the diagonal, cutting through the meat and rib bones.

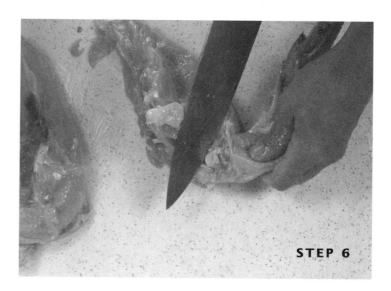

STEP 6

BUTTERFLYING OR SPATCHCOCKING

Split birds and butterflied, or spatchcocked, birds are handy for grilling and roast more quickly than whole birds.

To butterfly, or spatchcock, a bird is to cut out the backbone and flattening the breastbone, so the bird resembles an open book (or, in my view, a cowskin rug). To butterfly a bird, cut the ribs away from the backbone on both sides and remove the backbone, using poultry shears or a sharp knife. Turn the bird over (breast side up, legs pointing toward you) and lean down on the breastbone with your palms to crack it and flatten the bird. Cut a small incision on both sides of the breastbone, just above the chicken's lower end. Poke the drumstick tips through the incisions, folding them across the skin and through to the underside of the bird. Spatchcocked birds are typically grilled or pan-fried with a weight on them (such as an iron skillet or foil-wrapped brick) to flatten the meat and crisp the skin.

SPLIT BIRDS

Split birds are halved whole chickens. Cut along the backbone and remove it. Crack the breastbone, then pull out the breastbone and cartilage; cut through the central point to separate the chicken into two halves.

Quick, Thinly Sliced Cutlets

Instead of pounding boneless, skinless chicken breasts (cutlets) until they're ultra-thin, which can be messy and cause the meat to tear, try this time-saving tip. Place the cutlet, with the tender removed, on the cutting board. Flatten the palm of your hand over the cutlet, pressing down gently. Using a sharp chef's knife or Chinese cleaver, carefully slice horizontally through the chicken breast, moving the knife back and forth in a sawlike motion. Depending on the thickness of the breast, you can end up with two or three thin slices. These cutlets can be quickly fried or breaded for Chicken Piccata or Parmigiana or rolled around a filling.

Boning and Skinning Chicken Breast Halves

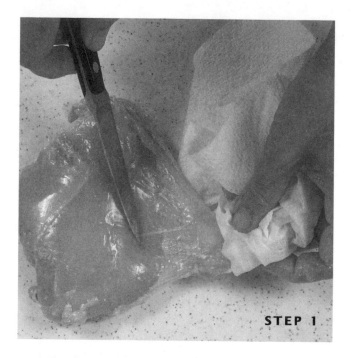

STEP 1

1. Pull the skin free with your fingers, using a paper towel to grasp it if the skin is slippery.

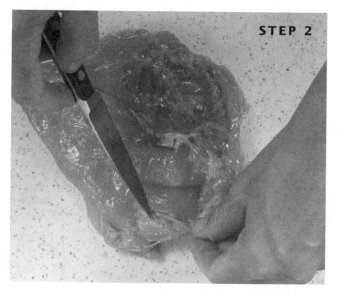

STEP 2

2. Start by removing the wishbone. Scrape the flesh away from the wishbone and pluck it out. (A paring knife works well for boning breasts.)

3. Wedge the knife blade as close to the breastbone as possible. Move it across the bone and the ribs, cutting the meat away. Guide your knife along the contours of the breastbone as you go, until the flesh is completely freed from the bone.

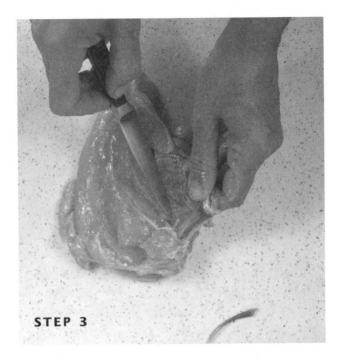

STEP 3

4. If desired, pull the tenderloin away and set aside to be cooked separately from the rest of the breast. To remove the white tendon, grasp the thicker end with one hand, then work the knife along the tendon, pulling as you go and wiggling the tendon from side to side until it is freed.

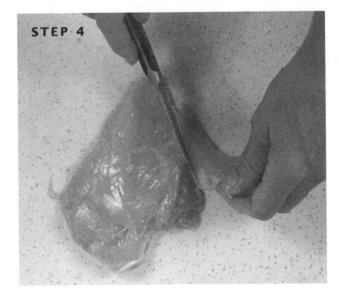

STEP 4

Brining for Flavor, Tenderness, and Texture

Brining for flavor is different from pickling. In the latter, food is preserved in a salty solution. But in brining, meats are immersed in a mild salt and water mixture for just a few hours, usually with herbs and other seasonings as well. The water is drained, and the food is then cooked. The meat turns out intensely moist, flavorful, and tender.

Here's how it works: When meats are submerged in a mild solution of water and salt, a chemical reaction occurs. The meat proteins relax and unwind, absorbing and capturing the brining solution. If the solution contains other flavorings, such as sugar, molasses, honey, wine, herbs, garlic, or spices, those seasonings are trapped in the meat fibers as well. Unlike dry rubs and marinades that season only the outer layer of meat, brining penetrates all of the flesh, so the salt and other flavors are absorbed throughout. And because the proteins have absorbed the liquid, the flesh plumps ups and stays juicier, preventing the problem of dried-out chicken meat.

Many poultry producers do the brining for you by injecting their products with a solution containing broth, stock, or water, along with butter or other fat, spices, flavor enhancers, and colorings. Raw poultry labels reading "basted," "marinated," or "added for flavoring" indicate some type of solution has been added before processing—up to 3 percent by weight for bone-in poultry and up to 8 percent by weight for boneless poultry. Don't brine these products at home; they'll become too salty.

BRINING TIPS

- The salt used is typically kosher or table salt, but kosher is preferred. Kosher salt dissolves more readily in water than table salt.
- Kosher and table salt differ in weight, and thereby in degree of saltiness. For every one and one-half cups of kosher salt use one cup of table salt.
- Brine in a nonreactive container that won't be harmed by the salt, such as glass, plastic, stainless steel, or ceramic (do not use aluminum).
- The stronger the brine, the less brining time needed. And don't brine too long or in too strong a solution, or the meat will be too salty. Even a short brining time improves flavor and juiciness.

- Remove chicken from the brine at the end of the recommended soaking period; dry the chicken and store it in the refrigerator until ready to cook.
- When cooking brined chicken, cut back on added salt or omit it completely, because the chicken will have absorbed enough salt from the brine.
- Sugar or other sweetener (such as honey, molasses, or maple syrup) is optional, but it balances the saltiness and enhances the chicken's natural sweetness.
- Add other flavorings to the brine, such as herbs, spices, and garlic, and substitute other liquids for all or part of the water, such as fruit juices, alcohol, tea, rice vinegar, or stock.
- Never reuse brine.

Testing for Doneness

How to tell when a chicken is "cooked until done"? Cook chicken until the juices run clear. Salmonella is completely wiped out when poultry heats up to a blushing 160 degrees (and kept at this temperature for three minutes), but most people prefer chicken that's not quite so pink. Breast meat that registers above 160 degrees for boneless, skinless pieces, and around 170 to 175 degrees for pieces with bone, will be moist with clear juices. Dark meat cooked to between 170 and 180 degrees will also be succulent and safe. At the perfect temperature, the juices will run clear, not pink or cloudy, and the meat will be moist and tender, not dried out. For greatest accuracy, use a meat thermometer.

BASIC RECIPES FOR BRINED CHICKEN, ON OR OFF THE BONE

After a quick dip in a salty bath chicken cooks up noticeably more juicy, plump, and flavorful than unbrined chicken.

Ingredients for Boneless, Skinless Breasts or Thighs

3¹/₂ TO 4 POUNDS BONELESS, SKINLESS PIECES

¹/₄ CUP KOSHER SALT

¹/₄ CUP SUGAR

2 CUPS WATER

BRINING TIME: 45 MINUTES TO 1 HOUR

Ingredients for Breasts, Legs, or Thighs with Bone and Skin

4 POUNDS CHICKEN PIECES, WITH BONE AND SKIN

³/₄ CUP KOSHER SALT

³/₄ CUP SUGAR

1 QUART WATER

BRINING TIME: 90 MINUTES TO 2 HOURS

Ingredients for a Whole Chicken

1 WHOLE CHICKEN (ABOUT 4 POUNDS), GIBLETS REMOVED

1 CUP KOSHER SALT

1 CUP SUGAR

1 GALLON WATER

BRINING TIME: 4 TO 8 HOURS

Note: For a crispier skin, let the chicken air-dry uncovered in the refrigerator overnight.

① In a deep container or gallon-size plastic zipper bag, mix together the salt, sugar, and water until salt and sugar are fully dissolved. Submerge chicken in the brine for the times indicated, refrigerated. If there's not enough brine, add extra water. (If the chicken insists on floating in the bowl, set a plate on top. If using a plastic bag, squeeze out the air until the chicken is completely immersed in the brine.)

② Rinse the chicken pieces and pat dry. Season as desired (watch that you don't over-salt), and grill, sauté, roast, or fry the pieces as you wish.

Meal-Morphing

Stretch your chicken and your kitchen time with what I call "meal-morphing." Leftover chicken doesn't have to be boring or simply reheated. Give it new life by morphing it into a completely new recipe, one that tastes fresh and different but saves time because you're not starting the dish from scratch. For instance, you can grill up a jumbo pack's worth of Scandinavian chicken marinated in sour cream, dill, and cucumber, then transform cooked pieces into a cooling pasta salad that uses the same basic marinade as a dressing but tastes entirely different. Watch for meal-morphing tips in selected recipes throughout this book.

The Royal Bird

Chicken can be a symbol of coziness and humble hospitality, as in a chicken pot pie or a Sunday roast. Yet, while chickens aren't as glamorous as caviar or truffles, they're perfectly at home with royalty and celebration. For her 1953 coronation, Queen Elizabeth II was honored with a chicken dish, known appropriately as Coronation Chicken. Chicken Marengo was whipped up on the battlefield by Napoleon's chef to commemorate the French victory at Marengo in 1800. And the classic Chicken Tetrazzini was named in honor of opera diva Luisa Tetrazzini by the man known as the "emperor of chefs," Auguste Escoffier, in 1894.

About These Recipes

Keep these tips in mind when cooking from this book.

Ingredients
- Garlic is always peeled unless otherwise indicated. Same for onions.
- Green onions include both green and white parts.
- Fresh ginger may be used peeled or unpeeled if the skin is soft.
- Soy sauce is Kikkoman, unless otherwise noted.
- Canola oil is preferred for its clean, neutral flavor, but you may use any neutral-flavored vegetable oil with a fairly high smoking point.
- For salt, sea salt is preferred unless kosher salt is specified.
- Eggs are large.
- If Asian, Indian, and Middle Eastern ingredients aren't available in regular super-markets, you'll find them in their respective ethnic markets.

Chickens
- Whole birds have lumps of fat just inside the cavity. Pull these lumps off and discard before cooking.
- Whole birds come with giblets, stuffed inside the cavity either loose or in a bag. If the recipe says "without giblets," remove them and set aside or freeze for another use.
- Unless the ingredient list specifies "boneless" or "skinless," use chicken pieces with bone and skin.
- Packaged ground chicken typically contains a blend of dark and light meat, perfect for these recipes. All-light meat is too lean, and all-dark meat too fatty. If desired, substitute ground turkey, such as a lean and dark meat blend with from 7 to 15 percent fat.
- When a recipe says to "cook until done," see the section in chapter 3, "Testing for Doneness."
- Every palate is different, and both fresh and packaged ingredients can vary in flavor. Adjust salt, pepper, and seasonings to taste, but never taste a dish with uncooked or partially cooked chicken in it.

Equipment
- You'll need a large, heavy skillet, preferably nonstick, with a lid.
- "Nonreactive" cookware is lined with a surface that won't react negatively to foods cooked in it such as acids like lemon juice or vinegar or salty brines. Stainless steel and glass are nonreactive, but aluminum, copper, and cast iron can "react" and discolor foods or create a metallic taste.
- Hand blenders and food processors are the mortar-and-pestles of the modern age. For ease and speed, many recipes call for ingredients to be chopped or whizzed together in the work bowl of a hand blender or food processor (full-size or mini versions). If you prefer, you may chop, grind, and combine the ingredients by hand.
- Grind spices in a clean coffee mill or spice grinder. Clean the mill or grinder out by whizzing pieces of bread in it.
- Poultry shears aren't necessary if you have a sharp, heavy chef's knife, but they can be handy.
- Use an instant-read meat thermometer to ensure safe and complete cooking.
- Keep loads of paper towels around when working with raw chicken, to avoid contaminating cloth dish towels. Use clean paper towels to dry washed counter surfaces and washed hands.

CHAPTER 4

Whole Birds

There's nothing simpler than cooking a whole chicken, although a chicken split into two halves comes pretty close. These one-bird recipes, roasted or cooked on the stove-top, are designed for simple satisfaction, with flavors that travel from China to Spain.

For more split-chicken recipes, flip to Chapter 9:
> Aromatic Anise Chicken
> Texas Barbecue Dry-Rub Chicken

Barcelona Brown-Bag Chicken and Vegetables

SERVES 6 Amaze your family and friends with this succulent, moist chicken and tender vegetables baked in a plain brown paper bag. This bag-o-chicken recipe (an oddball American technique that somehow really works) cooks chicken, carrots, and potatoes to perfection. Use any flavorings, but in this recipe the bird roasts in the sunny flavors of Spain—tomatoes, olives, dry sherry, marjoram, almonds, and red bell pepper. In 25 minutes you can prepare the whole meal, then relax for 1¼ hours of unattended cooking time.   *continued*

Barcelona Brown-Bag Chicken and Vegetables *continued*

1 WHOLE CHICKEN (ABOUT 4 POUNDS), WITHOUT GIBLETS

3 CLOVES GARLIC, MINCED

2 TABLESPOONS DRY SHERRY

2 TEASPOONS PAPRIKA

1 TEASPOON DRIED MARJORAM

1 TEASPOON SALT

1 RED BELL PEPPER, CUT INTO 1-INCH CHUNKS

1/2 RED OR YELLOW ONION, CUT INTO 1-INCH CHUNKS

1 CARROT, CUT INTO 1-INCH CHUNKS

2 RUSSET POTATOES (ABOUT 1 POUND), CUT INTO 1-INCH CHUNKS (LEAVE SKIN ON)

1 CUP GREEN OLIVES STUFFED WITH PIMIENTO

1/4 CUP BLANCHED WHOLE ALMONDS

1/2 CUP OIL-PACKED SUN-DRIED TOMATOES, CHOPPED, OIL RESERVED

① Place the oven·rack in the lower third of the oven. Be sure to allow plenty of space so the brown bag doesn't come in contact with the sides, top, or bottom of the oven. (Avoid bags with printing on them or glued-on handles.)

② Heat oven to 450 degrees. Fold the wing tips back and tuck them under the bird. Place the chicken in a 13 x 9 x 2-inch baking dish.

③ In a large bowl, mix together the garlic, sherry, paprika, marjoram, and salt to create a spice mixture. Rub the spice mixture all over the chicken and inside the chicken cavity, reserving about 1 tablespoon in the bowl.

④ Toss the red bell pepper, onion, carrot, and potatoes in the bowl with the remaining spice mixture. Add the olives, almonds, and sun-dried tomatoes, with a spoonful of the oil from the tomatoes, and mix all to coat thoroughly.

⑤ Lift the chicken, and spoon the vegetables around and under the bird. Carefully slide the pan into a clean, brown paper grocery bag. Today's markets are using shorter bags, so if the bag isn't long enough to fold the end over, carefully turn the pan around 90 degrees in the bag, then fold the end and staple it shut.

⑥ Place the bag in the oven (make sure the bag doesn't rest against the top or sides of the oven). Bake for 1 hour and 15 minutes.

⑦ Carefully remove the bag from the oven and cut it open. Let the chicken stand for 10 minutes. Spoon the vegetables onto a platter, top with chicken pieces, and serve.

Char Shu Cornish Hens

SERVES 2 TO 4 Slightly sweet and aromatic, Chinese roast pork (or char shu) is usually served in small slices or chopped bits. It's prized for its ability to season other dishes, such as fried rice, noodles, and soups. This recipe marinates Cornish hens in char shu seasonings. Serve one small whole or one large half Cornish hen per person, or use the meat as you would pork char shu, in small amounts to flavor and enhance other dishes. Note that the marinade is also sufficient for 2 whole broiler chickens, which may be jointed and cooked as pieces. Boil residual marinade for 3 minutes (or longer to thicken), then serve as a sauce, or refrigerate for up to 1 week and reuse as a marinade. You can buy shao-hsing wine in Chinese markets, or substitute dry sherry.

2 CORNISH HENS

Char Shu Marinade

1/2 CUP SOY SAUCE

1/4 CUP DRY SHERRY OR SHAO-HSING WINE

2 CLOVES GARLIC, MINCED

2 GREEN ONIONS, WHITE AND GREEN PARTS MINCED

1-INCH PIECE FRESH GINGER, MINCED

3 TABLESPOONS BROWN SUGAR

2 TABLESPOONS HONEY

1/2 TEASPOON CHINESE 5-SPICE POWDER (OPTIONAL)

1 TEASPOON TOASTED SESAME OIL

① Spatchcock the hens (see chapter 3), or split in half, or cut into pieces.

continued

Char Shu Cornish Hens *continued*

② Mix the marinade ingredients together in a container large enough to hold the hens. Add the and coat thoroughly with the marinade. Cover and refrigerate overnight, or at least 4 hours turning the hens in the marinade occasionally.

③ To cook the hens, heat the broiler or grill. Cook the hens on a rack at least 5 inches from the heat, allowing them to cook slowly, turning and basting with the marinade every 10 minute until done. This should take about 30 minutes. Make sure the skin doesn't burn. If the hens cooking too fast on the outside, move them farther from the heat (covering the grill can help too). When the hens are done, the skin should be a rich mahogany color, and the juices shou run clear.

④ Serve hot or at room temperature. If desired, chop the birds into 2-inch pieces, bones and al and serve Chinese-style with hot mustard and soy sauce for dipping.

Citrus-Brined Chicken, Roasted with Near East Rub

SERVES 4 A whole roasted chicken is ultra-easy, but too often it turns out dry instead of mois and juicy. Two to four hours of brining solves that problem, and this mixed-citrus-juice brine is almost like giving the bird a passport to the world. The brine readily complements flavorings fro the Mediterranean, Mexico, the Caribbean, the Middle East, and North Africa. You can roast the bird without additional seasonings, but a splash of the "Sesame and Sumac" rub before roasting adds an exotic Near East touch. (For brining instructions, see chapter 3.)

Tip: Fresh is always best, but in a pinch I use the canned fruit juices I keep on hand for brining or for an impulse-driven marinade.

Citrus Brine

²/₃ CUP KOSHER SALT

1¹/₂ CUPS ORANGE JUICE (FRESH OR 2 5.5-OUNCE CANS)

1¹/₂ CUPS GRAPEFRUIT JUICE (FRESH OR FROM CONCENTRATE)

1¹/₂ CUPS WATER

1 WHOLE CHICKEN (ABOUT 4 POUNDS), WITHOUT GIBLETS

2 TABLESPOONS MILD OLIVE OR CANOLA OIL

2 TABLESPOONS NEAR EAST "SESAME AND SUMAC" RUB (CHAPTER 12)

① Mix together the salt, juices, and water until salt is fully dissolved. Pour the mixture into a deep container or a gallon-size plastic zipper bag. Submerge the chicken in the brine for 2 to 4 hours, refrigerated; 3 hours is ideal. (If the chicken insists on floating, set a plate on top. If using a plastic bag, squeeze out the air until the chicken is completely immersed in the brine.) After brining, rinse the chicken and pat dry.

② Heat the oven to 450 degrees. Place the chicken on a rack in a roasting pan. Rub half of the oil all over the bird, inside and out. Rub the inside and outside with the spice rub. Leave the chicken to roast breast side up.

③ Roast uncovered 15 minutes. Turn the heat down to 375 degrees, rotate the pan in the oven so the bird cooks more evenly, and pour any juices collected in the bird's cavity into the pan (this prevents the pan bottom from burning). Continue to roast the bird until done, about 45 minutes. Baste the bird 2 or 3 times with the remaining oil during roasting. If the skin starts to brown too quickly, tent loosely with foil. Wait 10 minutes before carving the chicken into pieces. Serve warm.

China

Such a huge landmass as China makes generalizations difficult, but some ingredients do form a foundation of cooking there, including soy products, ginger, and rice, although in the northern plains and highlands, noodles and wheat doughs replace rice as the main starch. Food in China was vastly changed in the sixteenth century, when traders introduced chiles and tomatoes from the Americas, Dutch snow peas, and Portuguese watercress. But dairy products are rare in China, except for yogurt in the Muslim-influenced northwest. In Szechuan and Hunan provinces, dishes are spiced hot, sweet, and sour, often fried, refried, and deep-fried. The mild Cantonese cooking is most familiar to Americans, with oyster sauce, black beans, and chicken stock playing key roles. The Mandarin cooking of Beijing enjoys liberal garlic use and ample wine as seasonings.

adzuki beans	coriander	rice
bamboo shoots	cucumber	seaweed
bean sprouts	duck	sesame
black beans	garlic	shao-hsing wine
black vinegar	ginger	shiitake mushrooms
bok choy	golden tiger lily	shrimp
broccoli	needles	soy sauces
chiles	green onion	star anise
Chinese 5-spice powder	hoisin sauce	sugar
Chinese, or napa, cabbage	miso	Szechuan peppercorns
cilantro	noodles	tofu
cinnamon	oyster sauce	water chestnuts
cloud ear mushrooms	peppers	wonton wrappers

Ginger-Poached Chicken and Broth

SERVES 4 TO 6 In this Chinese poaching method, chicken simmers for a short time immersed in seasoned water, then the flame is turned off and the chicken continues to cook gently in the hot liquid. The meat is far more tender and moist than if boiled until done, and the resulting chicken broth is lightly seasoned with hints of ginger, green onion, and sherry.

You can make this dish just before serving, but I prefer to cook it a day before so the fat is easier to remove. Refrigerating it overnight allows the fat to harden, and it lifts off more easily than by skimming while hot. Also, the chicken meat stays moist in the broth and is easier to shred when cool. Use the broth for Wonton Soup or to replace regular chicken broth. The chicken can be used wherever cooked chicken is called for, or serve it warm or cold with soy sauce or a dipping sauce.

1 WHOLE CHICKEN (ABOUT 4 POUNDS), WITHOUT GIBLETS

2³/₄ TEASPOONS SALT

1¹/₂ INCHES FRESH GINGER, CUT INTO 6 SLICES

5 GREEN ONIONS, GREEN AND WHITE PARTS DIAGONALLY CUT INTO 2-INCH LENGTHS

2 TABLESPOONS DRY SHERRY

① Rub the chicken all over with the salt, including inside the cavity.

② Place the chicken and neck (if available) in a pot just large enough to hold them. Add the ginger, green onions, and sherry to the pot. Fill the pot with enough water to just cover the chicken by ¹/₂ inch.

③ Bring the water to a boil on high heat. Using a slotted spoon, skim away the brown scum that rises to the top and discard. Cover the pot and reduce the heat. Simmer the chicken 20 minutes.

④ Turn off the heat. Leave the chicken covered in the pot for 1 hour. Serve the meat and broth as a soup or separately in other recipes. If desired, refrigerate overnight before use. Before serving, skim or remove the fat and discard the cooked ginger, garlic, and green onions.

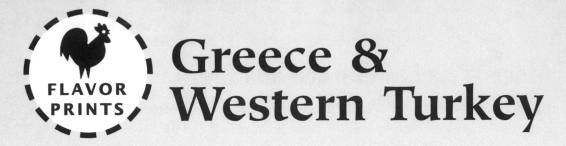

Greece & Western Turkey

Lemons, olives, and fresh herbs and vegetables, simply cooked, are the hall-marks of Greek and Turkish cooking around the Aegean Sea. Pictures of Greece emphasize islands, but most of the country is riverless, rugged mountain terrain, difficult for farming. Turkey, though, enjoys the Tigris, Euphrates, and other rivers. Meat and chicken, basted or marinated with lemon and olive oil, are grilled or spit-roasted. Cold appetizers precede a meal, typically including feta cheese, pepper salads, olives, rice-stuffed grape leaves, peppers, cucumbers, yogurt, and squid and octopus salads. Oregano marries lemon and olive oil, while cinnamon is wed to tomatoes. Breads are both leavened and unleavened, as in braided Easter breads and pita breads, respectively. Ingredients may be combined in the cooking process and also served as condiments at table, such as yogurt, olive oil and olives, cheeses, and vegetables.

Aleppo pepper	kasseri and kefolatiri	pine nuts
allspice	cheese	pistachios
bell peppers	lamb	pita bread and yeast breads
cinnamon	lemon	retsina wine
cucumber	marjoram	rice
dill	mint	seafood
eggplant	olives and olive oil	sesame
fennel	onion	spinach
feta cheese	oregano	tomato
garlic	ouzo	white beans
grape leaves	pasta	yogurt

Lemon-Rubbed Roaster
with Six Garlic Heads

SERVES 6 If you're going to roast a chicken, you might as well roast a large one, especially when it will have such a golden, crisp skin as this one does. The flavorings of lemon, rosemary, wine, and garlic are typical of Greece, Italy, and Provençe.

1 (6-POUND) ROASTING CHICKEN

6 HEADS (WHOLE BULBS) GARLIC

1 LEMON, HALVED

2 SPRIGS FRESH ROSEMARY

COARSE SALT AND FRESHLY GROUND PEPPER

1 TABLESPOON EXTRA-VIRGIN OLIVE OIL

1/2 CUP DRY WHITE WINE

① Heat the oven to 450 degrees. Rinse the chicken and pat dry. Remove the giblets and reserve for another use (or toss them into the roasting pan with the chicken).

② Slice the ends off the garlic heads to expose the interior cloves. Remove any loose papery peel from the bulb, but leave most of the peel on.

③ Set the chicken on a rack in a shallow roasting pan. Squeeze the lemon halves all over the chicken, rubbing the juice into the skin. Season generously all over, and inside, with salt and pepper. With the chicken breast side up, stuff the squeezed lemon halves into the cavity, along with the rosemary and 1 garlic head. Stuff another garlic head into the neck cavity of the bird, under the flap of skin. Surround the bird with the remaining 4 heads of garlic, cut side up. Drizzle the olive oil over the cut end of the garlic heads in the pan, and pour the wine into the pan.

④ Roast the chicken 30 minutes. Lower the heat to 375 degrees and continue roasting until cooked through, about 45 to 60 minutes. The skin should be crisp and golden, and the interior temperature in the thickest part of the leg should

continued

Lemon-Rubbed Roaster with Six Garlic Heads *continued*

register 170 degrees. The thickest part of the breast should register 155 degrees. (Remember that the chicken will continue to cook to another 5 to 10 degrees after it's out of the oven; this is known as carry-over cooking.)

⑤ Let the chicken rest 5 to 10 minutes before carving. Serve with the pan juices and crusty bread, letting guests squeeze the roasted garlic cloves onto the bread.

Lemongrass Roast Chicken

SERVES 4 Marinate this Vietnamese-seasoned chicken several hours or overnight, then roast whole until golden and fragrant with lemongrass, green onion, and the sweet-salty-hot flavors typical of Southeast Asian cuisine. Serve with a minty cucumber salad and cooked rice or Asian noodles.

Meal-Morphing Tip: Use leftover meat in Vietnamese Glass Noodles Soup (chapter 8) or in salads.

1 WHOLE CHICKEN (ABOUT 4 POUNDS), WITHOUT GIBLETS

3 STALKS LEMONGRASS

4 GREEN ONIONS

4 CLOVES GARLIC

3 TABLESPOONS FISH SAUCE

2 TEASPOONS SOY SAUCE

1 TABLESPOON SUGAR

2 TEASPOONS CANOLA OIL

1 1/2 TEASPOONS RED CHILE FLAKES

GARNISH: CHOPPED CILANTRO (OPTIONAL)

① Rinse the chicken and pat dry. Set in a bowl or in a plastic zipper bag for marinating.

② Peel off the tough 2 or 3 outer layers of the lemongrass. Slice the tender bulbous part (the lower 3 or 4 inches of the lemongrass) into 1-inch-long pieces for the marinade. Dump the pieces into the work bowl of a mini-chopper, hand blender, or food processor. Slice the lower part of the remaining upper stalks into a half-dozen 2-inch pieces and bruise or flatten with the side of a knife. Set aside for stuffing into the bird's cavity.

③ Chop the green onions, white and green parts, into 1-inch lengths. Reserve about half of the chopped green parts for stuffing into the cavity. Dump the remaining chopped pieces into the work bowl with the lemongrass.

④ Coarsely chop the garlic and dump into the work bowl as well. Add the fish sauce, soy sauce, sugar, and oil. Pulse or process until the ingredients are chopped and the mixture forms a thick paste. Pulse in the red chile flakes until just combined but not pulverized.

⑤ Slather the chicken inside and out with the marinade. Stuff the cavity with the reserved lemongrass pieces and green onion tops. Marinate refrigerated all day (at least 6 hours) or overnight, turning the chicken in the marinade midway through.

⑥ To cook, heat the oven to 375 degrees. Place the chicken in a roasting pan. Roast about 1 hour, basting occasionally with pan juices, until chicken is cooked through. (Chicken is done when a meat thermometer inserted in the thickest part of the thigh registers 170 to 175 degrees and the juices run clear.)

⑦ Let chicken rest 10 minutes, tented with foil, before carving. Carve into serving pieces, sprinkle with cilantro, and serve with cooked rice or noodles drizzled with the pan juices.

Southwest Skinny Chicken
A Pressure Cooker Recipe

SERVES 4 I love the ease of a whole chicken—and the thriftiness! A whole chicken takes an hour or so to roast in the oven, but in a pressure cooker, the bird can be cooked in about the time it takes to whip up a salad.

In this recipe, the skin of a whole chicken is pulled off (it takes just a minute). The bird is marinated for 15 minutes in lime juice and Mexican spices. Once brought to

continued

Southwest Skinny Chicken *continued*

pressure, the bird takes only 10 minutes to cook, and with the skin removed, it's very low in fat. The spices not only add a zesty flavor, but they give the bird an attractive red-yellow glow. This is a terrific year-round dish, but the citrusy lime taste is especially good in summer, when it can be far too hot to even consider roasting a chicken in the oven.

1 WHOLE CHICKEN (ABOUT 4 POUNDS), WITHOUT GIBLETS

5 CLOVES GARLIC, PEELED

3 LIMES, HALVED

1 TEASPOON GROUND CUMIN

1 TEASPOON DRIED OREGANO

1/4 TEASPOON DRIED THYME

1 TEASPOON GROUND DRIED RED CHILE (SUCH AS PASILLA)

1/2 TEASPOON SALT

1 CARROT, SLICED DIAGONALLY INTO 1-INCH LENGTHS

1 ONION, SLICED INTO RINGS

2 RIBS CELERY, SLICED DIAGONALLY INTO 1-INCH LENGTHS

① Skin the chicken by pulling the skin off with your hands, using a knife if needed (don't worry about the little bit of skin on the wings, which is almost impossible to remove easily). Holding the skin with a paper towel helps to keep it from slipping.

② Stab the chicken about 20 times all over with a fork and place in a pressure cooker. In the work bowl of a mini-chopper, hand blender, or food processor, process the garlic until chopped. Squeeze in the juice from the limes and process with the cumin, oregano, thyme, chile, and salt. (Or chop and combine the ingredients by hand.) Rub this mixture all over the chicken, pouring any excess into the pot. Let marinate for 15 minutes.

③ Scatter the carrot, onion, and celery around the chicken in the pot. Lock the lid in place and bring the pressure to high. Cook at this pressure, adjusting the flame as needed, for 10 minutes. Use the natural release method, as described by your pressure cooker manufacturer. When the chicken is cool enough to handle, carve into pieces and serve with the vegetables and juices. Cornbread, tortillas, rice, and beans make excellent side dishes.

Whole Chinese Red-Cooked Chicken

SERVES 4 In China, chicken simmered in soy sauce is referred to as "red-cooked," while chicken simmered in a nonsoy liquid (such as broth or water) is known as "white-cooked."

In this homey, nearly effortless, and warmly inviting dish, a whole chicken is first rubbed with Chinese 5-spice powder—an aromatic blend of star anise, cinnamon, cloves, fennel seed, and Szechuan peppercorns. It then simmers for 40 minutes in a concentrated mixture of soy sauce, sherry, ginger, and green onions, sweetened with brown sugar. The sauce, which turns the chicken a deep mahogany color, can be saved and reused as a classic "master sauce," the foundation for more main and side dishes.

1 WHOLE CHICKEN (ABOUT 4 POUNDS), WITHOUT GIBLETS

1¹/₂ TEASPOONS CHINESE 5-SPICE POWDER

4 GREEN ONIONS, GREEN AND WHITE PARTS SLICED INTO ¹/₂-INCH PIECES

¹/₂ CUP PACKED DARK BROWN SUGAR

1 CUP SOY SAUCE

1 CUP DRY SHERRY OR SHAO-HSING WINE

1 CUP WATER

2 SLICES FRESH GINGER

¹/₂ TEASPOON SESAME OIL

GARNISH: TOASTED SESAME SEEDS (OPTIONAL)

① Rinse chicken and pat dry. Rub chicken with Chinese 5-spice powder, inside and out.

② Place remaining ingredients except garnish in a pot just large enough to hold the chicken. Bring to a boil over medium heat. Set chicken in the pot breast side down. Spoon the liquid inside the cavity and over the chicken to coat completely.

③ Bring to a boil again, then cover and simmer 40 minutes. Turn the bird 2 or 3 times during this period to ensure even cooking.

④ Remove the pot from the heat and uncover. When the bird is cool enough to handle, carve into serving pieces or chop through the bones into bite-size pieces. Serve

continued

Whole Chinese Red-Cooked Chicken *continued*

warm with the sauce or at room temperature. Garnish with toasted sesame seeds if desired. Reserve excess sauce for use as a master sauce.

Master sauce: Strain the sauce through cheesecloth. Refrigerate and then remove congealed fat, leaving a small amount for flavor and sheen. To reuse the sauce, bring it to a rapid boil, then add raw chicken pieces (or cubed and seared pork, beef, or lamb) to it; cover and simmer until cooked through. Freeze or refrigerate remaining sauce. Bring refrigerated sauce to a rapid boil once a week and whenever it's reused. To retain the balance of flavors over time, taste the sauce and add smaller amounts of the original ingredients as needed.

Serving suggestions: Serve with steamed rice. For a complete dish, top rice with finely julienned fresh napa cabbage, top with warm chicken and sauce, and garnish with slivered green onions. This chicken also pairs well with noodles. For vegetable side dishes, use the sauce to flavor stir-fried vegetables, especially eggplant, mushrooms, and Asian luffah squash, which readily soak up the liquid.

CHAPTER 5

Chicken Packages Piece by Piece

Try these quantity recipes for thrifty chicken buys—great for those jumbo packs! These recipes cook from four to six pounds of chicken pieces. Serve as many as eight persons, or feed just a few mouths and save some pieces for encore performances.

Check out these chapters for more big cooking recipes:

Chapter 8
    African Chicken and Peanut Stew
    Hungarian Chicken Paprikás

Chapter 9
    Barbecued Korean Drums
    Chicken Churrasco in Chimichurri Sauce
    Cuban Sour Orange Chicken
    Filipino Coconut Barbecued Chicken
    Grilled Chicken in Minty Chutney
    Jamaican Jerk Chicken
    Juicy Grilled Grapefruit Chicken
    La Tunisia Chicken and Grilled Onions
    Portuguese Grilled Chicken Oporto
    Texas Barbecue Dry-Rub Chicken

continued

Chapter 10
   Chicken Adobo
   Chicken in Wine with Balsamic-Herb Gravy
   Coq au Vermouth

Bangladesh Drums

SERVES 4 TO 6 The Republic of Bangladesh, formerly East Pakistan, is bordered on three sides by India and by the Bay of Bengal and Burma to the south. Bengali and Bangladeshi cooking may seem unfamiliar, but many Indian restaurants in the West are actually run by Bangladeshi families, who make chicken dishes similar to this platter of golden, baked drumsticks. Look for garam masala where Indian spices are sold, or make your own (see chapter 12 for the recipe).

1/4 TEASPOON SAFFRON THREADS

1 TABLESPOON BOILING WATER

6 CLOVES GARLIC

2 INCHES GINGER, PEELED AND THICKLY SLICED

1/3 CUP FRESH LEMON JUICE

1 TABLESPOON GROUND HALF-SHARP PAPRIKA (OR MIX SWEET PAPRIKA WITH GROUND CHILE)

1 1/2 TEASPOONS SALT

1 TABLESPOON GARAM MASALA

4 POUNDS DRUMSTICKS OR OTHER CHICKEN PIECES

① Crumble the saffron into the water. Let soak 15 minutes.

② In the work bowl of a hand blender or food processor, combine the garlic, ginger, lemon juice, paprika, salt, and garam masala. Add the saffron liquid and pulse until blended.

③ Rub the spice mixture over the chicken pieces. Marinate, refrigerated, 1 hour to overnight.

④ Heat oven to 400 degrees. Arrange chicken pieces in a single layer in a baking dish.

Cook about 30 minutes, turning halfway through, or until the inside is done and the outside is golden and crispy. Serve hot.

Boneless Breasts for a Crowd

SERVES 6 TO 8 This recipe uses jumbo packs of boneless, skinless breasts, which seem to go on sale every other week. Most packs contain at least 6 huge and sometimes up to 8 average-size split breasts. A quick swirl in the marinade and a fast hot grill are all you need to cook up enough tasty meat to serve a crowd—but the real key to deep flavor is scoring with a sharp knife (see chapter 3).

This marinade is intensely seasoned, so the scored chicken needs only about 10 minutes of marinating time to be full of flavor. Opt for a very fruity or spicy olive oil, rather than a mild one. The "Italian Seasoning" called for here is just a convenient mix of dried herbs (rosemary, savory, sage, marjoram, and oregano, but no salt or processed flavorings) and is found in the spice aisle of supermarkets, under various brand names. Substitute your own blend of dried herbs if you like.

ABOUT 4 POUNDS BONELESS, SKINLESS CHICKEN BREAST HALVES

3 TABLESPOONS EXTRA-VIRGIN OLIVE OIL

1 TEASPOON ITALIAN SEASONING

2 LARGE CLOVES GARLIC, MINCED

1 TABLESPOON SOY SAUCE

① Score the chicken pieces on both sides (see chapter 3). Place in a baking dish or large bowl for marinating.

② Combine the remaining ingredients, crumbling the herbs in your palm to crush them before adding. Rub the chicken all over with the marinade, making sure to coat the scored areas well.

③ Grill over very high heat on both sides until the chicken is just cooked through; do not cook too long or the meat will dry out. Or pan fry in a large skillet (you may need to do two batches), over very high heat. Serve hot, at room temperature, or even cold.

Buckets of Oven-Fried Chicken

SERVES 6 TO 8 This easy recipe oven-bakes up to 6 pounds of chicken pieces in about an hour—with a coating as crisp and crunchy as if they were deep-fried. For 3 pounds of chicken, use half the ingredients and bake at the same temperature. Note that you'll need two baking sheets with low sides for this recipe. I've found the method described below to be the easiest, quickest, and least messy for dipping and breading all types of foods in large quantities.

1 1/2 CUPS CORN FLAKE CRUMBS

1 TEASPOON GRANULATED GARLIC

1 TEASPOON PAPRIKA

1/2 TEASPOON DRIED HERBS, SUCH AS THYME, OREGANO, BASIL, OR A MIX

1/2 TEASPOON SALT

1/2 CUP BUTTERMILK

5 TO 6 POUNDS MIXED CHICKEN PIECES, WITH OR WITHOUT SKIN OR BONE

① Position 2 racks evenly in the oven. Heat oven to 375 degrees. For easy cleanup, line 2 baking sheets with foil, then lightly coat with nonstick cooking spray.

② Dump the crumbs, garlic, paprika, dried herbs (crumbled), and salt into a small paper bag; shake to distribute. Pour the buttermilk into a large mixing bowl. Drop 4 or 5 pieces of chicken into the buttermilk and coat completely.

③ Shake out a single layer (about 1/4-inch deep) of crumbs from the paper bag into a baking dish. Shake the dish to distribute the crumbs evenly. Using tongs, place as many buttermilk-coated chicken pieces as will fit comfortably on the layer of crumbs. (Let any excess buttermilk drip back into the bowl before you add the chicken to the crumbs.)

④ Gently shake enough crumbs out of the bag to coat the tops of the pieces. Use a dry spoon to scoop up crumbs already in the pan to coat the sides of the pieces. With another dry set of tongs or a fork, pick up the crumb-coated pieces and arrange them top side up on one of the baking sheets.

⑤ Shake the crumb dish gently to redistribute the crumbs into a single layer, adding more crumbs if necessary. Repeat the coating process (dipping chicken in buttermilk, placing on crumbs, coating tops and sides with crumbs), until all chicken is breaded and arranged on the pans. If the bag runs out of crumbs, pour excess crumbs from the dish back into the bag. When all pieces are coated, discard excess crumbs (do not reuse for reasons of food safety).

⑥ For better browning, lightly spritz the tops of the chicken with nonstick cooking spray. Bake 20 minutes for boneless, skinless breasts; bake 45 to 60 minutes for pieces with bone, or until juices run clear. (Larger pieces and dark meat will take the most time.) For more even cooking, swap the positions of the baking sheets halfway through cooking. Serve hot or at room temperature.

Roasted Chicken Breasts for Sandwiches and Salads

MAKES 8 BREAST HALVES Sometimes you need a large quantity of moist, simply cooked chicken meat for salads, sandwiches, soups, and creative cookery. I discovered this pain-free, mess-free method in a *Barefoot Contessa* cookbook by Ina Garten and agree with her assessment—the meat is moist, flavorful, and perfect for absorbing other flavors. Be sure to leave the skin and bone on the pieces during cooking; they add flavor, and you can remove them later if desired. You may also serve these cooked pieces whole, as they are, with a spot of garlicky mayonnaise or a blue-cheese dressing on the side.

> 8 CHICKEN BREAST HALVES
> EXTRA-VIRGIN OLIVE OIL
> SALT AND FRESHLY GROUND PEPPER

① Heat the oven to 350 degrees.

continued

Roasted Chicken Breasts for Sandwiches and Salads *continued*

② Place the chicken on a baking sheet. Rub the pieces all over with olive oil. Generously salt and pepper. Roast 30 to 35 minutes, until just cooked through (don't overcook; the hot pieces will continue to cook after they come out of the oven).

③ When the pieces are cool enough to handle, shred or slice as needed, or refrigerate until ready to use.

Sesame-Seeded Teriyaki Wings

SERVES 6 AS AN ENTRÉE, OR 10 TO 12 AS AN APPETIZER Is there anything that Japanese teriyaki sauce doesn't taste good on? In Los Angeles and other cities, teriyaki stands teem with customers chowing down on burgers, steak sandwiches, grilled vegetables, chicken, and shrimp, all lightly charred and splashed with this classic Japanese sauce. Teriyaki wings, delightfully sticky and crunchy with sesame seeds (not traditional but good), are one of my favorite meals or appetizers. Frequent basting and even cooking at a moderate temperature produce a gorgeous mahogany glaze. Mirin, a Japanese sweet cooking wine, and sake make this dish authentic, but you can substitute honey and white wine, respectively.

Teriyaki Sauce (makes about 1 cup)

$1/2$ CUP MIRIN (OR HONEY)

$1/2$ CUP SAKE (OR WHITE WINE)

$1/2$ CUP SOY SAUCE

2 TABLESPOONS SUGAR

2 ($1/4$-INCH) SLICES FRESH GINGER

$4^1/2$ TO 5 POUNDS CHICKEN WINGS (20 TO 25 WINGS)

2 TABLESPOONS HONEY (OPTIONAL)

2 TABLESPOONS TOASTED SESAME SEEDS (OPTIONAL)

① Heat the teriyaki sauce ingredients in a small saucepan over medium-low heat. Stir to dissolve the sugar. Bring to a boil and simmer on low another 10 minutes to thicken the sauce. Cool. Remove ginger and discard. (Sauce may be stored sealed in a jar, refrigerated, up to 1 week.)

② To cook the wings whole, tuck the wing tips under the drummette to form a triangle. For smaller pieces (good for appetizers and snacks), cut the wings through their joints; you may leave the tips attached or cut them off and save them for stock. (I like to nibble on the crisp tips, so I leave them on.)

③ Marinate the chicken: Combine chicken with the teriyaki sauce; cover and refrigerate 4 hours or up to overnight. Turn the wings occasionally so all pieces absorb flavor evenly.

④ Heat the oven to 350 degrees. Line a baking sheet with foil for easy cleanup. Lightly spritz the foil with nonstick vegetable spray or grease with vegetable oil. Arrange the wings on the foil with the more attractive side facing down and the underside facing up. Mix 2 tablespoons of the leftover marinade with the honey and set aside.

⑤ Bake for 10 minutes, then remove the pan from the oven. Baste the underside with the marinade, and return the pan to the oven, rotating it front to back so the chicken cooks evenly. Cook 10 minutes. Remove the pan, baste, flip the pieces over so the presentation side now faces up. Baste the presentation side. Return the pan to the oven, rotating it again. Cook 10 more minutes. Baste the wings and rotate the pan. Cook 10 minutes.

⑥ Finally, remove the pan from the oven. Baste the presentation side once with the marinade, and again with the honey-marinade mixture. Sprinkle the sesame seeds on top and drizzle any remaining honey-marinade over the seeds. Bake another 5 minutes, or until wings are a deep mahogany color. Serve warm or at room temperature. As a meal, these wings pair well with rice and a cucumber salad. Or serve as an appetizer or snack.

Japan

Japan is actually four large islands and thousands of smaller ones, characterized by mountains, lush forests, and heavy rainfall. With so little land, agriculture and livestock are limited, and chicken (wakadori, chikin) is quite popular. Fish dominates, and dried bonito (tuna) often anchors other flavors in broths, stews, and sauces, as does miso (fermented soybean paste).

Japanese cooking uses almost no spices. Instead, the emphasis is on the pure, clean flavors of principal ingredients. A few condiments add contrast, such as shichimi togarashi (seven-pepper spice) and furikake (seaweed flakes, sesame seeds, and bonito). In cooking, mirin, a sweet wine, is the preferred sweetener, while sake is comparable to dry white wine. Some vegetables such as cucumber are served raw, but most are pickled, preserved, simmered, or deep-fried in batter. Root vegetables like carrots, burdock root, daikon radish, and yams are common. Mushrooms range from the fairy-sized enoki to fresh and dried shiitake, to autumn's pine-scented matsutake. The seemingly un-Japanese batter-fried foods of tempura and pork and chicken cutlets were influences of Portuguese and Dutch traders.

Rice is the main grain, but noodles are also popular. Udon (wheat noodles) and mung bean noodles are served in soups, while soba, or buckwheat noodles, are commonly served cold, but these are not hard-and-fast delineations. Overall, dishes are simply prepared, but the combination of flavors, textures, and colors creates the elegance and variety that so typifies Japanese eating style.

bean thread noodles	lotus root	sansho
bonito flakes	matsutake mushrooms	seaweed
burdock	mirin	sesame seeds and oil
chestnuts	miso	shichimi
Chinese, or napa, cabbage	panko bread crumbs	shiitake mushrooms
cloud ear mushrooms	persimmon	soba (buckwheat noodles)
daikon	plum	soy sauce
dashi	quail eggs	sweet potato
eggplant	red beans	taro
ginger	rice	tofu
green onion	rice vinegar	udon (wheat noodles)
green tea	sake	wasabi

CHAPTER 6

Chicken Plus Six Ingredients (or Less!)

From pantry to table, these meals feature chicken and just a few select ingredients. Salt, pepper, and chicken aren't counted in the "six" components, but the few ingredients that join them are tossed together effortlessly to make meals that arc cxotic and worldly, without being complicated or time-consuming.

Want more Chicken Plus Six or Less recipes? Find them here:

Chapter 7
    Chicken in 5 Minutes' "Thyme"
    Herbed Bistro Chicken Breasts
    Parmesan-Crusted Chicken

Chapter 9
    Grilled Chicken in Minty Chutney
    Grilled Lemon-Dill Chicken

Chapter 10
    Basic Breaded Chicken Cutlets, or Scallopine

continued

Chapter 12
Chicken Wontons
Fried Chicken Drummettes with Hot Pomegranate Honey
Rumaki
Napa-Hazelnut Chicken Salad

Chicken in Saffron Cream Sauce

SERVES 2 TO 4   Serve this "chicken plus three ingredients" recipe over buttered egg noodles or rice. If you want to stretch the number of servings, increase the amount of pasta or rice. For more sauce, add extra chicken and cream, and don't reduce the mixture quite as much.

$1/2$ CUP CHICKEN STOCK OR CANNED LOW-SODIUM BROTH

$1/4$ TEASPOON SAFFRON THREADS

1 CUP HEAVY CREAM

$1^1/2$ TO 2 CUPS SHREDDED, COOKED CHICKEN MEAT

① Over high heat, bring the chicken stock to a boil in a saucepan. Crush the saffron threads in your palm and crumble them into the stock. Gently boil the stock for 2 to 3 minutes. Stir in the cream and bring the mixture back up to a boil.

② Reduce the heat to medium low. Simmer until the sauce reduces to $2/3$ cup, about 8 to 10 minutes. Stir in the chicken meat and cook until heated through. Serve over noodles or steamed rice.

Crispy Comino Chicken Wings

SERVES 3 TO 4 AS A LIGHT MEAL, OR 4 TO 6 AS A SNACK Finger lickin' great! Golden, slightly crisp, and perfect as snacks or a light main course, these chicken wings can be addictive. They taste as good cold as they do hot out of the oven. Serve them instead of fried chicken or as picnic fare. With a texture similar to that of Buffalo Chicken Wings, these treats are well-spiced with garlic, cumin, and paprika without being fiery hot.

Note: You can double the recipe and bake on two trays.

1 TEASPOON GRANULATED GARLIC

1 TEASPOON GROUND CUMIN (COMINO)

1/2 TEASPOON DRIED OREGANO, PREFERABLY MEXICAN, CRUSHED

1/4 TEASPOON PAPRIKA

1/2 TEASPOON SALT

2 POUNDS CHICKEN WINGS (ABOUT 10)

1 TO 2 TABLESPOONS CANOLA OIL

① Heat the oven to 425 degrees. Line a baking sheet with foil for easy cleanup. Mix together the garlic, cumin, oregano, paprika, and salt in a small bowl.

② To prepare the wings, cut the drummette section off each wing. Leave the wing tips attached to the middle wing section. (Some folks prefer to cut away and discard the wing tips, but I like the way they get crisp in this recipe.) Or cook the wings whole by simply folding the wing tip under the drummette section to form a triangle.

③ Pour 1 tablespoon oil onto the baking sheet. Rub the wing pieces with the oil, coating thoroughly, and adding up to 1 more tablespoon oil if needed. Arrange the pieces on the baking sheet in a single layer but not touching. Sprinkle the spice mixture on the wings and rub in thoroughly.

④ You can bake the pieces immediately, or allow them to rest for up to 30 minutes before cooking. Bake 20 minutes. Flip the pieces over and bake another 20 to 25 minutes. They should be slightly crisp and golden on the outside. Serve hot or at room temperature.

Mediterranean and Iberian Europe

The countries of the coastal Mediterranean and the Iberian Peninsula—Italy, southern France, Spain, Portugal, and the Basque—have FlavorPrints that differ not so much in the ingredients used, but in the ways they are combined, or the degree to which certain ingredients dominate all other flavors. Every country uses garlic, for instance, but the closer you get to sunshine and the sea, as in Provence, the more garlic you'll taste.

Olive oil and olives dominate southern pots, while butter is the favorite northern fat, even in Italy. Southern regions combine garlic with anchovies and parsley. Basil appears mostly in Italy and France, while sweet and hot peppers and paprika season Spanish and Portuguese dishes. Italians thrive on pasta and risotto. Spaniards enjoy sherry, ham, and tapas (small appetizers). Provençal French specialize in a multitude of fresh herbs and vegetables. Portuguese season foods with cilantro, parsley, vinegar, dry wines, and incendiary piripiri peppers.

almonds
anchovy
asparagus
bacon and pancetta
capers
eggplant
garlic
ham (serrano,
  prosciutto)
liqueurs
mushrooms
olives and olive oil
onion
paprika
pasta

pâtés
peppers
potato
rice
saffron
salt cod
sardines
shallot
tomato
variety meats
wines and fortified
  wines

Dairy: butter, cream,
  cheese

Fresh and
  dried herbs:
basil
bay leaf
dill
lavender
oregano
marjoram
parsley
rosemary
sage
tarragon
thyme

Fingerling and Rosemary-Smoked Chicken Hash

SERVES 3 TO 4 Delicate fingerling potatoes have such a lovely flavor, I hate to overspice them. They meld especially well with just a few fresh herbs. This simple but upscale hash (great for dinner, breakfast, or lunch) puts leftover Rosemary-Smoked Chicken Halves (also in this chapter) to good use in an easy meal morph. The chicken meat is fried until crisp with potatoes, shallots, and bell pepper, then finished with a light touch of earthy truffle oil. You may substitute other cooked chicken meat (half-a-bird's worth) and use new red potatoes or Yukon Golds instead of fingerlings. I find that corn oil harmonizes sweetly with potatoes, but canola or vegetable oil work fine, too.

1¹/₄ POUNDS FINGERLING POTATOES, SCRUBBED

SALT

1 ROSEMARY-SMOKED CHICKEN HALF (SEE RECIPE IN THIS CHAPTER)

3 TABLESPOONS CORN OIL

8 LARGE SHALLOTS (ABOUT 6 OUNCES), PEELED AND THINLY SLICED

1 TEASPOON FRESH THYME LEAVES (OR OTHER FRESH HERB)

¹/₂ GREEN BELL PEPPER, DICED

1 TEASPOON TRUFFLE OIL (OPTIONAL)

FRESHLY GROUND PEPPER

① Cook the potatoes whole or halved: If necessary, cut the potatoes so they're all of uniform size. Place the potatoes and 1 teaspoon salt in a pot. Pour in just enough water to cover, and bring to a boil over high heat. Lower the heat and simmer until potatoes are just tender enough to be pierced with a fork, about 15 minutes for small to medium fingerlings. Drain and rinse with cold water. Let the potatoes dry thoroughly before frying. Slice the potatoes into bite-size rounds or chunks, about ¹/₂ inch thick.

② Remove the cooked meat from the chicken half. Dice into pieces the same size as the cut-up potatoes.

continued

Fingerling and Rosemary-Smoked Chicken Hash *continued*

③ Heat 2 tablespoons corn oil on medium high in a large nonstick skillet. Brown the potatoes, shallots, and thyme, cooking for about 10 minutes and stirring only occasionally, to encourage crisp edges. Remove the mixture from the pan.

④ Pour the remaining 1 tablespoon corn oil into the pan and turn the heat to high. When the oil is hot, stir in the chicken and bell pepper. Cook 2 to 3 minutes to brown. Dump the thyme and cooked potato mixture into the pan. Pour in the truffle oil. Stir to mix. Cook until chicken and potatoes are nicely browned and a bit crisp on the edges, about 2 minutes. Season well with salt and pepper and serve.

Miso-Chicken Yakitori

SERVES 4 AS AN APPETIZER, OR 2 AS AN ENTRÉE Yakitori are the most addictive little Japanese skewers of grilled, seasoned chicken. Some versions of yakitori require the glaze to be cooked until thickened. In this version, the miso thickens, sweetens, and adds body to the sauce, eliminating the need to precook it before grilling. Miso is soybean paste that comes in several varieties, mirin is a sweet cooking wine, and both are found in Japanese or Asian markets. Miso is also sold in supermarkets, and you can substitute honey for the mirin if you like. Also, you'll need bamboo, wooden, or metal skewers for this dish. Be sure to soak bamboo and wooden skewers in water for 30 minutes before cooking to prevent them from burning.

3 TABLESPOONS WHITE MISO

3 TO 4 TABLESPOONS MIRIN (OR HONEY)

1 TABLESPOON SOY SAUCE

1½ POUNDS BONELESS, SKINLESS CHICKEN MEAT (PREFERABLY DARK MEAT)

Optional Vegetables

3 THICK GREEN ONIONS, GREEN AND WHITE PARTS CUT INTO 1-INCH LENGTHS

6 OUNCES CLEANED MUSHROOM CAPS (SUCH AS CRIMINI, SHIITAKE, OR BUTTON MUSHROOMS)

1 GREEN, RED, OR YELLOW BELL PEPPER, CUT INTO 1-INCH PIECES

① Combine the miso, 3 tablespoons of mirin or honey, and soy sauce in a mixing bowl. Taste—the mixture should be sweet and salty. If it's overly salty, however, add another tablespoon of mirin. If you're planning to cook vegetables, set aside 2 tablespoons of the marinade.

② Cut the chicken into 1-inch cubes. Dump into the bowl with the miso mixture and coat thoroughly. Cover and refrigerate for 3 to 5 hours.

③ Pat the chicken pieces dry. Loosely thread them onto skewers, leaving enough space in between the pieces for the heat to penetrate. To cook, heat a grill or broiler until very hot. Cook the yakitori fairly close to the heat source, turning and basting occasionally, until golden and cooked through. To cook vegetables, first coat the vegetables with the reserved marinade. Thread the vegetables in between the chicken pieces; grill or broil until chicken and vegetables are cooked through.

Moo-shu Chicken Wraps

MAKES 4 MOO-SHU ROLLS Here's another way to morph cooked chicken into an exotic new meal. This tasty four-ingredient recipe, a quick take on traditional Chinese moo-shu, literally comes together in minutes. You'll need a microwave oven, a microwave-safe dish, a cutting board, and a knife.

2 CUPS COOKED, SHREDDED CHICKEN MEAT (PREFERABLY DARK MEAT)

2 TABLESPOONS HOISIN SAUCE

2 CUPS FINELY SHREDDED NAPA CABBAGE

4 FLOUR TORTILLAS, HEATED (SEE METHOD BELOW)

2 GREEN ONIONS, GREEN AND WHITE PARTS CHOPPED

① In a microwave-safe bowl (such as a Pyrex® casserole with lid), toss the chicken meat with the hoisin sauce. Sprinkle the cabbage on top.

② Cover and microwave 1 minute on high. Stir the mixture. The chicken should be just heated through, and the cabbage slightly wilted but not yet limp. If the

continued

cabbage is too crunchy for your taste, microwave another 15 seconds or until the desired consistency is reached.

Note: The chicken and cabbage will release liquid as they heat, so avoid overcooking them.

③ Spoon the mixture into warm flour tortillas, sprinkle with chopped green onions, roll up, and enjoy.

Heating flour tortillas: Run your hand under the faucet and lightly dampen one side of each tortilla. Stack the tortillas on a microwave-safe plate (it helps to spritz nonstick spray in between each tortilla). Cover with another plate, inverted, and microwave 1 minute on high. Check to see if the tortillas are warm. If not, microwave for another minute, or until tortillas are soft, pliable, and warmed through.

Nutty Pounded Paillards

SERVES 4 Forget breading and frying to get a crunchy crust: These boneless, skin-less breasts are flattened thin (into what the French call "paillards"), and nut pieces are pounded directly into them. You don't really need to make a sauce, but I can't resist deglazing the pan to catch every luscious little bit. In the summer, these make great snacks and picnic items, served cold or at room temperature, with or without a sauce or garnish.

> 4 BONELESS, SKINLESS CHICKEN BREAST HALVES
>
> SALT AND FRESHLY GROUND PEPPER
>
> ABOUT 1/2 CUP COARSELY CHOPPED TOASTED HAZELNUTS, ALMONDS, OR PECANS
>
> 1 TEASPOON BUTTER

1 TEASPOON CANOLA OIL

¹⁄₃ CUP CHICKEN STOCK OR CANNED LOW-SODIUM CHICKEN BROTH

2 TABLESPOONS CHOPPED PARSLEY

① Pound the breasts until about ¹⁄₃ inch thick. Salt and pepper both sides of each breast.

② Spread 1 tablespoon or so of chopped nut pieces on the cutting board surface. Place a chicken breast on top. Pound lightly until nut pieces adhere to chicken breast surface. Repeat with the other side of the chicken breast. Set aside and continue with the remaining breasts.

③ Heat butter and oil in a large skillet until very hot. Add as many paillards as will fit in the pan without crowding. Cook on one side about 1 minute (the chicken should cook quickly enough to begin browning, without stewing in its own juices). Flip the paillards and cook until just cooked though. Place the cooked paillards on a platter and tent with foil to keep warm (or place in a low oven), until ready to serve. Repeat with any remaining paillards, adding more butter and oil as needed.

④ Remove the pan from the heat and pour in the chicken stock. Reduce slightly over high heat, scraping up any browned bits, to make a sauce. Serve the paillards drizzled with the sauce and garnished with chopped parsley.

One-Pot Chicken, Mushrooms, and Saffron Rice

SERVES 4 Though this recipe uses saffron and aromatic basmati rice, two common Indian ingredients, it isn't particularly Indian in flavor. In fact, it's more like a quick-and-easy Spanish paella or a South American arroz con pollo, which also feature rice, saffron, and chicken as the main players. Passport and pedigree aside, this particular

continued

One-Pot Chicken, Mushrooms, and Saffron Rice *continued*

one-pot dish captures what makes similar recipes so appealing—it's simple and satisfying. For a change of pace, sauté bell pepper, sausage, ham, tomato, olives, peas, or other ingredients with the onion.

3 CUPS CHICKEN STOCK OR CANNED LOW-SODIUM CHICKEN BROTH

GENEROUS PINCH SAFFRON THREADS

2 TABLESPOONS OLIVE OIL

1 LARGE ONION (ABOUT 7 OUNCES), DICED

8 OUNCES SLICED MUSHROOMS, ANY TYPE OR A MIX

1½ CUPS BASMATI RICE

SALT AND FRESHLY GROUND PEPPER

6 BONELESS, SKINLESS CHICKEN THIGHS (ABOUT 1½ POUNDS)

GARNISH: MINCED PARSLEY (OPTIONAL)

① In a small pot, bring the chicken stock just to a boil. Turn off the heat and crumble in the saffron.

② While the stock heats, warm the olive oil in a heavy, large skillet over medium-high heat. Cook the onion in the oil 2 to 3 minutes, until soft. Stir in the mushrooms and cook until they soften, another 3 to 5 minutes.

③ Stir the rice into the onion mixture until all grains are coated with oil. Toast 1 to 2 minutes on medium low, stirring occasionally.

④ Generously salt and pepper the chicken pieces. Nestle the chicken pieces into the rice. Pour in the hot saffron broth. Cover and cook on medium-low heat until the water is absorbed, the chicken cooked through, and the rice tender, about 20 minutes. Turn off the heat. Stir with a chopstick or fork. Cover and let steam another 10 to 15 minutes. Garnish with parsley and serve.

Pollo alla Diavola
"Devil-Style Chicken"

SERVES 4 Simplicity at its finest. In Italy, cooks may add crushed red pepper flakes, sage, or other herbs, and some recipes include mustard (a French influence), but lemon juice, olive oil, salt, and heaps of pepper ultimately define this dish—that and a crisp, grilled, deep brown skin. The spicy pepper is what makes it "devilish"—the more you use, the hotter it gets. Baste with fresh sage or rosemary sprigs for authenticity. Marinate for as little as 30 minutes or as long as overnight, but about 4 hours produces ideal flavor.

This recipe uses chicken pieces or halves, but traditionally, Italians season a whole spatchcocked chicken, then grill it outdoors or fry it in a heavy pan, weighted with a brick. (To spatchcock a chicken, see chapter 3.) Follow the marinating instructions below, then wrap a brick in foil, and grill the spatchcocked bird weighted down with the brick.

1 CHICKEN (3 TO 3^1/$_2$ POUNDS), IN PIECES OR HALVES

2^1/$_2$ TEASPOONS KOSHER SALT OR COARSELY-GROUND SEA SALT

2 TO 3 TABLESPOONS FRESH COARSELY-GROUND PEPPER, TO TASTE

^{1}/$_3$ CUP FRESH LEMON JUICE

^{1}/$_3$ CUP EXTRA-VIRGIN OLIVE OIL

GARNISH: LEMON WEDGES

① Rinse and dry the chicken pieces. Place the pieces in a nonreactive dish to marinate. Generously season chicken on all sides, pressing the coarse bits of salt and pepper into the flesh. Combine the lemon juice and olive oil. Coat the chicken well with the olive oil mixture. Cover and refrigerate about 4 hours, or from 30 minutes up to overnight.

② When ready to cook, prepare the grill or broiler. Cook on a medium-hot grill or broil, basting occasionally with the marinade, until cooked through. Chicken is done when skin is well browned and juices run clear. Serve garnished with lemon wedges.

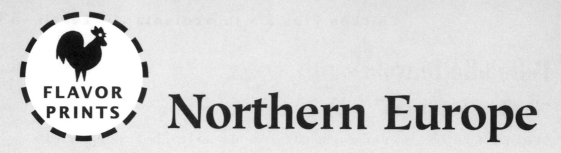

Northern Europe

Because of geography and climate, Northern European countries can be differentiated as mainly meat-based or fish-based, and the FlavorPrints vary accordingly. These cold-weather peoples specialize in preserved meats, fish, and pickles, put up in the fall to carry families through winter. Game is popular and may include wild boar, rabbit, deer, and duck. Pork reigns supreme in Germany and its neighboring countries and appears as ham, roasts, bacon, and sausages. Olive oil is replaced in these countries by rich butter, lard, and bacon fat. For the most part, onions, leeks, and chives supersede garlic. Sweet and sour together flavor many stews and roasts, and beer and wine are poured into the pot as well as the glass.

Meat-based—Northern France, Belgium, Holland, Austria, Germany, Switzerland

apple	fondue	rice (Dutch rijsttafel)
asparagus	garlic	rye breads
bacon	ham	sage
baguettes	horseradish	sauerkraut
bay leaf	liqueurs	sausages
beet	mayonnaise	tarragon
bell peppers	mushrooms	thyme
Belgian endive	mustard	vinegar
cabbage	nutmeg	wine
cardamom	onion	
cherry	parsley	Dairy: plenty—milk,
chocolate	pasta	cream, butter, goat
cinnamon	poppyseeds	cheeses, cow cheeses
cream	potato	
dark breads	pork	

Fish-based—Scandinavia

apple	cod	potato
berries	dill	salmon gravlax
cardamom	eel	sour cream
cinnamon	mackerel	

Roasted Thighs with Apples, Normandy Style

SERVES 4 Cooks in Normandy traditionally cook this dish on the stovetop, by browning the chicken pieces in a heavy pan and deglazing with a favorite French ingredient: heavy cream.

Browning chicken on the stove can be messy, so in this recipe, I roast the pieces in a scorching hot oven until they're a pale golden brown. I also lighten the richness of the dish: The Cognac (another French favorite) effectively carries the crisp, fresh flavors of apples and onions with just a touch of sugar, so there's no need for cream. Green peppercorns (the dried kind, not in brine) zip up the dish with their mild pungency, but the recipe also works well with black peppercorns. If you have fresh thyme, toss on a few sprigs as garnish before serving.

8 CHICKEN THIGHS (ABOUT 2 POUNDS)

3 TABLESPOONS COGNAC

1¹/₂ TEASPOONS SUGAR

2 GRANNY SMITH APPLES

1 SMALL TO MEDIUM ONION

COARSE SEA OR KOSHER SALT

COARSELY GROUND GREEN OR BLACK PEPPERCORNS

GARNISH: FRESH THYME SPRIGS (OPTIONAL)

① Place a rack in the center of the oven. Heat the oven to 500 degrees. Rinse the thighs and pat dry. Trim any excess flaps of skin and fat from the thighs.

② Pour the Cognac and ¹/₂ teaspoon sugar into a mixing bowl. Peel, core, and dice the apples. Toss them into the Cognac bowl as you go, and stir them to coat. (This prevents them from darkening.) Dice the onion and stir into the apples.

③ Arrange the chicken skin side up in a roasting pan or large baking dish (13 x 8 x 2-inches or equivalent). Make sure the pieces aren't touching. Generously season the surface with coarsely ground salt and peppercorns.

continued

Roasted Thighs with Apples, Normandy Style *continued*

④ Roast 10 minutes. Flip the pieces over. Season this side with more salt and pepper. Roast 10 more minutes.

⑤ Flip the pieces over (skin side up again). Nestle the apple-onion mixture between the pieces. Sprinkle another $1/2$ teaspoon of sugar over the apples. Roast another 10 minutes.

⑥ Stir the apple-onion mixture, keeping it between the thighs (not on top of them). Sprinkle the remaining $1/2$ teaspoon sugar over the apples. Roast a final 5 minutes, until chicken is cooked through. The mixture will give off juices and that yield a lovely sauce with apple bits for texture.

⑦ To serve, remove the chicken from the pan. Stir the apples and collected juices together. Serve the chicken pieces with some of the apple mixture spooned over or under them. Garnish with fresh thyme.

Rosemary-Smoked Chicken Halves

SERVES 4 If you grow your own rosemary bushes, you're in luck, but even a small bunch of fresh rosemary sprigs from the market will work in this recipe. Soak the rosemary branches or sprigs in water beforehand to keep them from flaming. (Weight the branches down with a plate if they insist on floating.) Rosemary is an evergreen bush rich in natural oils, and if not presoaked, it will ignite in the same way that dry trees do in forest fires.

I typically smoke the chicken on a gas grill with a lid, an upper rack, and two burners, so I can control the heat more easily. Whether you use a charcoal or gas grill, you'll need to set aside two cooking areas—one with direct heat for the initial smoking process, and one with indirect heat to cook the chicken through slowly. I often smoke red potatoes, eggplant, and other vegetables at the same time on their own bed of rosemary and finish cooking them with the chicken over indirect heat.

8 TO 10 SPRIGS FRESH ROSEMARY (6 TO 8 INCHES LONG)

3 CLOVES GARLIC, FINELY CHOPPED

3 TABLESPOONS EXTRA-VIRGIN OLIVE OIL

1 (4-POUND) CHICKEN, SPLIT INTO 2 HALVES

COARSE SEA OR KOSHER SALT AND FRESHLY GROUND PEPPER

① Soak the rosemary in water for at least 30 minutes. Drain just before using.

② While the rosemary soaks, mix together the garlic and olive oil in a pan or baking dish large enough to hold the chicken halves. Set the halves on top. Generously season the chicken on all sides with salt and pepper. Rub the garlic and oil mixture all over the chicken to coat. (You can do this in advance, from 30 minutes to overnight; refrigerate if marinating for longer than 1 hour.)

③ Next, heat up a gas or charcoal grill with a lid, keeping the lid closed to retain the heat. Bring one area to medium-low to low heat, and set aside another area for indirect heat. After the rosemary is consumed on the hot side, you'll need to finish cooking the chicken over indirect heat.

④ Using tongs, remove the rosemary from the water and arrange into two loose beds on top of the grilling rack, over direct heat. Immediately place the chicken halves, skin side up, directly on the rosemary beds. Cover the grill and let the rosemary smoke for about 10 minutes. If you notice any flare-ups of the rosemary or chicken, open the lid and adjust as needed.

⑤ After about 10 minutes, most of the rosemary will be blackened and burned away. Move the chicken to indirect heat, on the same grill rack or a higher rack, and close the lid. Let any remaining green rosemary continue to smoke over direct medium-low heat.

⑥ Continue to cook the chicken, with the lid closed, until done. After 10 minutes, baste the halves with the residual oil and garlic mixture, and flip them so they're skin side down. Turn them over again after another 10 to 15 minutes, and keep turning and cooking as needed until the skin is golden and the meat cooked through evenly. From start to finish (smoking to final cooking), the halves will take

continued

Rosemary-Smoked Chicken Halves *continued*

about 50 to 60 minutes. Serve hot or room temperature. Leftovers make delicious sandwiches and salads, and can be morphed into Fingerling and Rosemary-Smoked Chicken Hash (earlier in this chapter).

Saffron Poached Chicken

SERVES 4 Moist, succulent chicken breasts, infused with saffron's golden hues and elegant flavor, come together here almost effortlessly. Serve them with buttered egg noodles or rice drizzled with some of the broth, and a crisp green salad or steamed vegetable.

For an elegant entrée, reduce the broth and drizzle it over the warm chicken. You can also enrich the sauce by stirring in a tablespoon of butter or a splash of heavy cream. If desired, garnish with finely chopped parsley or cilantro, finely diced sweet red peppers, or freshly cracked peppercorns.

4 CHICKEN BREAST HALVES

1 (14-OUNCE) CAN LOW-SODIUM CHICKEN BROTH

2 TABLESPOONS DRY SHERRY

1 TABLESPOON EXTRA-VIRGIN OLIVE OIL

2 CLOVES GARLIC, MINCED

1 BAY LEAF

$1/8$ TEASPOON CRUSHED AND CRUMBLED SAFFRON THREADS

① Arrange the chicken breasts snugly in a small pot. Cover with chicken broth (if necessary, add a little water just to cover the breasts). Add the remaining ingredients. Cover, and bring to a boil over medium heat. Turn down heat and simmer 2 minutes.

② Move the pot off the heat and let stand 30 minutes. Remove the chicken from the broth before serving. Broth can be saved for soup or for cooking rice or reduced into a sauce. Serve chicken warm or cold.

Eastern Europe, Poland, and Russia

Onions, mushrooms, sour cream, yogurt, and paprika (originally from Turkey) dominate the overall FlavorPrint for this region. Horseradish, dill, parsley, bay leaves, and cloves are also common, but so are coriander, cinnamon, allspice, cardamom, ginger, basil, and other eastern seasonings, courtesy of caravans stopping in Georgia on their journeys between Baghdad and Venice. Grains—bulgur wheat, kasha, rye, and oats—come from the central steppes, which also support dairy herds. Potatoes, beets, barley, and corn grow on the fertile plains along the Danube. European chefs, with their French sauces, minced meats, pastries, asparagus, and potatoes, made a permanent impact, introduced by Russia's Peter the Great. The Black Sea territories contribute a mix of eggplants, tomatoes, and peppers to the regional FlavorPrint.

bacon	cucumber	sausages
beans	dill	sorrel
bell peppers	eggplant	sour cream
breads	fennel	tarragon
buckwheat	garlic	tomato
cabbage	mushrooms	walnuts
caraway	onion	
caviar	paprika	Dairy: yogurt, sour
celery	potato	cream, cheese
chicken fat or pork lard	sauerkraut	

Ukrainian Portobellos and Garlic-Laced Livers

SERVES 4 From July through September, Ukrainian forests softly rumble with the gentle footsteps of mushroom gatherers. Throngs of them. Women, men, grandparents, and children from toddlers to teens—all take part in the hunt. It's practically a national sport, and most decidedly a culinary obsession.

continued

Ukrainian Portobellos and Garlic-Laced Livers *continued*

Ukrainians, and their Russian neighbors, go wild for wild mushrooms. Morels, chanterelles, and untold other varieties are plucked, picked, and plunked into baskets and buckets, before being carted off to the *dacha*, or summer cabin. Once in the kitchen, the earthy little fungi may be tossed into garlicky marinades; strung together and dried; baked in sour cream; fried in butter; or simmered into soups. They're cooked alone, as the main ingredient, or combined with cheese, yogurt, beef, or chicken.

Chicken livers in particular are naturally compatible with mushrooms. In this recipe, chicken livers are fried in butter and an extravagant amount of garlic. They're then mounded on meaty, grilled portobello mushrooms and served. Noodles are a good side dish, or better yet is a rustic, flavored bread—any kind will do: Sour, potato, rye, sesame, dill, flaxseed, onion, challah, and caraway are all fine picks for sopping up the garlicky mushroom juices.

Mushrooms

> 4 PORTOBELLO MUSHROOMS, CAPS ABOUT 5 INCHES IN DIAMETER (ABOUT 1 POUND)
>
> 2 TABLESPOONS MILD OLIVE OIL
>
> 1 TABLESPOON SOY SAUCE
>
> 1 CLOVE GARLIC, MINCED

Livers

> 2 TABLESPOONS BUTTER
>
> 2 TABLESPOONS MILD OLIVE OIL
>
> 5 LARGE CLOVES GARLIC, THINLY SLICED OR COARSELY CHOPPED
>
> 1 POUND CHICKEN LIVERS, TRIMMED AND PATTED DRY
>
> SALT AND FRESHLY GROUND PEPPER
>
> GARNISH: LEMON WEDGES AND CHOPPED PARSLEY (OPTIONAL)

Cook the mushrooms:

① Heat a grill or broiler until very hot. Pluck or cut the stems from the mushrooms. Coarsely chop the stems and set aside for cooking with the livers.

② Combine the olive oil, soy sauce, and garlic. Baste the mushroom caps on both sides. Grill or broil the mushrooms until just cooked, turning over halfway through. Set the caps gill side up on four plates or a serving platter. Tent with foil to keep warm.

Cook the livers:

① In a large skillet heat the butter and olive oil over medium-high heat. When the butter starts to foam, toss in the garlic. Stir and cook it about 30 seconds. Add the livers, salt, and pepper. Cook, stirring occasionally, until lightly brown on the edges but still pink in the center. Dump in the reserved chopped mushroom stems. Stir and cook until mushroom pieces are soft and chicken livers just cooked through. Taste and add more salt or pepper as needed.

② Spoon the livers and their pan juices on top of the mushroom caps and serve warm. If desired, garnish with lemon wedges and chopped parsley.

Holiday Shopping Sprees

If you're looking to stock up on or sample new spices and seasonings, a good time to shop at ethnic markets is just before a major holiday—not necessarily Christmas or Thanksgiving, but holidays celebrated by the cultures that frequent such markets. In the weeks before India's Diwali, or Festival of Lights, you can usually find great buys on saffron, masalas, dals, chutneys, mustard oil, ajowan, and seasonings you may have always wanted to try. To anticipate the best bargain times at Asian, Mexican, and other ethnic markets, find out when the most popular feasting holidays are held by searching the country pages on the Internet or looking in travel books.

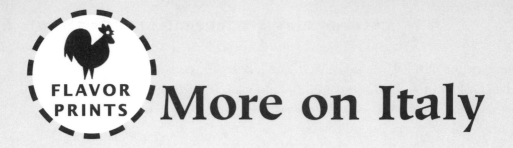

FLAVOR PRINTS More on Italy

Italy's fertile soil, sunny skies, and long coastline produce just about every ingredient a cook—and a chicken—could want. It's probably the world's favorite cuisine and, thus, deserves its own FlavorPrint.

The FlavorPrint starts with green herbs: oregano, rosemary, basil, bay leaves, fennel, parsley, marjoram, thyme, sage, tarragon. Other ingredients include garlic, onion, olive oil and olives, saffron, anchovies, capers, wine and balsamic vinegars, red and white wines, liqueurs, pasta, polenta, and risotto, among others.

Besides cayenne, Arab traders introduced warm spices like cinnamon, clove, allspice, nutmeg, and ginger, which may appear in savory sauces as well as sweets. Vegetables include tomatoes (used less commonly in the north), artichokes, eggplant, truffles and mushrooms, escarole, radicchio, endive, broccoli and broccoli rabe, cabbage, green beans, asparagus, zucchini and squash, spinach, and sweet and hot peppers. Legumes include cannellini beans, green peas, chickpeas, and fava beans. Chicken, chicken livers, and game birds are common, often cooked in combination with pork products like pancetta (Italian bacon), sausages, salami, and prosciutto. Wherever there's coastline, you'll find a vast array of seafood: squid, octopus, shellfish, tuna, sardines, swordfish, lobster, cod, and more.

Northern Italy reflects Swiss/Bavarian and French influences. It's the home of Italian fondue (fonduta), Chicken Marengo, cioppino fish stew, and Parmigiano-Reggiano, Gorgonzola, mascarpone, and Asiago cheeses. Butter is more commonly used in the north than olive oil. Southern Italy reflects Middle Eastern influences, with citrus fruits (lemons and oranges), raisins, hot chiles, mint, and pine nuts. Each of Italy's many central provinces reflects the same degree of diversity as those in the northern and southern regions, but in all cases, the hallmark of Italian cuisine is the use of fresh, local ingredients, cooked simply.

CHAPTER 7

Thirty-Minutes-or-Less Chicken Meals

Beat the midweek madness—make these meals in almost no time (most can be prepared in only twenty minutes). They're quick to fix, but they certainly don't skimp on flavor. You just get to enjoy 'em sooner.

Fast food never tasted so good. Whip up these other quick recipes:

Chapter 6
> Moo-shu Chicken Wraps
> Nutty Pounded Paillards

Chapter 10
> Basic Breaded Chicken Cutlets, or Scallopine

Chapter 12
> Chicken "Salad" in Rice Paper Rolls
> Napa-Hazelnut Chicken Salad
> Southeast Asian Chicken Salad with Spring Onion Oil
> Thai Minced Chicken Salad (Larb)
> Warm Chicken-Mushroom Medley on Mixed Greens

Chicken in 5 Minutes' "Thyme"

SERVES 2 For this recipe, slice boneless, skinless breasts very thin laterally, almost wafer-thin, into cutlets about 1/4 inch thick—a technique that's quicker than pounding them thin. This basic recipe is simple and flavorful and takes just minutes to prepare.

> 1 POUND WAFER-THIN CHICKEN CUTLETS
>
> 1¹/₂ TABLESPOONS FRESH LEMON JUICE
>
> 1¹/₂ TABLESPOONS SOY SAUCE
>
> 1¹/₂ TEASPOONS FRESH THYME LEAVES OR ¹/₂ TEASPOON DRIED THYME
>
> FRESHLY GROUND PEPPER
>
> 1 TEASPOON CANOLA OIL
>
> 1 TEASPOON OLIVE OIL

① Rub the chicken cutlets on both sides with the lemon juice and soy sauce. Crumble or chop the thyme and sprinkle it and the pepper over both sides of the cutlets. Marinate 10 minutes.

② Heat the oils in a large skillet over medium-high heat until very hot. Add the cutlets and brown for 1 to 2 minutes on each side until cooked through. Remove the cutlets to a serving platter. Quickly deglaze the pan with any leftover marinade and pour the resulting sauce over the cutlets. Add more pepper to taste, and serve.

Chicken, Scampi-Style

SERVES 3 TO 4 I've always felt that the classic Italian dish known as Shrimp Scampi is loved more for the garlicky, buttery pool of juices (so good sopped up with crusty bread) than for the shrimp itself. So in this dish, I've replaced the shrimp with skinless chicken thighs. The garlic simmers in the butter sauce while the chicken thighs cook on a hot grill or in a large nonstick skillet. In just 20 minutes, the dish is done, ready for those crusty pieces of bread.

6 CHICKEN THIGHS, WITHOUT SKIN

SALT AND FRESHLY GROUND PEPPER

1/2 TEASPOON GROUND DRIED SAGE OR POULTRY SEASONING

3 TABLESPOONS COGNAC OR BRANDY

2 TABLESPOONS EXTRA-VIRGIN OLIVE OIL

6 TO 8 CLOVES GARLIC

1 LEMON

1 CUP LOOSELY PACKED FRESH PARSLEY

2 TABLESPOONS BUTTER

① Heat the grill or set out a large skillet for frying the pieces.

② Rub the chicken pieces with salt, pepper, and sage. Marinate 5 minutes in 2 tablespoons Cognac and the olive oil.

③ While the chicken marinates, prepare the sauce ingredients: Mince the garlic. Halve the lemon. Squeeze 2 tablespoons juice from one lemon half, and cut the other half into 4 wedges for garnish. Finely chop the parsley.

④ When the grill is hot (or after heating the skillet over high heat), add the chicken pieces presentation side down, reserving the marinade. Cook until golden brown, about 7 minutes. Flip the pieces over and brown the other side until the pieces are cooked through (about 7 minutes more). After the initial browning, adjust the heat or move the pieces around so they cook evenly without burning. Remove the chicken to a platter when done.

⑤ While the chicken cooks, melt the butter in a small skillet over medium-low heat. Cook the garlic in the butter, stirring, until soft but not brown. Pour in the reserved marinade, remaining 1 tablespoon Cognac, and 2 tablespoons lemon juice. Bring to a boil. Turn off the heat and stir the parsley into the sauce. Pour the sauce over the chicken pieces, grind on more pepper, garnish with lemon wedges, and serve.

Herbed Bistro Chicken Breasts

SERVES 4 My husband could eat these five nights a week, as long as they're served with buttered egg noodles. I agree. These delicate pan-fried cutlets and their herby wine sauce taste even better with comforting noodles and a salad or steamed vegetable, but they're also good with rice, couscous, or crusty bread. It's a simple bistro-style meal that's always a winner.

Note: You can also use chicken pieces with bones and skin; just cook them longer, and for larger pieces, add a tad more liquid.

2 TEASPOONS GLOBAL GOURMET HERB SEASONING (CHAPTER 12)

2 TABLESPOONS ALL-PURPOSE FLOUR

$1/4$ TEASPOON SALT

4 BONELESS, SKINLESS CHICKEN BREAST HALVES

1 TABLESPOON CANOLA OIL

$1/4$ CUP DRY VERMOUTH (OR WHITE WINE)

2 TEASPOONS BUTTER

GARNISH: CHOPPED FRESH HERBS, SUCH AS PARSLEY OR CHIVES

① Combine Global Gourmet Herb Seasoning, flour, and salt in a bag (such as a clean, plastic produce bag). Shake to mix well. Toss in the chicken breasts and shake again, making sure all surfaces are coated.

② Heat the oil in a large skillet (preferably nonstick) over medium-high heat until very hot. Shake off excess coating from chicken. Arrange the chicken pieces in a single layer in the pan. Cook about 3 minutes, letting the bottom side brown slightly before turning. Cook another 2 to 3 minutes.

③ When the bottom side shows signs of browning, pour in the vermouth and quickly cover. Cook 3 to 5 minutes, until chicken is cooked through. Uncover and remove chicken to a platter. Stir the butter into the pan juices, scraping up any browned bits. Pour the juices over the chicken and serve. If desired, garnish with chopped fresh herbs, such as parsley or chives.

Parmesan-Crusted Chicken

SERVES 4 I'm addicted to these delicate, thin chicken pieces, pan-fried with a crisp, golden cheese crust. This recipe works best with small, thin pieces of chicken meat, such as boneless breast halves sliced laterally to create thin cutlets or scallopine. It's also a great way to turn small tidbits, such as chicken tenders, into irresistible crunchy nuggets, for snacks or finger food. The pieces are dipped in seasoned egg, then dredged in Parmesan and Romano cheese (no bread crumbs, just cheese). A quick sauté in olive oil, and they're done. Serve these crunchy gems alone or with Summer Fresh Tomato Sauce.

1 LARGE EGG

1/2 TEASPOON GRANULATED GARLIC

1/2 TEASPOON FRESHLY GROUND PEPPER

ABOUT 2 POUNDS THINLY SLICED, BONELESS, SKINLESS CHICKEN CUTLETS OR TIDBITS

ABOUT 2 CUPS GRATED PARMESAN OR ROMANO CHEESE, OR MIXTURE OF BOTH

1 TABLESPOON CANOLA OIL

1 TABLESPOON EXTRA-VIRGIN OLIVE OIL

OPTIONAL: SUMMER FRESH TOMATO SAUCE (SEE CHAPTER 12)

① Beat the egg lightly with 1 teaspoon water, the garlic, and pepper.

② Dip the chicken cutlets into the beaten egg to coat, draining off excess. Dredge them in the grated cheese to coat. Let rest 5 minutes before cooking.

③ Heat the oils in a large skillet over medium-high heat until hot but not quite smoking. Add the cutlets and cook until browned on one side, about 2 minutes. Turn the cutlets over and brown the other side until chicken is cooked through. The cheese crust should be golden, crisp, and crunchy. Cook the cutlets in batches as needed so as not to crowd the pan, adding more oil if necessary. Serve plain or with Summer Tomato Sauce on the side.

Pollo Rojo
A Pressure Cooker Recipe

SERVES 4 Serve with warm tortillas, rice, or hominy to absorb the rich, red juices of this quick chicken dish. Instead of making the Concentrated Red Chile Sauce from scratch, you can take a shortcut by reducing a canned red chile or enchilada sauce in a separate saucepan until very thick, before cooking with the chicken. The canned sauce won't taste as fresh or rich, but it does fine in a pinch.

> 4 CHICKEN BREAST HALVES, ON BONE BUT WITH SKIN REMOVED
>
> 2 CARROTS, CUT DIAGONALLY INTO 1-INCH LENGTHS
>
> 1 RIB CELERY, CUT DIAGONALLY INTO 1-INCH LENGTHS
>
> 1 CUP CONCENTRATED RED CHILE SAUCE (CHAPTER 12)
>
> GARNISH: CHOPPED FRESH CILANTRO

① Place the chicken, carrots, celery, and sauce in a pressure cooker. Stir until all ingredients are coated with the sauce. Lock the pressure cooker lid onto the pot.

② Over medium-high heat, bring to the pot to high pressure. Maintain the pressure for 5 minutes, then remove from heat. Use the natural release method (as described by your pressure cooker manufacturer). Serve the chicken, with the sauce and vegetables spooned on top, and garnish with cilantro.

Spicy Eggplant and Chicken with Sesame

SERVES 3 TO 4 This stir-fry is actually not very spicy, but lean a tad more heavily on the chili paste, and it will be. Japanese or Asian eggplants are best for this dish; they're sweet, tender, and rarely bitter, though you can use other types. (Also, the fresher the eggplant, the less bitter it's likely to be.) Many Chinese recipes call for dry sherry as a substitute for the amber-colored shao-hsing rice cooking wine, which early emigrants from China couldn't find here. You may use either, but if you can pick up a bottle of shao-hsing (also called shao-xing) in your local Chinese market, you'll find it has a light smokiness and full body that magically enriches the dish.

Tip: Prepare the chopped veggies first, before slicing the chicken, to keep your cutting board clean and help prevent cross-contamination.

Sauce

²/₃ CUP CHICKEN BROTH

3 TABLESPOONS HOISIN SAUCE

3 TABLESPOONS DISTILLED WHITE VINEGAR

1 TABLESPOON DRY SHERRY OR SHAO-HSING WINE

1 TABLESPOON SOY SAUCE

2 TEASPOONS BOTTLED ASIAN CHILI GARLIC SAUCE, OR TO TASTE

2 TEASPOONS SUGAR

1 TEASPOON TOASTED SESAME OIL

Thickener

1 TABLESPOON CORNSTARCH

1 TABLESPOON WATER

Eggplant, Chicken, and Aromatics

1 POUND CHINESE OR JAPANESE EGGPLANTS (ABOUT 3)

2 LARGE BONELESS, SKINLESS CHICKEN BREAST HALVES

1 TABLESPOON CORNSTARCH

¹/₂ CUP CANOLA OIL

1 HEAPING TABLESPOON MINCED GARLIC (ABOUT 3 LARGE CLOVES)

1 HEAPING TABLESPOON MINCED PEELED GINGER (ABOUT A 1-INCH PIECE)

2 GREEN ONIONS, GREEN AND WHITE PARTS SLICED DIAGONALLY INTO ¹/₂-INCH LENGTHS

1 TABLESPOON TOASTED SESAME SEEDS (CHAPTER 12)

① *Sauce:* Combine all sauce ingredients and set aside.

② *Thickener:* Stir the cornstarch and water together and set aside.

③ *Eggplant:* Slice the eggplants lengthwise into quarters, then slice these strips in half

continued

Spicy Eggplant and Chicken with Sesame *continued*

and then half again (each eggplant is now cut into 16 strips). Slice the strips on the diagonal into bite-size pieces, about 1½ inches in length.

④ *Chicken:* Slice the chicken into thin strips, then into bite-size pieces the same size as the eggplant. Toss with 1 tablespoon cornstarch. (This can be done as much as 3 hours in advance; store covered, refrigerated).

⑤ *To cook:* Heat ¼ cup of the canola oil in a wok or large skillet until hot, about 375 degrees. Quickly stir in the eggplant, which will soak up all the oil instantly. Let the eggplant cook undisturbed for 2 to 3 minutes until surfaces turn golden brown. Stir and brown another 2 minutes or until almost cooked through. Scoop out of the pan and set aside.

⑥ Pour in the remaining ¼ cup canola oil into the pan. Heat on high until hot. Dump in the garlic and ginger. Stir-fry a few seconds until aromatic and soft. Stir in the chicken. Stir-fry until almost cooked through but just pink in the center.

⑦ Pour in the sauce and eggplant. Stir-fry 2 to 3 minutes to blend flavors and cook chicken through. Stir the thickener mixture again to mix, then pour into the pan. Boil for 1 to 2 minutes to cook cornstarch through and thicken sauce. Stir in the green onions and sesame seeds. Serve hot, with cooked rice or Asian noodles.

Summer Chicken and Eggplant Parmigiana

SERVES 8 AS AN APPETIZER, OR 4 AS A MEAL WITH PASTA

This main course or appetizer is a fresh, warm-weather approach to classic Chicken and Eggplant Parmigiana. Chicken tenders are so small and delicate they don't need to be pounded thin like full breasts do, allowing you to skip a traditional step. They fry quickly in a coating of herbed bread crumbs and Parmesan cheese. Instead of oven-baked in a cooked sauce and mozzarella, they're broiled with a light layer of cheese, then served with thin slices of fried eggplant on a bed of Summer Fresh Tomato Sauce. The sauce is uncooked and can be made as much as four hours in advance, so plan accordingly, and the eggplant and tenders can be fried in advance, then warmed with a layer of cheese just before serving.

2 JAPANESE EGGPLANTS (10 OUNCES)

ABOUT 4 TABLESPOONS OLIVE OIL

3/4 CUP DRY ITALIAN SEASONED BREAD CRUMBS

1/4 CUP GRATED PARMESAN CHEESE OR ROMANO-PARMESAN CHEESE MIX

SALT AND FRESHLY GROUND PEPPER

1 POUND CHICKEN TENDERS

ALL-PURPOSE FLOUR FOR DREDGING

ABOUT 2 TABLESPOONS CANOLA OIL

2 EGGS, BEATEN WITH 2 TEASPOONS WATER

1/2 POUND SHREDDED CHEESE (EMMENTALER, PROVOLONE, OR MOZZARELLA) (ABOUT 1 3/4 CUP)

1 RECIPE SUMMER FRESH TOMATO SAUCE (CHAPTER 12)

① Cut the eggplants diagonally into oval slices about the same length as the tenders and 1/4 inch wide. Brush both sides with olive oil. Heat a skillet over medium-high heat. Brown the slices on both sides until the eggplant is just tender. Remove the eggplant to a plate. (You may need to cook the eggplant in 2 batches.

Note: You may also grill the eggplant slices in advance, instead of frying.

② Mix together the bread crumbs and Parmesan cheese. Salt and pepper the chicken tenders. Dredge the tenders in flour and shake off excess. Dip each piece into the egg mixture, draining off excess, then coat in the bread crumb mixture.

③ In the same skillet, heat 1 tablespoon olive oil and 1 tablespoon canola oil over medium-high heat. When a few bread crumbs sizzle in the pan, fry half the tenders,

continued

Summer Chicken and Eggplant Parmigiana *continued*

or as many will fit in the pan without crowding. Brown the tenders on both sides, about 1 minute per side, until cooked through and coating is crisp and golden brown. Remove from the pan and drain on paper towels. Repeat with the remaining tenders, adding more oil as needed.

④ While the tenders cook, or when you're ready to serve them, heat the broiler until very hot. Arrange the eggplant and tenders on a sheet pan. Sprinkle the shredded cheese over each piece and grind fresh pepper on top. Broil about 8 inches from the heat until the cheese melts.

⑤ To serve as an appetizer, spoon the Summer Fresh Tomato Sauce around the edges of a platter. Arrange the tenders and eggplant slices in the center, alternating and overlapping them in spoke pattern. Finish with a few spoonfuls of sauce in the center and serve. To make this into a full entrée, serve with cooked pasta tossed with olive oil, spooning the sauce, chicken, and eggplant on top.

Tipsy Chicken Paillards

SERVES 4 This can be an elegant dish for guests or a quick and easy weeknight meal. Who would turn down chicken, mushrooms, Swiss cheese, and wine? A side dish of egg noodles and a simple salad round out the meal.

You can adapt this basic paillard (French for thinly pounded cutlets) recipe any way you want. Try adding herbs, such as tarragon, basil, or rosemary. The liquid can be broth, juice, any type of wine, or even an exotic liqueur, such as Grand Marnier. For an Italian meal, top the paillards with a fresh tomato sauce and mozzarella, then broil until the cheese melts. Use bell peppers, paprika, and sour cream for a Hungarian touch. Use the paillards as a bed for holding a matchstick zucchini and carrot sauté.

Check to see what's lurking in the fridge, waiting to be used up. Got mustard? Toss it into the pan and you're ready for Chicken Dijon. Experiment!

4 BONELESS, SKINLESS CHICKEN BREAST HALVES

SALT AND FRESHLY GROUND PEPPER

3 TEASPOONS BUTTER

1 TEASPOON EXTRA-VIRGIN OLIVE OIL

3 TABLESPOONS GRATED SWISS CHEESE

2 TABLESPOONS FINELY CHOPPED ONION

1 CLOVE GARLIC, MINCED

4 OUNCES MUSHROOMS, SLICED

$1/4$ CUP MARSALA WINE

SPLASH OF COGNAC

GARNISH: MINCED PARSLEY OR CHIVES

① Pound the chicken breast halves to about $1/3$-inch thickness. Season each side with salt and pepper.

② Heat 1 teaspoon butter and the oil in a large skillet over high heat. Quickly add the chicken. Cook about 1 minute, then flip the breasts over to cook the other side. Sprinkle with the cheese, and cook 45 to 60 seconds on this side, until just cooked through. Remove from the heat and keep warm by either tenting with foil or placing the cooked breasts in a low oven. (If necessary, cook the chicken in batches, adding more butter and oil as needed.)

③ Melt the remaining 2 teaspoons butter in the same skillet over medium heat. Cook the onion and garlic until the onion turns slightly brown on the edges. Stir in the mushrooms and cook until soft but still a bit firm. Pour in the marsala wine, cooking until the sauce thickens slightly. Finally, splash in a bit of Cognac, cooking briefly to burn off the alcohol. Pour this sauce over the chicken. Garnish with minced herbs and serve.

Africa

Apart from North Africa, which has a completely different FlavorPrint, the African countries of Ethiopia, Nigeria, and South Africa and the nations of West Africa offer the continent's most distinctive and intriguing FlavorPrints. Rain is rare in all but a few areas. West Africa and Central Africa do enjoy rain, so rice is a staple crop. In dry areas, millet, sorghum, and corn take precedence. Stews stretch what little meat exists, with root vegetables like cassava and sweet potatoes filling up the iron pots. Peanuts, or "ground nuts" as they're called there, appear as protein and flavoring in many dishes. Lentils, peas, and beans enrich the meal, and chickens and their eggs are popular everywhere, or at least wherever they're able to be raised. While recipes can border on being bland, some of the hottest chile dishes on the planet are created by African cooks.

banana	date	palm oil
banana leaves	dried shrimp and fish	peanuts
beans	eggplant	peppers
black-eyed peas	garlic	periperi sauce
cardamom	ginger	pineapple
cassava	injera bread	plantain
chiles	lemon	rice
cinnamon	mango	sweet potato
coconut	melon seeds	tomato
corn	okra	yam

La Tunisia Chicken and Grilled Onions

Miso-Chicken Yakitori

Rustic Tortilla Soup

Bangladesh Drums

Chicken, Scampi-Style

Barbecued Korean Drums

Parmesan-Crusted Chicken

Barcelona Brown-Bag Chicken and Vegetables

CHAPTER 8

Chicken in a Bowl: Soups, Stocks, and Stews

Everyone knows chicken soup is good for what ails you. Serve it Asian-style with ginger and wontons. Sup on comforting winter warmers like chowder, gumbo, stews, and even the folk cure for the common cold: Jewish chicken soup with pleasantly plump matzo balls.

African Chicken and Peanut Stew

SERVES 4 TO 6 From Ghana to the Caribbean, there are as many variations of this dish as there are iron pots in Africa. It's traditionally made with chicken or lamb and is usually as hot as the midday equatorial sun. This version tames the heat to a mild bite, though you can always add more red pepper for extra heat. Redolent with warm spices, this stew echoes the complex flavors of a nutty curry, and a squeeze of fresh lemon juice balances the rich peanut taste. Serve with steamed basmati or other rice and a simple salad on the side.

This recipe produces a good deal of liquid, so it works as well for 2½ pounds to as much as 4 pounds of chicken. If the broth seems too thin, reduce it at a fast boil.

continued

African Chicken and Peanut Stew *continued*

I prefer to keep the skin on the white meat pieces to prevent them from drying out, though I do remove it from the thighs and dark meat.

$^1/_2$ TEASPOON SALT OR TO TASTE

ABOUT 3 POUNDS CHICKEN PIECES, WITH OR WITHOUT SKIN

1 TABLESPOON PEANUT, CANOLA, OR OTHER NEUTRAL OIL

$^1/_3$ CUP CREAMY PEANUT BUTTER (NATURAL, UNSWEETENED)

$1^3/_4$ CUPS CHICKEN STOCK OR CANNED LOW-SODIUM BROTH (PREFERABLY ROASTED CHICKEN BROTH)

1 ONION, CHOPPED

2 CLOVES GARLIC, MINCED

$^1/_2$ TEASPOON CURRY POWDER

$^1/_2$ TEASPOON GROUND CORIANDER

$^1/_2$ TEASPOON GROUND CUMIN

$^1/_2$ TO 1 TEASPOON RED PEPPER FLAKES, TO TASTE

$^1/_2$ TEASPOON GROUND GINGER

$^1/_4$ TEASPOON GROUND CINNAMON

1 (14.5-OUNCE) CAN DICED TOMATOES WITH JUICE

$^1/_2$ RED BELL PEPPER, CUT INTO THIN STRIPS

$^1/_2$ GREEN BELL PEPPER, CUT INTO THIN STRIPS

3 TABLESPOONS FRESH LEMON JUICE

Garnishes

$^1/_4$ CUP CHOPPED CILANTRO

$^1/_4$ CUP CHOPPED TOASTED PEANUTS (OPTIONAL)

① Salt the chicken. In a large heavy pot or Dutch oven, heat the oil on high. When hot, add the chicken pieces and brown on all sides. Remove the chicken from the pot and set aside.

② While the chicken browns, stir the peanut butter into the chicken broth until combined (mixture will be grainy until cooked). Set aside.

③ Cook the onion in the same pot, uncovered, over medium heat, until soft. Stir in the garlic, curry powder, coriander, cumin, and red pepper flakes. Cook 1 minute. Add the ginger, cinnamon, tomatoes with their juices, and the peanut butter–broth mixture. Mix the chicken back into the pot. Bring the liquid to a boil, then partially cover and simmer on low until the chicken is tender and cooked through, about 30 minutes, stirring occasionally.

④ Stir in the bell pepper strips and 2 tablespoons of the lemon juice. Boil rapidly, uncovered, for 3 to 5 minutes, just until the bell peppers soften but still retain some texture. Before serving, stir in the remaining 1 tablespoon lemon juice and taste to correct the seasonings (it may need more salt). Garnish with cilantro and peanuts. If desired, pass additional red pepper flakes on the side. Serve with cooked rice.

Basic Chicken Stock

MAKES ABOUT 2 QUARTS In this stock version, a whole chicken is used. After the first hour, you may remove the flavored meat from the carcass and reserve for another use, then return the carcass to the pot and continue cooking. Or just leave the whole bird in and let everything simmer for the full time.

1 (4- TO 5-POUND) WHOLE CHICKEN, WITHOUT GIBLETS

1 TABLESPOON SALT

2 MEDIUM ONIONS, QUARTERED

2 CARROTS, CHOPPED

2 RIBS CELERY, CHOPPED

continued

Basic Chicken Stock *continued*

    3 SPRIGS PARSLEY

    2 BAY LEAVES

    5 BLACK PEPPERCORNS

① Place all ingredients in a large pot. Fill with 3 quarts water or enough to cover the chicken. Bring the water almost to a boil over high heat. Reduce heat to low. Simmer partially covered, 1 hour, skimming off any foam or scum that rises.

② Remove the chicken and pick off the meat. Return carcass to the pot. Simmer uncovered another 1 to 1½ hours. (Or continue to simmer the whole bird, meat and all.)

③ When the stock is cool enough to work with, strain it through cheesecloth, discarding the carcass, herbs, and vegetables. Refrigerate, covered, for up to 3 days, or freeze for 6 months. Fat will congeal on the surface when cold, which actually helps to preserve the stock; remove and discard it before use.

Variation: Chicken Stock from Bones and Pieces

Instead of a whole chicken, substitute 5 to 6 pounds chicken wings, backs, ribs, and other bony parts (including feet if you can find them). Simmer for 2 hours.

Belgian Chicken Braised in Beer

SERVES 4 This is good, hearty food on a cold night. To serve six, just add more chicken pieces and adjust the seasonings accordingly. Use any full-flavored, slightly sweet, dark beer. My personal favorite for cooking and drinking is Samuel Smith's Nut Brown Ale; it's not too bitter and not too sweet, a rich and nutty blend. It's also easier to find in supermarkets than true Belgian ales. In this dish, the bacon adds salt and smokiness, while carrots and potatoes enrich the braising liquid with their own natural sweetness. A package of peeled baby carrots saves chopping time, and I leave potatoes in their jackets, unpeeled—the skin and the surface just below it is loaded with flavor and nutrients.

3 ONIONS (ABOUT 1¹/₂ POUNDS)

¹/₂ POUND PEELED BABY CARROTS OR CHOPPED, PEELED REGULAR CARROTS

1 RUSSET POTATO (ABOUT 12 OUNCES), UNPEELED OR PEELED

¹/₄ POUND SLICED BACON, IN ¹/₄- TO ¹/₂-INCH-WIDE PIECES

3 POUNDS CHICKEN PIECES, WITH OR WITHOUT SKIN

SALT AND FRESHLY GROUND PEPPER

1 TEASPOON SUGAR

1 TEASPOON DRIED THYME

2 TABLESPOONS ALL-PURPOSE FLOUR

1 BOTTLE (1 PINT, 2.7 OUNCES) SAMUEL SMITH'S NUT BROWN ALE OR OTHER DARK BEER (AMOUNT
     CAN BE APPROXIMATE)

2 TO 3 TABLESPOONS CIDER VINEGAR

2 TABLESPOONS CHOPPED PARSLEY

① Slice the onions into thin wedges, similar in width to the carrots for even cooking. Chop the potato into similar-size pieces. Set aside.

② In a Dutch oven over medium-high heat, cook the bacon until crisp; remove with a slotted spoon and drain on paper towels.

③ Season the chicken pieces with salt and pepper. Brown on all sides in the bacon fat. Remove the chicken and set aside. Spoon off all but 2 tablespoons of fat from the pot.

④ In the same pot over medium heat, cook the onions, carrots, potatoes, and sugar until the onions and carrots start to brown, about 10 to 15 minutes, stirring occasionally.

continued

Belgian Chicken Braised in Beer *continued*

⑤ Crumble in the thyme and stir in the flour. Allow the flour to cook through, about 2 minutes, stirring frequently. Stir in the beer and scrape up any browned bits from the bottom of the pot. Return the chicken to the pot and stir in 1/2 teaspoon salt.

⑥ Bring the liquid to a boil, then cover and simmer 30 minutes over low heat, or until chicken is just cooked through. Stir in 2 tablespoons of the vinegar and most of the bacon (reserve a few pieces for garnish). Bring to a boil and boil, uncovered, a minute or so until the mixture thickens slightly. Just before serving add the remaining tablespoon of vinegar and season with more salt and pepper as needed. Sprinkle the reserved bacon and parsley on top, and serve with hot, crusty bread.

Chilled Fire-Roasted Tomatillo and Grilled Chicken Soup

MAKES ABOUT 1 QUART; SERVES 4 AS A COOLING FIRST COURSE OR 2 AS A LIGHT MEAL As a base, chicken broth anchors the flavors in sauces and soups, in this case a cold soup. Tomatillos look like little green tomatoes (but they're not) wrapped in a papery husk, and are distantly related to the Cape gooseberry. Sold in Latino markets and some supermarkets, they have a tart lemon-apple flavor and a crisp texture. Raw, they're chopped into green salsas with lime and onion. Cooked tomatillos are often added to red salsas and Mexican moles, or stews. In this cold soup, they're fire-roasted on the grill to produce a rustic charring and sweet, smoky taste, blended with chicken broth, and accented with sour cream, lime juice, and chiles. As a garnish, raw, chopped tomatillos bring crunchy texture and tartness.

This quick-to-fix soup is an excellent way to use up leftover grilled or cooked chicken meat and makes a refreshing starter to a summer meal.

1 POUND TOMATILLOS (ABOUT 9 LARGE)

1 (14.5 OUNCE) CAN LOW-SODIUM CHICKEN BROTH

2 CLOVES GARLIC, PEELED

2 GREEN ONIONS, GREEN AND WHITE PARTS CUT INTO 1-INCH LENGTHS

1 TO 2 SERRANO CHILES, STEMMED AND SEEDED

3 TABLESPOONS FRESH LIME JUICE (ABOUT 3 LIMES), PLUS MORE AS NEEDED

2 TABLESPOONS SOUR CREAM

MEAT FROM 1 LARGE GRILLED CHICKEN BREAST HALF (OR OTHER COOKED CHICKEN)

SALT AND FRESHLY GROUND BLACK PEPPER

GARNISH: LIME WEDGES, CILANTRO SPRIGS (OPTIONAL)

① *To fire-roast the tomatillos:* Start heating a grill or broiler on high. Peel and remove the tomatillos' papery skins. Rinse well under running water until no longer sticky. Pat dry. Set aside 2 tomatillos for garnish. On the grill, roast the tomatillos over a high, hot flame until blackened on tops and bottoms and sides start to turn golden. If using a broiler, place the tomatillos on a pan and broil about 4 inches from the heat until blackened on top and bottom and sides start to brown. The insides should be soft, but it's okay if a few still have some firmness.

② Remove the tomatillos from the heat and plop into the work bowl of a food processor. Pour in half the can of broth. Pulse until finely chopped and mixture is almost puréed, but not quite—there should be some texture, with bits of blackened skin and seeds. Pour the tomatillo mixture into a 1-quart bowl.

③ In the same work bowl (don't rinse it out), pulse the garlic, green onions, and serrano chile (use 2 if you like it spicy) with a bit more broth, until the vegetables are finely chopped. Scrape the mixture into the tomatillo bowl. Stir in any remaining broth, the lime juice, and the sour cream. Cover and refrigerate until slightly chilled.

continued

Chilled Fire-Roasted Tomatillo and Grilled Chicken Soup *continued*

④ While the soup chills, finely chop the 2 reserved tomatillos for garnish. Shred or dice the chicken meat. Just before serving, taste for salt and pepper. Cold foods especially need more salt to bring out their flavor. To serve, ladle the soup into bowls, garnish with chopped tomatillo and chicken, and serve. If desired, pass some lime, cilantro sprigs, and quesadilla wedges or corn chips on the side.

Chunky Chicken, Corn, and Potato Chowder

SERVES 6 Large chicken chunks become the focus of this classic American chowder, enriched with the New World crops of potatoes and corn. A bounty of nutrition lies just under the skin of the potatoes. Peel them if you prefer, but with their jackets on, well-scrubbed unpeeled potatoes deliver much more flavor, texture, and visual interest than peeled potatoes.

Tip: Soups and stews profit from a last blast of flavor just before serving. In this case, extra thyme (fresh or dried) sprinkled on top refreshes the essence of thyme already simmered into the soup. Chopped celery leaves, with their fresh, slightly sharp accent, also act as tasty, pretty garnishes. The French often contrast the richness of cream soups and sauces with the tanginess of sorrel leaves—not always easy to come by, but if you have them, add them. A final light dusting of paprika colors the soup and brightens the flavors. Whether you're serving the soup freshly made or reheating it (some soups and stews taste even better the next day), be sure to sprinkle on a garnish or two as a flavor perk just before serving.

1/4-POUND SLAB BACON OR 4 THICK SLICES

1 ONION, CHOPPED

2 CLOVES GARLIC, MINCED

1 RIB CELERY, DICED

1/2 RED BELL PEPPER, DICED

31/2 CUPS CHICKEN STOCK OR CANNED LOW-SODIUM BROTH

11/2 POUNDS RUSSET POTATOES (ABOUT 2 LARGE), DICED

1 BAY LEAF

1 TEASPOON DRIED THYME

1/2 TEASPOON SUGAR

1/2 TEASPOON SALT

2 LARGE BONELESS, SKINLESS CHICKEN BREAST HALVES, CUT INTO 1-INCH CHUNKS

11/2 CUPS CORN KERNELS (FRESH, CANNED AND DRAINED, OR FROZEN)

1 CUP HEAVY CREAM

FRESHLY GROUND PEPPER

GARNISH: PAPRIKA, CHOPPED SORREL OR CELERY LEAVES (OPTIONAL)

① Chop the bacon into pieces about 1/3 inch wide. Heat a large, heavy pot over medium heat. Add the bacon and cook, stirring occasionally, until the bacon is crisp. Remove the bacon and set aside. Remove all but 2 to 3 tablespoons drippings from the pot.

② Add onion, garlic, celery, and bell pepper to the pot. Cook over medium heat, stirring occasionally, until onion is translucent, about 5 minutes. Add stock, potatoes, bay leaf, half the thyme (1/2 teaspoon), sugar, and salt. Cover and bring to a boil over high heat. Reduce heat and simmer, uncovered, 10 minutes.

continued

Chunky Chicken, Corn, and Potato Chowder *continued*

③ Stir in the chicken, corn, cream, cooked bacon, and pepper to taste. Simmer until chicken cooks through and potatoes are tender, about 10 minutes, stirring occasionally. Crumble in the remaining thyme. For best results, cover chowder and let stand off the flame for 30 to 60 minutes so the flavors can blend, or refrigerate overnight.

④ Reheat the chowder. Taste and adjust seasonings as needed. Serve hot, garnished with paprika. Sprinkle coarsely chopped sorrel leaves or celery leaves on top if desired.

Cock-a-Leekie

SERVES 4 This hearty Scottish chicken and leek soup takes the chill off cold winter or cool spring nights. Barley is a most pleasingly plump grain, absorbing enough liquid to triple in size. For a lighter soup, omit the barley or replace it with a lesser amount of cooked rice. Serve with warm crusty bread, such as whole wheat rolls.

2¹/₂ POUNDS CHICKEN PIECES, DARK AND LIGHT

¹/₂ CUP PEARL BARLEY

2 CARROTS, CUT INTO ¹/₂ INCH PIECES

1 RIB CELERY, CUT INTO ¹/₂ INCH PIECES

2 BAY LEAVES

¹/₄ TEASPOON DRIED THYME

2 TEASPOONS SALT

¹/₄ TEASPOON FRESHLY GROUND PEPPER, PREFERABLY WHITE PEPPER

4 LARGE LEEKS (ABOUT 2¹/₂ POUNDS)

3 TABLESPOONS CHOPPED PARSLEY

① Toss the chicken, barley, carrots, celery, bay leaves, thyme, salt, and pepper into a large pot. Add water to cover (about 1¹/₂ quarts). Bring to a boil over medium-high heat. Skim off any scum that rises to the top. Partially cover the pot, reduce the heat, and simmer 15 minutes.

② While the chicken simmers, rinse and trim the leeks, removing all dirt trapped in the layers (slice the leeks in half lengthwise and rinse the layers under running water). Chop the leeks into 1/2-inch pieces, including the white part and about 3 inches of the pale green part.

③ Stir the leeks into the pot. Bring the soup to a boil over high heat. Reduce the heat, partially cover, and simmer another 30 to 40 minutes, or until chicken and barley are cooked through.

④ Remove chicken pieces from the pot. When cool enough to handle, shred the meat; discard the skin and bones. Return the chicken meat to the pot with 2 tablespoons parsley. Reheat and simmer another 5 minutes. Serve hot with remaining parsley as a garnish on top.

Ginger-Wonton Soup with Spring Onion Oil

SERVES 4 In its simplest form—wontons and broth—this soup is wholesome and satisfying. With cabbage and shredded chicken, the soup becomes a meal in itself. But if you want to enhance either version, top with a spoonful of Spring Onion Oil, a Vietnamese staple. The nutty, charred bits of green onion fried in oil add sparkle to all sorts of dishes, and a jarful lasts two weeks in the fridge.

The recipe for Ginger-Poached Chicken and Broth is full of fresh flavors, and my husband and I always feel healthier just from eating it. Perhaps it's the ginger and green onions, the freshly cooked chicken, or the lack of preservatives or additives. It's the easiest way to prepare chicken for shredding into soup or salad that I know of, with the moistest, most flavorful results. Use it for making this recipe.

Note: When making wonton soup, don't be tempted to boil the wontons directly in the broth—you'll end up with an unpleasant, gooey mess. The texture turns out best if you first boil the wontons in water until they float, about 3 to 5 minutes. Drain them, then add them to the hot soup. If wontons are frozen, do not thaw before cooking; just plop them directly into the boiling water.

continued

Ginger-Wonton Soup with Spring Onion Oil *continued*

20 UNCOOKED WONTONS, FRESH OR FROZEN (CHICKEN WONTONS, CHAPTER 12)

4 CUPS CHICKEN BROTH FROM GINGER-POACHED CHICKEN AND BROTH (CHAPTER 4)

3 CUPS PACKED SHREDDED NAPA CABBAGE

1/2 TEASPOON TOASTED SESAME OIL

1 CUP SHREDDED COOKED CHICKEN MEAT FROM GINGER-POACHED CHICKEN AND BROTH
    (CHAPTER 4)

1 GREEN ONION, WHITE AND GREEN PARTS DIAGONALLY SLICED

1 TABLESPOON TOASTED SESAME SEEDS (CHAPTER 12)

OPTIONAL: SPRING ONION OIL (CHAPTER 12)

① Bring a large pot of salted water to a boil. Add the wontons and simmer gently until tender and cooked through. Using a slotted spoon, remove the wontons and evenly distribute them in 4 large soup bowls, or place in 1 large serving bowl.

② Heat the chicken broth until boiling. Stir in the cabbage and sesame oil. Cook until the cabbage softens, about 1 minute.

③ Ladle the soup evenly into the bowls of wontons. Garnish each bowl with equal amounts of the chicken, green onion, and sesame seed. Top each bowl with a spoonful of Spring Onion Oil, including some of the charred green onion bits. Serve hot.

Gumbo Ya-Ya

SERVES 4 My brother-in-law is a gumbo freak. If it's on the menu, he'll order it. He's had every kind of gumbo imaginable—crawfish, seafood, sausage, duck, and 'gator—but he always returns to chicken gumbo, his favorite. Of course, every Southern cook makes gumbo (chicken or otherwise) differently, and whatever's in the fridge or the pantry can be the deciding influence on how that day's gumbo will taste.

This basic chicken gumbo recipe stands on its own and is simpler to make than many gumbos, but don't be shy about adapting the dish to your own fixin's. Make it as spicy and flavorful as you like. Homemade broth adds richness, as does cooked dark meat chicken. Toss in a few more herbs, like oregano or marjoram, and more garlic for a robust gumbo. Using precooked chicken and sausage saves time, but you can cook these ingredients up fresh if you like.

The key flavoring agent in any gumbo, though, is the roux—it should be chocolate brown without being burned. Roux is a French term for flour and fat cooked slowly together (stirring constantly) until deeply flavored but not burned. If the roux burns, throw it out and start anew; it will only make the gumbo taste bitter.

Even though the word *gumbo* means okra in an African dialect, this is one of many gumbos that don't contain it. Instead of okra, this version uses filé powder (ground sassafras) to thicken the stew, a local ingredient introduced to Louisiana settlers by Native Americans. Look for it in supermarket spice aisles.

1/4 CUP VEGETABLE OIL

1/4 CUP ALL-PURPOSE FLOUR

2 MEDIUM ONIONS, DICED

2 RIBS CELERY, DICED, PLUS LEAVES FOR GARNISH

1 SMALL GREEN BELL PEPPER, DICED

1 BAY LEAF

1/2 POUND ANDOUILLE OR KIELBASA SAUSAGE (FULLY COOKED), CUT INTO 1/2-INCH SLICES

1 3/4 CUPS CHICKEN STOCK OR LOW-SODIUM CANNED BROTH

2 CUPS DICED COOKED CHICKEN

2 TEASPOONS FILÉ POWDER

SALT AND FRESHLY GROUND PEPPER

LOUISIANA-STYLE HOT SAUCE TO TASTE

① To make the roux, you need to stir constantly: In a heavy-bottom pan or pot, heat the oil over medium heat. Slowly stir in the flour (a wooden spatula works well), working out any lumps or clumps. Turn the heat to low and continue to stir the roux until it turns a dark, chocolate brown, about 35 to 45 minutes.

② When the roux is ready, toss in the onions, celery (not the leaves), green pepper, bay leaf, and sausage. Stir and cook over medium heat until the vegetables are cooked through.

③ Mix in the stock, stirring until the roux binds smoothly with the liquid. Simmer for about 20 minutes. Mix in the chicken and filé powder, and add salt and pepper to

continued

Gumbo Ya-Ya *continued*

taste. Simmer another 10 minutes, without boiling. Serve in bowls with rice and hefty doses of Louisiana-style hot sauce.

Hungarian Chicken Paprikás

SERVES 4 Chicken Paprikás has been eaten in Hungary and at the finer tables of the world since at least the early nineteenth century, making it a true culinary classic. It's hard to improve upon such a timeless recipe, and the only other common variation of this dish is to serve it without sour cream. At that point, it's still a classic, for it becomes Chicken Pörkolt, an equally famous paprika-based dish and one of the most traditional of Hungarian stews. Regardless of whether you serve the chicken as a "paprikás" or a "pörkolt," either dish will seem naked without a platter of egg dumplings or egg noodles on the side. As a further homage to tradition, serve the meal with a pickled or fresh cabbage salad.

1 TABLESPOON LARD OR BUTTER

1 ONION, THINLY SLICED

1 RED BELL PEPPER, CUT INTO STRIPS

1 GREEN BELL PEPPER, CUT INTO STRIPS

2 TABLESPOONS SWEET HUNGARIAN PAPRIKA

1/2 TEASPOON DRIED MARJORAM, CRUMBLED

DASH CAYENNE

1 TEASPOON SALT

2 PEELED, SEEDED, CHOPPED TOMATOES (FRESH OR CANNED)

1 CUP CHICKEN STOCK OR CANNED LOW-SODIUM BROTH

1 CHICKEN, CUT INTO 8 PIECES (OR 3 TO 4 POUNDS CHICKEN PIECES)

2 TEASPOONS FLOUR

1/2 CUP SOUR CREAM

2 TABLESPOONS MINCED PARSLEY

① Heat the lard or butter in a large, heavy skillet over medium-high heat. Add the onion, pepper strips, paprika, marjoram, cayenne, and salt. Cook until the vegetables are slightly limp, about 3 minutes.

② Add the tomatoes and stock. Bring the mixture to a boil. Add the chicken pieces, spooning some of vegetables and sauce over each piece. Cover and simmer over low heat until the chicken is tender, about 45 minutes to 1 hour.

③ Spoon off the grease from the stew. Stir the flour into the sour cream and add to the chicken. Stir. Simmer 5 minutes, uncovered. (Or make the stew without the sour cream and flour mixture.) Serve the chicken pieces topped with the vegetables and gravy and sprinkled with minced parsley.

Jewish Matzo Ball Soup

SERVES 8 What would a book on chicken be without the ubiquitous and delicious Matzo Ball Soup? Every Jewish cook tweaks the basic matzo ball (*knaidlach*) recipe with his or her own techniques. Some lighten the mix with club soda or seltzer as the liquid; others fold in stiffly beaten egg whites. Minced parsley, dill, or grated carrot may be tossed into the matzo mix, or a pinch of powdered ginger. Georgian Jews sometimes add ground walnuts.

4 EGGS

1/4 CUP SCHMALTZ (RENDERED CHICKEN FAT) OR VEGETABLE OIL

1 TEASPOON SALT

FRESHLY GROUND BLACK PEPPER

1 CUP MATZO MEAL

1/4 CUP LIQUID (WATER, CHICKEN STOCK, CLUB SODA, OR SELTZER)

2 QUARTS HOMEMADE CHICKEN STOCK, HEATED TO BOILING

① Beat the eggs in a mixing bowl until combined. Beat in the schmaltz, salt and pepper, matzo meal, and the liquid. Refrigerate until chilled, at least 1 hour.

② Bring a large pot of salted water to a boil. While the water heats, dampen your hands and shape the mixture into 16 balls about 1 inch in diameter. Drop the balls into the boiling water. Cover and reduce the heat. Simmer 30 to 40 minutes until

continued

Jewish Matzo Ball Soup *continued*

tender, keeping the lid on the pot. Remove with a slotted spoon and serve in hot chicken stock.

Note: You may also simmer the matzo balls directly in the chicken stock, though they'll absorb so much of it as they cook that you'll end up with about half the stock.

Lemony Garlic Chicken and Broth

MAKES 4 COOKED BREASTS AND ABOUT 1 QUART BROTH

This variation of seasoned poached chicken lends itself well to Mediterranean, Latin, Middle Eastern, and African recipes. You can shred the chicken into the broth, with additions like pasta, rice, vegetables, and so on, to make a quick and satisfying garlicky soup with a slight lemon tang.

The chicken meat is moist and delicate, perfect for shredding into Napa-Hazelnut Chicken Salad (chapter 12), for filling tortillas or pita bread, or sliced to make exceptionally flavorful sandwiches. Use the broth wherever you would use chicken stock, such as for cooking rice or couscous, making gravy, or as a soup base. Chicken may also be skinned and reheated and served with salt, pepper, or a simple sauce made from the thickened, reduced broth.

4 CHICKEN BREAST HALVES, WITH SKIN AND BONE (3^1/$_2$ TO 4 POUNDS)

2 TEASPOONS SALT

JUICE FROM ^{1}/$_2$ LEMON

1 RIB CELERY, PREFERABLY WITH LEAVES, CUT INTO THIRDS

3 LARGE CLOVES GARLIC, COARSELY CHOPPED

1 LARGE OR 2 SMALL BAY LEAVES

① Fit the chicken pieces snugly into a pot just big enough to hold them, allowing for 1 to 2 inches of space above the chicken. Add the remaining ingredients and water to cover the chicken by ^{1}/$_2$ inch. Bring to a boil over medium heat.

② Cover, reduce the heat, and simmer 5 minutes. Turn off the heat and leave the chicken immersed in the broth for at least 30 minutes. Chicken will continue to cook gently in the hot broth. (Don't worry: The chicken meat won't overcook, even if you let it cool completely in the broth.) Refrigerate the chicken in the broth, which helps keep it moist, and discard the layer of fat that solidifies when chilled. Remove the bay leaves, garlic, and celery before serving. To serve, see the recipe introduction above.

Mexican Poached Chicken

MAKES 4 HALF-BREASTS AND ABOUT 4 CUPS BROTH
This poaching method produces moist, tender meat that stays juicy, with a delicate melt-in-your-mouth texture. Serve it with warm tortillas, or shredded into tacos, burritos, sandwiches, salads, and enchiladas. The cooked broth makes a delicious soup or stew.

4 LARGE CHICKEN BREAST HALVES (ON BONE, WITH SKIN)

3 GREEN ONIONS, GREEN AND WHITE PARTS CUT INTO 2-INCH LENGTHS

1 CARROT, CUT INTO 2-INCH LENGTHS

2$1/4$ TEASPOONS SALT

$1/2$ TEASPOON MEXICAN OREGANO

$1/2$ TEASPOON GROUND CUMIN

1 BAY LEAF

1 CLOVE GARLIC, CRUSHED AND SKIN REMOVED

① Place the chicken in a saucepan, fitting the pieces together snugly. Add the remaining ingredients. Just barely cover with water. Bring the water to a boil and remove any scum that rises to the surface. Cover and reduce the heat. Simmer 5 minutes.

② Let the mixture stand at least 30 minutes. Remove the fat and vegetables before using. (To remove the fat easily, refrigerate the broth and chicken until the fat hardens, then lift off.) Serve the chicken warm, with a bit of the juices, or shred into other dishes. Reserve the broth for soup, stew, or wherever a seasoned chicken stock is called for.

Mexico, Central America, and Southwestern United States

Two main cultures collided in Mexico and in her neighbors to the north and south: Native Indians, with their chiles, tomatoes, corn, tortillas, and beans; and the Spanish, with chicken, beef, pork, lard, cheese, and rice. Combine these ingredients with geographical influences and you have the essentials of this region's FlavorPrint. Chiles (some hot, some sweet and mild) are combined with tomatoes or lime (sometimes both) and may be augmented with some combination of garlic, onion, cumin, cinnamon, oregano, and saffron. Cilantro leads the fresh green herbs. The Yucatan Peninsula reflects more coastal flavors common to the Caribbean, including cooking in leaves, sour orange, and achiote.

achiote (annatto)	hominy	pumpkin seeds
avocado	huitlacoche	rice
banana and leaves	jicama	salsas
black beans	lard	sesame seeds
bolillos (rolls)	lemon	squashes
chiles	lime	tamarind
chocolate/cacao	mango	tomatillo
cilantro	masa harina	tomato
cinnamon	moles	tortillas (corn and
corn	nopales (cactus pads)	wheat flour)
cumin	olives	turkey
dried shrimp	onion	vanilla
epazote	orange	vinegar
garlic	oregano	
green onion	papaya	Dairy: cheese, crema,
guava	pinto beans	sour cream

Rustic Tortilla Soup

SERVES 4 I love all kinds of soup, but my husband is a bit more picky. This, though, is the one soup he readily requests and enjoys to no end. No wonder, for this savory meal consists of boiling hot chicken broth, aromatic with cumin and chile and laced with lime, ladled over a mound of crisp fried tortillas, cheese, chicken, tomatoes, and avocado. The ingredients are just barely cooked by the hot broth, allowing their pure flavors and natural textures to be tasted distinctly from the rest of the soup.

This is a festive soup to serve to guests, and much of it can be done in advance. The raw ingredients can be chopped (preferably in large, coarse chunks) and set aside, then sprinkled into soup bowls just before serving. Be sure to bring the ingredients to room temperature before use. The chicken broth and its ingredients can be prepared the day before, then reheated before pouring into the bowls. Pass extra chips on the side to round out this satisfying meal in a bowl.

CORN TORTILLA CHIPS, ABOUT 4 LARGE HANDFULS OR MORE

2 CUPS SHREDDED CHEDDAR CHEESE

1 CUP COOKED CHICKEN MEAT, SHREDDED

2 ROMA TOMATOES, COARSELY CHOPPED

1 RIPE AVOCADO, PEELED AND COARSELY CHOPPED

1 TABLESPOON OLIVE OIL

1/2 ONION, SLICED INTO THIN RINGS

2 CLOVES GARLIC, MINCED

1 1/2 TEASPOONS GROUND CUMIN

1 TABLESPOON GROUND RED CHILE

2 CUPS CHICKEN STOCK OR CANNED LOW-SODIUM BROTH

2 LIMES, HALVED

2 GREEN ONIONS, GREEN AND WHITE PARTS CHOPPED

FRESH CILANTRO SPRIGS

① Before cooking the soup, prepare the soup bowls with the raw ingredients. In each of 4 deep bowls, place a handful of tortilla chips; you may use store-bought ones,

continued

Rustic Tortilla Soup *continued*

but the flavor is better if they are freshly fried. On top of the chips, place ¼ of each of the following ingredients, in this order: shredded cheese, chicken, tomatoes, and avocado.

② Heat the olive oil in a large saucepan over medium heat. Add the onion and cook until translucent. Add the garlic, cumin, and chile, and cook another 2 minutes. Pour in the chicken stock. When it is boiling hot, squeeze in the juice from the limes.

③ Ladle the chicken broth over the ingredients in each bowl. Top with green onions and sprigs of fresh cilantro and serve immediately; pass additional chips on the side.

Thai Hot 'n' Sour Chicken Soup
"Tom Yam Kai"

SERVES 2 AS A LIGHT MEAL, OR 4 AS A STARTER

This may be the most popular of all Thai soups. The broth is a potent blend of spicy chile heat, tart lime, and saltiness from the fish sauce. It's also very simple and quick to prepare and often is served with shrimp instead of chicken. Look for the lemongrass, galangal, kaffir lime leaves, fish sauce (*nam pla*), and straw mushrooms in Southeast Asian markets.

If you don't happen to have Thai chile paste, any chile paste can be used, such as Chinese chile-garlic paste, which is often sold in supermarkets. If you want to make a larger batch of this soup, increase the chile paste sparingly. A little goes a long way, and even if you double the other ingredients in the recipe, you'll likely not need to double the chile paste, unless you're a fire freak.

Note: Do not eat the lemongrass, lime leaves, galangal or ginger slices, or the chiles. Thais serve these chunky pieces with the soup in the bowl, pushing them aside as they eat. If you prefer, you can remove them with a slotted spoon before serving.

1 STALK LEMONGRASS

1 (2-INCH) PIECE FRESH GALANGAL OR 1-INCH PIECE FRESH GINGER

2 FRESH RED OR GREEN CHILES, SUCH AS THAI OR SERRANO

1 GREEN ONION

8 OUNCES BONELESS, SKINLESS CHICKEN BREAST

3 CUPS CHICKEN STOCK OR LOW-SODIUM CANNED BROTH

3 KAFFIR LIME LEAVES, OR 1 TEASPOON LIME JUICE

1 TEASPOON THAI CHILE PASTE, OR TO TASTE

1 (15-OUNCE CAN) STRAW MUSHROOMS, RINSED AND DRAINED

1/4 CUP LIME JUICE, OR TO TASTE

2 TO 3 TABLESPOONS FISH SAUCE (*NAM PLA*), TO TASTE

GARNISH: FRESH CILANTRO SPRIGS

① Prepare the lemongrass: Remove the tough outer layers and slice the inner section into 5 or 6 1-inch pieces. Smash the pieces with the side of the knife to flatten.

② Slice the galangal or ginger on the diagonal into thick pieces. Slice the chiles in half, lengthwise. Thinly slice the green onion (green and white parts) on the diagonal. Slice the chicken into thin strips, about 2 inches in length. Set each ingredient aside separately.

③ In a large pot over medium-high heat, bring the stock to a boil. Stir in the lemongrass, galangal, and lime leaves. Boil 3 minutes. Add the chile paste, chiles, and mushrooms. Bring to a low boil and cook another 2 to 3 minutes to allow the flavors to blend.

④ Stir in the chicken and simmer until almost cooked through, about 2 minutes. Add the 1/4 cup lime juice, fish sauce, and green onion. Taste and correct the seasonings. The soup should have a balance of spiciness, sourness, and saltiness. Pour the soup into bowls, garnish each bowl with several fresh cilantro sprigs, and serve.

Vietnamese Glass Noodles Soup with Lemongrass Roast Chicken
"Mien Ga"

SERVES 2 AS A LIGHT LUNCH OR DINNER, 4 AS A STARTER

When I was a kid, my mother made a succulent dish of "glass noodles"—bean thread noodles flavored with chicken broth, soy sauce, garlic, and cooked ground beef or pork. Hers was a Korean dish, but glass noodles are found in many Asian cultures, and in this Vietnamese-flavored soup.

Bean thread noodles are white, brittle noodles made from mung beans. When softened in hot liquid, they turn silky and translucent, hence the name, "glass noodles" or "cellophane noodles." Sold in Asian markets and some supermarkets, bean thread noodles come in small nests of about one ounce, usually bundled with six to ten nests per package, or in larger bundles. The smaller nests are more convenient. When dry, bean thread noodles are virtually impossible to break or cut up, so if you can only find the larger packages, cook a whole nest and use as much as you prefer, reserving the remainder.

This soup is a handy meal morph of Lemongrass Roast Chicken (chapter 4); be sure to enrich the stock with any leftover pan juices from the roast. If you don't have Lemongrass Roast Chicken leftovers, make it with any cooked shredded chicken.

2 (1.32-OUNCE OR SO) BUNDLES BEAN THREAD NOODLES

10 DRIED CLOUD EAR OR SHIITAKE MUSHROOMS, OR A MIXTURE OF THEM

1 QUART CHICKEN STOCK OR CANNED LOW-SODIUM BROTH

1 1/2 TEASPOONS SUGAR

1 1/2 TABLESPOONS FISH SAUCE (*NAM PLA* OR *NUOC MAM*), OR TO TASTE

SALT

ABOUT 1 CUP PACKED SHREDDED COOKED CHICKEN MEAT (PREFERABLY FROM LEMONGRASS ROAST CHICKEN)

2 GREEN ONIONS, GREEN AND WHITE PARTS SLICED THIN

ABOUT 1/4 CUP COARSELY CHOPPED CILANTRO SPRIGS

1 LARGE LIME, QUARTERED

1 SMALL GREEN CHILE, MINCED, OR DRIED RED CHILE FLAKES TO TASTE

① Soak noodles in hot water to cover until soft, about 20 minutes. Drain thoroughly and snip several times with scissors to cut into shorter lengths (about 3 to 4 inches). Soak the mushrooms in hot water to cover until soft, about 15 minutes. Rinse to remove any grit, squeeze dry, and snip into bite-size strips, discarding tough stems.

② Bring the stock to a boil. Stir in sugar, fish sauce, noodles, mushrooms, and salt to taste. Simmer a few minutes to warm all ingredients. Ladle into bowls. Sprinkle shredded chicken over noodles and top with green onions and cilantro sprigs. Serve with lime wedges and chile on the side.

CHAPTER 9

Broiled and Grilled Chicken

Outdoor grills and indoor broilers cook chicken quickly, with savory recipes for Chicken Churrasco with Chimichurri Sauce, Cuban Sour Orange Chicken, Tandoori Chicken, and Portuguese Grilled Chicken Oporto, and stops at a few other countries along the way.

Need to perfect your grilling and broiling skills? The first two recipes in this chapter provide the basics of grilling and broiling chicken.

Basic Grilling:
Cooking Chicken on an Outdoor Grill

Grilling chicken is far from an exact science. It requires much more intuition, attention, and practice than other cooking methods, but the advantages are well worth the effort: smoky flavor, mahogany skin, tasty charred bits, and a fun-filled excursion to the great outdoors . . . not to mention the social aspects of a grill-out in the backyard or favorite park.

But grilling is also not rocket science. It's likely humankind's oldest form of cooking—we surely ate our first chickens hot off the open fire rather than from any skillet or oven. The trick, though, is cooking the meat until it's no longer pink inside, without blackening the skin or exterior or drying the meat out. So you need to grill not over a blast-furnace flame, but over a more gentle medium-hot to medium-low range of heat.

Basic Grilling and Broiling, Simplified

Broiling

Heat the broiler until very hot. Arrange the chicken skin side down on a lightly oiled broiling pan and broil 4 to 6 inches from the flame, about 10 to 15 minutes. Turn, baste, and broil the pieces until cooked through, basting often. Be careful not to scorch the skin.

Direct Grilling

Heat the grill. Lightly coat the chicken surface with nonstick spray or brush with oil to help prevent sticking. Place the chicken skin side down on the hot grill directly over medium heat. Cook 6 to 8 minutes, making sure not to burn the skin. Turn and cook another 10 to 12 minutes, basting often, until cooked through. For boneless, skinless pieces, cook for about half the time.

Indirect Grilling

Heat the grill. Place the chicken pieces on the grill in an area away from the heat source (not directly over it), skin side up (you will not need to turn them). Cover the grill. During cooking, baste often and check to make sure the chicken is not scorching. Cook the chicken about 30 minutes, or until cooked through, moving the pieces around to cook evenly. For a crisper skin, grill the chicken skin side down directly over the heat for about 5 minutes.

The grilling recipes in this book all adhere to basic instructions that follow. If you keep these rules of thumb in mind and pay attention to the fire, you'll end up with a decently grilled bird. But because outdoor conditions of wind and air temperature affect every grill, you'll also need to be flexible and use your own judgment about when to move the chicken around, when to baste, and when to flip the pieces over.

Remember that the ultimate goal is a moist, tender interior, a handsomely browned exterior, and meat that's perfectly cooked (not raw or dry). Use a meat thermometer to check for doneness: 170 to 175 degrees for white meat, and 175 to 180 degrees for dark meat, measured in the thickest portions (away from the bone). Even without a thermometer, you can visually see if the chicken is done: Juices will run clear, not pink or cloudy.

Method:
Indirect Grilling, or Grill-Roasting

This method uses a covered grill, which functions as both an oven and a broiler. Cook chicken not directly over the heat, but to the side. For charcoal grills, pile white-hot coals at opposite sides of the grill, in the center only, or just around the edges—the point is to leave an area away from direct heat so the chicken can cook, or roast, without charring. Leave the vents partially open, but close them slightly if the chicken cooks too quickly or open them wider if it cooks too slowly. For gas grills, ignite both sides of the grill (covered) until they heat up, then turn off one burner and cook the chicken over that side of the grill, on the same level or on an upper rack, with the lid down. For a crisper skin or exterior, brown the pieces directly over the heat, uncovered, or flip the pieces occasionally while they cook to help them brown.

What are the best pieces for indirect grilling? Whole birds, halves, quarters, and large to medium pieces with bone. Do keep the skin on, as it adds flavor, protects the meat from drying out, and can be removed later if you so desire. Any thick piece of chicken should be cooked primarily on indirect heat, but you can do a quick stint over direct heat to add color and crispness.

Method:
Direct Grilling, Covered and Open

This is the same technique you would use for cooking steaks—setting the meat on the grill directly above the heat source, whether it be gas or charcoal. It uses a close, high heat similar to cooking in a broiler, only the heat cooks from below rather than from above.

You can grill directly with the lid closed (vents open) to help cook the interior, but watch that the chicken doesn't flare up and burn. Cooking open, without a lid, works well for small or thin pieces, such as wings, boneless breasts, and kebabs. For thicker pieces, you run the risk of cooking the outside but not the inside. You can combat this problem by finishing the pieces farther away from the heat source, such as on a higher rack, either covered or uncovered or a bit of both.

Basic Broiling:
Cooking Chicken in a Broiler

Your oven's broiler is the original indoor grill. It's a quick method: cooking at high heat from above the chicken rather than below it. Broiling works best with pieces of chicken similar in size and not too large, otherwise the exterior cooks faster than the interior. For best results:

- Get the broiler really hot before putting the chicken in. Allow at least 10 minutes of preheating.
- Line a pan with foil for easy cleanup, and place a broiling rack on top. Some cooks recommend heating the pan and rack in the broiler before adding the chicken, so the skin gets grill-type marks on it, and the heat bouncing off the pan bottom helps to sear the skin more quickly. This works well, but you may also just place the chicken skin-side down on an unheated rack and pan and slide it into a hot broiler.
- Cook the chicken pieces skin side down first, and always broil pieces with skin on. Skinless pieces just dry out and cook unevenly.
- Broil close to the heat source, but not so close that the chicken flares up or burns. Small pieces (wings and drumsticks) do fine when their surface is about 4 inches from the heat source, while larger ones (breasts and thighs) need more distance, some 5 to 8 inches from the heat. (Some broilers are not adjustable, so small pieces are best for them.) For mixed pieces, arrange the larger ones in the center and the smaller ones around the edges of the broiling pan, and broil the chicken surfaces about 6 inches from the heat.
- Cooking times vary with the broiler's heat output and the pieces being cooked. Because the skin cooks more quickly, broil the pieces with the skin side down for about two thirds of the total cooking time, then flip them over.
- Plan on about 15 to 20 minutes with skin side down, then flip pieces over and cook another 10 to 15 minutes, checking to make sure the skin is browning but not burning. If the chicken seems to be cooking too quickly, move it farther away from the heat source.

Aromatic Anise Chicken: Roasted, Grilled, or Spatchcocked

SERVES 4 TO 6 Aniseed has a sweet, mildly licorice taste and combines well with celery, coriander, and green peppercorns. These and a few other ingredients envelop the chicken in a cozy Mediterranean glow, finished with a lemony olive oil baste. I usually make extra pieces of this chicken because the cold leftovers are so good as picnic fare or in sandwiches. The rub can be used for a roast chicken or for grilled chicken halves, pieces, or a whole spatchcocked bird.

    1 (4-POUND) WHOLE CHICKEN, WITHOUT GIBLETS

Anise Rub (makes ¹/₃ cup)

    1 TABLESPOON WHOLE ANISEED

    2 TEASPOONS GRANULATED GARLIC

    2 TEASPOONS CELERY SEED

    1 TEASPOON DRIED OREGANO (GREEK OR TURKISH PREFERRED)

    1¹/₂ TEASPOONS WHOLE GREEN PEPPERCORNS (DRIED, NOT BRINED)

    2 TEASPOONS WHOLE CORIANDER SEEDS

    2 TEASPOONS SUGAR

    2 TEASPOONS SALT

Anise Baste

    JUICE OF 1 LEMON (2 TABLESPOONS)

    3 TABLESPOONS EXTRA-VIRGIN OLIVE OIL

    2 TEASPOONS ANISE RUB

① Rinse and pat the chicken dry. If roasting whole, leave the bird uncut. If grilling, cut the chicken as for spatchcocking, cut in half, or cut into 8 pieces. (See chapter 3 for instructions).

② *Make the Anise Rub:* Measure the ingredients into a spice grinder or clean coffee mill and whir until ground. Rub the bird all over with 3 tablespoons of the spice rub, including under and on top of the skin. Allow at least 1 hour or as long as overnight

continued

Aromatic Anise Chicken *continued*

for the spices to be absorbed. (Refrigerate the chicken if waiting longer than 1 hour before cooking.) Reserve any remaining rub.

③ *Prepare the Anise Baste:* Mix together the lemon juice, olive oil, and 2 teaspoons of the remaining rub. (You'll have a tad more rub left over; use it to season other meats, vegetables, or salads.)

④ When ready to cook, grill or broil the chicken according to the instructions at the beginning of this chapter. As the chicken cooks, baste every 10 to 15 minutes with the Anise Baste. Serve hot or at room temperature.

Barbecued Korean Drums

SERVES 4 TO 6 Good 'n' garlicky, the way Koreans like them! Serve for dinner with steamed rice and a grilled eggplant salad, and keep leftovers available as snacks. A dish of pickled kimchi on the side would be mandatory in Korea. This marinade works with all types of chicken parts and is especially handy when jumbo packs go on sale.

4 POUNDS CHICKEN DRUMSTICKS (OR OTHER PIECES)

4 GREEN ONIONS

$1/3$ CUP PACKED DARK BROWN SUGAR

$1/2$ CUP SOY SAUCE

5 CLOVES GARLIC, MINCED

2-INCH PIECE FRESH GINGER, MINCED

1 TABLESPOON SESAME OIL

2 TABLESPOONS TOASTED SESAME SEEDS, PLUS MORE FOR GARNISH (CHAPTER 12)

2 TABLESPOONS DRY SHERRY

DASH RED PEPPER FLAKES

① Slash the drumsticks diagonally in 2 or 3 places on one side, cutting to the bone. Repeat on the opposite side. Slice the green onions (green and white parts) on the diagonal into 1-inch lengths.

② In a shallow dish or glass pan, mix remaining ingredients. Stir in the green onions. Add the chicken, coating well with the marinade. Marinate at least 1 hour, preferably overnight, refrigerated.

③ When ready to cook, grill or broil the chicken according to the instructions at the beginning of this chapter. Turn and baste occasionally with the marinade. Cook until the drums have a deep mahogany glaze and the meat is cooked through. (If the chicken browns too quickly, move it from direct heat to indirect heat and cook with the lid closed.) Garnish with more sesame seeds. Serve hot or at room temperature.

Note: If desired, boil the remaining marinade in a saucepan for at least 3 minutes. When it's reduced and syrupy, serve on the side to spoon over cooked rice.

Chicken Churrasco with Chimichurri Sauce

SERVES 4 TO 6 In Argentina, bowls of chimichurri sauce, a pungent parsley-garlic-vinegar mix, grace the tables of grill restaurants, awaiting hot, smoky platters of churrasco—grilled steaks, sausages, chops, and meat, meat, meat. Robust chimichurri sauce accents any grilled food, from chicken to vegetables. You can whip it up in just a few minutes using a hand blender, mini-chopper, or, for larger amounts, a food processor. Fresh ingredients vary in intensity, so taste and adjust the seasonings to your preference.

    1 RECIPE CHIMICHURRI SAUCE (SEE BELOW)

    2 CLOVES GARLIC, COARSELY CHOPPED

    3 TABLESPOONS EXTRA-VIRGIN OLIVE OIL

    SALT AND FRESHLY GROUND PEPPER

    3 TO 4 POUNDS CHICKEN PIECES, WITH OR WITHOUT SKIN

① Make the Chimichurri Sauce as directed below. Empty the sauce from the food processor's work bowl into another container, but don't rinse out the bowl (it's okay of you do, but not necessary).

continued

Chicken Churrasco with Chimichurri Sauce *continued*

② Process the garlic and olive oil together in the work bowl until the garlic is finely chopped. Salt and pepper the chicken and coat it with the garlic-olive oil mixture. Allow the chicken to absorb the flavors at least 20 minutes, preferably 1 hour, covered and refrigerated.

③ Grill or broil according to the instructions at the beginning of this chapter. Serve with Chimichurri Sauce on the side.

Chimichurri Sauce

MAKES ABOUT 1 1/3 CUPS

> 6 CLOVES GARLIC, PEELED
>
> 2 BAY LEAVES
>
> 2 CUPS DENSELY PACKED FRESH PARSLEY, TOUGH STEMS CUT AWAY AND DISCARDED
>
> 1/2 CUP EXTRA-VIRGIN OLIVE OIL
>
> 1/4 CUP (OR MORE TO TASTE) SHERRY WINE VINEGAR OR RED WINE VINEGAR
>
> 1 TEASPOON SALT
>
> 1/2 TEASPOON FRESHLY GROUND PEPPER

Finely chop the garlic and bay leaves in the work bowl of a food processor. Add the parsley to the work bowl. Pour the olive oil, 1/4 cup vinegar, salt, and pepper on top of the parsley to weigh it down for easier chopping. Process until the mixture is finely chopped but not totally puréed. Taste and adjust the seasonings (you may need more vinegar). Serve at room temperature. To store, cover and refrigerate; the sauce will last several days, but the flavors will weaken over time.

Chicken of the Moors

SERVES 4 TO 6; MAKES 1 CUP SAUCE In this dish, hot red pepper and leafy green cilantro, influences of the Moors in Spain, punch up traditional Mediterranean ingredients—tart lemons and capers, garlic, bay leaves, olive oil, and wine vinegar. Cilantro was actually introduced to the New World by the Spanish Moors. It was the predominant green herb used in Spain until it was eventually replaced by parsley, gradually favored by most other Mediterranean countries over cilantro. This is a spicy, tart, and tangy dish, with a marinade that doubles as a sauce or salad dressing. A mini-food processor or hand blender with work bowl (one of my favorite kitchen tools) whips up the marinade in minutes.

Moorish Marinade

5 CLOVES GARLIC, PEELED

1/2 TEASPOON SALT

2 LARGE OR 4 SMALL BAY LEAVES

3/4 CUP PACKED FRESH CILANTRO

3/4 TEASPOON RED PEPPER FLAKES

2 TABLESPOONS CAPERS

1/4 CUP EXTRA-VIRGIN OLIVE OIL

1/4 CUP FRESH LEMON JUICE

1/4 CUP RED WINE VINEGAR

2 POUNDS BONELESS, SKINLESS CHICKEN THIGHS (OR OTHER CHICKEN PIECES)

① Using a food processor, hand blender with work bowl, or blender, purée together all of the marinade ingredients. Set aside and refrigerate 1/2 cup of the marinade for later use as a sauce.

② Place the chicken in a nonreactive dish. Stab the pieces in several places with a fork or knife tip to help the marinade penetrate. Coat the chicken with the marinade. Cover and refrigerate for 2 hours up to overnight, turning once or twice.

③ When ready to cook, grill or broil the chicken according to the instructions at the beginning of this chapter. Baste occasionally with the marinade. Bring the reserved, refrigerated marinade to room temperature or warm it in a saucepan. Serve the chicken with the marinade as a sauce on the side.

Serving suggestion: Arrange the chicken on a bed of lettuce and tomatoes drizzled with the sauce. Or serve with grilled vegetables, also drizzled with sauce. Crusty sourdough or French bread sops up the sauce nicely.

Cuban Sour Orange Chicken

SERVES 4 TO 6 A peculiar, rumpled-skin orange grows in Cuba, with an intensely tart juice that's more like lime juice than the sweet citrus taste we associate with oranges. Few U.S. markets outside of Florida carry the fresh *"naranja agria,"* though bottled juice is sometimes found in Hispanic markets. The Seville orange is similar and also quite sour.

If you do have fresh sour oranges available, by all means use them instead of the orange and lime juice mixture in this recipe. If not, the combined juices approximate the taste of authentic *naranja agria.* Sliced kumquats, golden in color with edible flesh and skin, make a good garnish for this dish, as do orange and lime wedges.

Cuban Sour Orange Marinade

> 3/4 CUP PACKED FRESH CILANTRO
>
> 3 CLOVES GARLIC
>
> 1 CUP FRESH ORANGE JUICE
>
> 1/3 CUP FRESH LIME JUICE
>
> 2 TABLESPOONS EXTRA-VIRGIN OLIVE OIL
>
> 2 TEASPOONS GROUND CUMIN
>
> 1 1/2 TEASPOONS DRIED MARJORAM, CRUMBLED
>
> 1 TEASPOON SALT
>
> 1/2 TEASPOON RED PEPPER FLAKES
>
> 4 TO 6 CHICKEN BREASTS (OR PIECES OF CHOICE)
>
> GARNISH: ORANGE AND LIME WEDGES OR SLICED KUMQUATS; CILANTRO SPRIGS

① Using the work bowl of a hand blender or food processor, or working by hand, coarsely chop the cilantro. Dump the cilantro into a nonreactive baking dish (or plastic zipper bag) large enough to hold the chicken pieces.

② Finely chop the garlic (in the same work bowl or by hand). Combine the garlic with the orange and lime juices, olive oil, cumin, marjoram, salt, and red pepper flakes.

③ Pour the mixture into the baking dish and stir to mix. Place the chicken in the marinade, coating completely. Cover and refrigerate at least 4 hours or overnight, turning the chicken in the marinade once or twice.

Caribbean

When you think Caribbean cuisine, think warm breezes, warm water, endless coastline, and a wild cultural mix. First, you have the native foods of the Americas—corn, beans, root vegetables, chiles, pineapple, guava, and allspice. When Spanish conquistadors; African slaves; English, French, Portuguese, and Dutch traders; and Asian laborers arrived, they brought such additions as pork and ham, olives, capers, garlic, cilantro, rice, dairy products and Edam cheese, sweets, ginger, soy sauce, tamarind, coconut, and curry. Creole people and Creole cooking were born when Europeans, Africans, and native islanders inter-mixed. Middle Eastern and Indian foods came courtesy of the European trade empires. Spicy Jamaican jerk dishes, rum and molasses, tropical fruits, seafood and shellfish, beans, cassava, roti bread, stews, and one-pot meals typify the Caribbean FlavorPrint, which is as diverse as the cultures that settled there.

ackee	chives	mango	Scotch bonnet and
allspice	cilantro	molasses	habañero chiles
annatto	cinnamon	okra	shrimp
bananas	cloves	onion	soy sauce
black beans	coconut	papaya	squashes
breadfruit	conch	peppers	sweet potato
callaloo	curry powder	pigeon peas	tamarind
cassava	garlic	plantain	thyme
chayote	ginger	rice	turmeric
chiles	lime	saffron	yam

④ Grill or broil according to the basic instructions at the beginning of this chapter. Baste often during cooking. Before serving, boil the marinade for 3 minutes to kill bacteria and thicken the sauce. Transfer the chicken to a platter. Garnish with cilantro sprigs, orange sections, lime wedges, or kumquats, and serve with the boiled marinade as a sauce.

Filipino Coconut Barbecued Chicken

SERVES 5 TO 8 Kecap manis is a thick, sweet soy sauce found in Filipino and other Asian markets. Be sure to use unsweetened coconut milk, also found in Asian markets, for this sweet-spicy-salty-tart marinade. If you don't have kecap manis for this recipe, substitute ¼ cup regular soy sauce plus 1 tablespoon brown sugar. You may also broil the chicken pieces instead of grilling.

Filipino Coconut Marinade (makes about 2 cups)

    1 CUP CANNED UNSWEETENED COCONUT MILK

    10 CLOVES GARLIC, PEELED

    1 CUP LOOSELY PACKED FRESH CILANTRO

    ½ CUP PACKED DARK BROWN SUGAR

    ¼ CUP KECAP MANIS

    3 TABLESPOONS FISH SAUCE (*NAM PLA*)

    2 TABLESPOONS FRESH LIME JUICE

    1 (1½-INCH) PIECE FRESH GINGER, COARSELY CHOPPED

    2 GREEN ONIONS

    2 SERRANO CHILES (OR JALAPEÑOS), STEMMED (REMOVE SEEDS IF DESIRED)

    1 TEASPOON SALT

    4 TO 5 POUNDS CHICKEN PIECES

① Combine marinade ingredients in a food processor. Pulse until all ingredients are finely chopped. Marinate the chicken pieces in 1 cup of the marinade, reserving the remaining marinade for basting and serving. Cover and refrigerate chicken at least 4 hours, preferably overnight.

② When ready to cook, grill or broil the chicken according to the instructions at the beginning of this chapter. Baste occasionally with the marinade. Serve hot or at room temperature. If desired, boil any remaining marinade for 3 minutes to use as a sauce, especially if serving with rice.

Grilled Chicken Fajitas

SERVES 6 TO 8 Traditional Tex-Mex fajitas consist of charcoal-grilled beef skirt steak, but chicken, cooked the same way with the same seasonings, can be just as outstanding. Boneless, skinless chicken works best. I like to cook half breasts and half thighs, slice them thinly, and mix them together for a balanced mix of lean and dark meat. Use whichever pieces you prefer; just don't overcook them (especially the breasts). The meat should be moist and tender inside, sporting a gloriously grilled exterior. Serve with warm flour tortillas and Pico de Gallo (chapter 12). If you plan to serve all of the fajitas at once, you may want to make a double batch of Pico de Gallo so you have plenty to go around.

3 POUNDS BONELESS, SKINLESS CHICKEN PIECES

1 SMALL TO MEDIUM ONION

2 TEASPOONS GROUND CUMIN

2 TEASPOONS GROUND RED CHILE

2 TEASPOONS GRANULATED GARLIC

1/2 TEASPOON SALT

1/3 CUP FRESH LIME JUICE

1/4 CUP OLIVE OIL

4 PICKLED JALAPEÑOS, CHOPPED, PLUS 2 TABLESPOONS JALAPEÑO ESCABECHE (PICKLING) LIQUID

FOR SERVING: WARM FLOUR TORTILLAS AND PICO DE GALLO (CHAPTER 12)

① Score the chicken breasts. Thinly slice the onion. Place the chicken in a nonreactive container to marinate. Combine the cumin, red chile, garlic, and salt in a small dish. Rub the mixture all over the chicken. Pour the lime juice, olive oil, jalapeños, and jalapeño liquid over the chicken. Slosh the pieces around to coat all surfaces. Place the onion slices under, on top of, and between the chicken pieces. Cover and refrigerate at least 2 hours or overnight.

② Prepare the grill; heat until very hot. Grill the chicken over a high, direct heat, according to the basic instructions at the beginning of this chapter. Cook quickly and for a very short time, so as not to overcook. To serve, slice the chicken into

continued

Grilled Chicken Fajitas *continued*

small, thin strips. Take a warmed flour tortilla, load it with the meat, then spoon some Pico de Gallo on top. Tex-Mex heaven!

Note: To cook the onions, use a foil pie tin or make a small tray out of aluminum foil, pour in the residual marinade and onions, and set the tray on the hot part of the grill until the mixture cooks through completely. Most of the marinade will evaporate but the onions and jalapeño bits will remain. Stir the mixture occasionally as it cooks. Toss together with the sliced fajita meat before serving.

Grilled Chicken in Minty Chutney

SERVES 6 Indian flatbreads make an ideal accompaniment to this chicken, marinated in and served with a heavenly lemon-mint chutney.

    4 POUNDS CHICKEN THIGHS, SKIN REMOVED
    1/2 CUP PUDINE KI CHUTNEY (CHAPTER 12), PLUS MORE FOR SERVING
    1/2 CUP PLAIN YOGURT
    2 TEASPOONS GARAM MASALA (CHAPTER 12)

① Stab chicken pieces all over on both sides with a fork to allow marinade to penetrate. Place in a nonreactive dish for marinating.

② Stir together the chutney, yogurt, and garam masala. Smear all over the chicken. Cover and refrigerate at least 1 hour, preferably overnight.

③ Grill (or broil) the chicken until completely cooked, turning halfway through. Serve with additional chutney on the side.

FLAVOR PRINTS

India, Pakistan, and Sri Lanka

One word best describes cooking in and surrounding India: spices—not necessarily spicy hot, although this can be the case, but the complex use of multiple spices in a single dish. Even the breads are spiced. Indians also recognize that a spice may impart distinctively different flavors when used raw, toasted, whole, or freshly ground. Spices are valued for their medicinal properties as much as for their seasoning abilities.

Invading armies, traders, and immigrants, including Alexander the Great, have contributed to Indian cooking. Greeks and Middle Easterners brought ingredients and techniques. Moghul invaders in the sixteenth century introduced meat and rice dishes. Portuguese ships brought chiles to the southern shores. The more recent British introduced baked goods, puddings, cakes, and ice cream, and Westernized Indian families began eating at formal tables with forks, knives, and full British-style place settings. Huns, Arabs, Turks, Afghans, and the Dutch have also left culinary marks.

Distinct cooking styles exist within the region's vast geography, climate, and cultures. Wheat grows in the temperate north, close to the Himalayas, and meat dishes can be elaborate. In the south, dishes become hotter, sometimes fiery. Rice and a vegetarian lifestyle predominate. Jungles in India and Sri Lanka yield mangoes, guava, papaya, bananas, and coconuts. Vegetarian Hindus, Buddhists, and Jains rely on grains, legumes (dals), and vegetables, while Muslims cook beef, lamb, and poultry. Rice or bread, a vegetable, a meat, and dal are all part of the typical meal. No table is complete for any Indian, though, without an array of condiments—chutneys, raitas, sambals, and pickles, which further season, temper, and balance the overall meal.

ajowan or ajwain
almonds
amchoor (mango powder)
asafetida
black cumin
cardamom
cauliflower
chickpeas and flour
chiles

chutney
cilantro
cinnamon
coconut
coriander
cucumber
cumin
curry leaf
eggplant
fennel seed
fenugreek
garam masala

garlic
ginger
lentils (dal)
lime
mango
mint
mung beans
mustard oil
mustard seeds
nigella
onion
panch phoron

peas
pickles
poppyseeds (white)
potato
raita
rice (basmati)
saffron
sesame seeds and oil (til)
spinach
tamarind

tomato
turmeric

Dairy: ghee, yogurt, paneer cheese

Bread: naan, poppadum, pakoras (fritters), samosas (stuffed pastries)

Grilled Lemon-Dill Chicken

SERVES 4 A fresh, light marinade infuses this chicken with sour cream, dill, cucumber, and lemon essences. Ironically, this flavor package reflects the seasonings of very diverse cultures: Scandinavia (where they would use fish rather than chicken) and Turkey and Eastern Europe (for which would substitute yogurt for the sour cream in the dressing). The chicken is equally at home in a smorgasbord with dark rye bread as it is with toasted pita bread or a Georgian green bean–walnut salad. Serve warm or cold.

> 4 BONELESS, SKINLESS CHICKEN BREAST HALVES
>
> 1/2 CUP SOUR CREAM, DILL, AND CUCUMBER DRESSING (CHAPTER 12)
>
> 2 TABLESPOONS FRESH LEMON JUICE
>
> 1 TEASPOON ANCHOVY PASTE
>
> FRESHLY, COARSELY GROUND PEPPER
>
> NONSTICK VEGETABLE OIL SPRAY

① Score the chicken breasts for more even cooking. Mix together the dressing, lemon juice, and anchovy paste. Marinate the chicken in the mixture at least 1 hour, preferably 4 hours, or up to overnight, refrigerated.

② Heat a grill to medium-high. Before placing the chicken on the grill, spray the chicken surface with nonstick vegetable oil spray to prevent sticking. Grill until the surface is charred with grill marks, then spritz the top of the chicken with more spray and flip. Cook just until chicken is done, to avoid drying it out. Serve with a liberal grind of pepper and additional dressing on the side. You may also broil the chicken according to the basic instructions at the beginning of this chapter.

Ground Chicken Kebabs

SERVES 2 AS A MEAL, OR 6 AS AN APPETIZER Textured with subtly sweet, shredded coconut, these ground-meat kebabs pair well with minty Pudine Ki Chutney (chapter 12) and flatbread. You can shape the mixture around bamboo or metal skewers for grilling, or pat it into small patties and pan-fry in a bit of oil.

Make sure the mixture is well chilled before shaping. Here's an easy way to form the meat: Place a sheet of plastic wrap on your work surface. Spread a length of the mixture in a strip down the plastic. (For a 12-inch-long skewer, use 1/4 of the mixture, spreading it in an 8- to 10-inch-long strip.) Lay a skewer on top of the mixture. Pull the plastic up so the meat wraps around the skewer like a sausage. Tighten the plastic, pushing the meat back against the skewer to firm up and flatten slightly. You can refrigerate the plastic-wrapped skewers until ready to grill. Remove the plastic before grilling.

1 EGG

1 POUND GROUND CHICKEN

1/2 CUP SHREDDED DRIED COCONUT (UNSWEETENED)

1/2 CUP FINELY CHOPPED RED ONION

1-INCH PIECE FRESH GINGER, PEELED AND MINCED

3 CLOVES GARLIC, MINCED

1 TEASPOON SALT

1 TEASPOON GROUND CUMIN

1 TEAPOON GROUND CORIANDER

1 TABLESPOON TOASTED SESAME SEEDS (CHAPTER 12)

1 TABLESPOON BESAN (CHICKPEA) FLOUR OR ALL-PURPOSE FLOUR

① Break the egg into a mixing bowl. Beat with a fork until blended. Dump in the remaining ingredients and mix until combined.

② Cover and refrigerate the mixture until well chilled. Shape the mixture around skewers and grill (as described above), or form into patties for pan-frying. When grilling, gently place the skewers on a hot grill. Cook one side completely before turning and grilling the other side, so the mixture firms up around the skewer. Serve hot, preferably with 1 cup of Pudine Ki Chutney (chapter 12) on the side.

Jamaican Jerk Chicken

SERVES 4 TO 6 In Jamaica's signature dish, allspice, thyme, and fiery hot peppers mingle with warm spices for a complex and irresistible grilling sauce. Warning: Scotch bonnets and habañero peppers are among the world's hottest chiles, but people love them for their unique fruity flavor. Use them sparingly, and for safety's sake, wear gloves when handling them. One touch to your eyes with pepper-laced fingers and you'll be crying (literally). If you're intimidated by the prospect if such potent peppers, opt for mild jalapeños instead. Also, cut out the seeds and membranes to help tame a chile's heat.

4 TO 5 POUNDS CHICKEN PIECES, WITH SKIN

Jerk Marinade (makes ¹/₂ cup)

¹/₄ CUP FRESH THYME LEAVES

6 GREEN ONIONS, WHITE AND GREEN PARTS CUT INTO 1-INCH LENGTHS

1-INCH PIECE FRESH GINGER

3 GARLIC CLOVES

2 BAY LEAVES

1 SCOTCH BONNET OR HABAÑERO PEPPER, OR 2 JALAPEÑOS, STEMMED AND SEEDED

2 TEASPOONS FRESHLY GROUND PEPPER

2 TEASPOONS GROUND CORIANDER

1 TEASPOON GROUND ALLSPICE

1 TEASPOON SALT

¹/₂ TEASPOON FRESHLY GRATED NUTMEG

¹/₂ TEASPOON GROUND CINNAMON

¹/₄ CUP DISTILLED WHITE VINEGAR

2 TABLESPOONS SOY SAUCE

2 TABLESPOONS CANOLA OIL

① Place the chicken pieces in a nonreactive dish or plastic zipper bag. Combine all marinade ingredients in a food processor. Blend until smooth. Pour over chicken, coating chicken well. Marinate covered and refrigerated 3 hours to overnight, sloshing the chicken in the marinade occasionally.

② When ready to cook, grill or broil the chicken according to the instructions at the beginning of this chapter. Baste occasionally with the marinade. Serve hot or at room temperature.

Juicy Grilled Grapefruit Chicken

SERVES 4 TO 6 Among citrus fruits, grapefruit juice tenderizes best, without being as harsh as lemon or lime, or as sweet as orange juice. Texas-grown Ruby Reds are especially sweet, boosting the naturally delicate flavor of chicken. Italian seasoning, a mix of dried herbs manufactured by most spice brands, adds the right amount of herb flavor, and some onion, garlic, and vinegar punch up the whole dish. This is an all-purpose chicken recipe that works well with almost any side dish, especially buttered egg noodles and steamed vegetables.

> 4 TO 6 CHICKEN BREAST HALVES, WITH OR WITHOUT BONE AND SKIN

Grapefruit Marinade

> 2/3 CUP FRESH GRAPEFRUIT JUICE, OR 1 (5.5-OUNCE) CAN GRAPEFRUIT JUICE
>
> 1/4 CUP DICED ONION
>
> 3 CLOVES GARLIC, MINCED
>
> 1 TABLESPOON SOY SAUCE
>
> 1 TABLESPOON RED WINE VINEGAR
>
> 1 TEASPOON OLIVE OIL
>
> 1/2 TEASPOON ITALIAN SEASONING (MIXED DRIED HERBS)
>
> 1/2 TEASPOON SUGAR

① If using boneless, skinless breast halves, score them lightly for even cooking. Mix together all marinade ingredients. Add chicken and coat thoroughly. Marinate refrigerated 2 hours to overnight.

② To cook, grill or broil the chicken according to the instructions at the beginning of this chapter. Baste occasionally with the marinade. Serve hot or at room temperature.

La Tunisia Chicken and Grilled Onions

SERVES 4 TO 6 The heady spices of North Africa—cumin, cinnamon, caraway, and red pepper—turn plain chicken into a seductively exotic bird, especially when grilled. I find it easiest to grill whole pieces of chicken separate from the thickly sliced onions, but you can also skewer kebabs of boneless chicken and onion chunks, peppers, cherry tomatoes, and eggplant for a festive party dish. Thighs have the most flavor, but all parts taste fine in this dish. Use sweet paprika for a milder tone if you don't like hot foods. I use half-sharp paprika and the dish gets pleasantly spicy—not too much to break a sweat, just enough to be noticed.

> 1 POUND ONIONS
>
> 4 TO 5 POUNDS CHICKEN PIECES (SUCH AS THIGHS)

La Tunisia Marinade

> 3 TABLESPOONS EXTRA-VIRGIN OLIVE OIL
>
> 1/2 CUP RED WINE VINEGAR
>
> 2 TABLESPOONS SOY SAUCE
>
> JUICE OF 1 LEMON
>
> 6 CLOVES GARLIC
>
> 2 TABLESPOONS PAPRIKA
>
> 1 HEAPING TABLESPOON GROUND CUMIN
>
> 2 TEASPOONS CARAWAY SEEDS
>
> 1 TEASPOON GROUND CINNAMON
>
> 1/2 TEASPOON RED PEPPER FLAKES
>
> GARNISH: 1/4 CUP CHOPPED CILANTRO

① Slice the onions into thick rounds, about 1/2 inch wide. Skewer them, piercing through the diameter. Place the chicken pieces in a nonreactive baking dish large enough to hold the chicken and the skewered onions.

② Using a blender, food processor, or mortar and pestle, blend together the marinade ingredients. Coat the chicken pieces and skewered onions with the marinade. Marinate at least 2 hours, preferably overnight, refrigerated, turning once or twice.

③ When ready to cook, grill the onion skewers and chicken pieces over medium-high heat until cooked through, being careful not to burn them. Or cook in the broiler.

North Africa: Morocco, Algeria, Tunisia, and Libya

FLAVOR PRINTS

The FlavorPrint of North Africa could almost be mistaken for that of the Middle East. Rightly so, as Arab invaders brought their spices, wheat, lentils, and Islamic religion with them. Additionally, the Turkish Ottomans contributed their gift of paper-thin sheets of pastry. Europeans from across the Mediterranean brought pastas, lemons, oranges, and New World tomatoes, chiles, and potatoes. Put these cultures together and you have the ingredients for North African cuisine.

almonds
Arabic breads
black pepper
carrot
cardamom
cassia
chickpeas
chiles
cilantro
cinnamon
cloves
coriander
couscous
cumin

dried fruit (apricots, dates, raisins, prunes)
eggplant
fava beans
garlic
ginger
harissa
honey
lemon (fresh and preserved)
lentils
mint
nutmeg
olives and olive oil

onion
orange
paprika
parsley
peppers
pine nuts
phyllo dough (malsouga)
ras el hanouth
rosebuds
saffron
sesame
tomato
turmeric
zucchini

(See the grilling and broiling instructions at the beginning of this chapter.) Baste occasionally as the chicken and onions cook.

④ Serve the chicken and onions on a platter. Sprinkle with chopped cilantro before serving. Serve with couscous or saffron rice, warm flatbread, and a cooling cucumber salad, if desired.

Portuguese Grilled Chicken Oporto

SERVES 4 TO 6 Oporto, Portugal's second-largest city, is the primary source of the famous fortified wine known as "port." Port is named after the town, which is also a leading supplier of wine corks. Port comes in many varieties, including a luscious blended Tawny Port. While some Tawny Ports can be expensive, inexpensive versions work fine for this recipe, or use a Ruby Port.

The history of Oporto precedes ancient Rome, and at one time it was called Portus Cale, whence the name Portugal is derived. Overrun by the Moors and later by the Spaniards and the French, Portugal has retained bits and pieces of each conqueror's culinary traditions. As in this dish, the cooking is flavorful but simple, with a fondness for garlic, sweet paprika, olive oil, and, of course, port.

4 CLOVES GARLIC

1 TEASPOON SALT

2 LARGE OR 4 SMALL BAY LEAVES

1 TABLESPOON SWEET PAPRIKA

1/4 TEASPOON RED PEPPER FLAKES

2 TABLESPOONS EXTRA-VIRGIN OLIVE OIL

2 TABLESPOONS CIDER VINEGAR

6 TABLESPOONS TAWNY OR RUBY PORT

4 POUNDS CHICKEN BREAST HALVES, OR 1 CHICKEN QUARTERED (OR PIECES OF CHOICE)

① Grind the garlic, salt, bay leaves, paprika, and red pepper flakes in the work bowl of a hand blender or food processor or by hand using a mortar and pestle. Blend in the olive oil, vinegar, and port. Place the chicken in a nonreactive dish or plastic zipper bag and coat completely with the marinade. Cover and refrigerate 2 hours to overnight, turning once or twice.

② To cook, grill or broil the chicken according to the instructions at the beginning of this chapter. Baste occasionally with the marinade. Serve hot or at room temperature.

Tandoori Chicken

SERVES 4 This tender, moist tandoori chicken, full of warm spices, is adapted from classic Indian cooking specifically for Western kitchens and weekday meals. By using a premixed garam masala, you spend just a few minutes preparing the marinade one day, then simply grill or broil the chicken the next day. Garam masala can be found in Indian markets, or you may prefer to make your own fresh mix using the Global Gourmet's Garam Masala recipe (chapter 12). Ghee is Indian clarified butter, but vegetable oil may be used instead. Try this chicken with garlic naan, an Indian flatbread, or basmati rice, and a minty yogurt raita.

2¹/₂ POUNDS CHICKEN THIGHS OR OTHER PIECES, WITH OR WITHOUT SKIN

3 TABLESPOONS FRESH LIME JUICE

¹/₂ TEASPOON SALT

¹/₂ CUP YOGURT

3 TABLESPOONS GARAM MASALA

1 TEASPOON TURMERIC

1 TABLESPOON MINCED GARLIC

1 TABLESPOON MINCED GINGER

¹/₄ CUP GHEE OR CANOLA OIL

¹/₄ TEASPOON SAFFRON THREADS

① Using a small knife, pierce the chicken pieces all over with deep slits every half inch or so. Place the chicken in a large bowl or baking dish. Pour the lime juice over the chicken pieces and sprinkle with salt. Let stand 20 minutes.

② Meanwhile, mix the yogurt with the garam masala, turmeric, garlic, and ginger. Pour the yogurt mixture over the chicken, coating thoroughly, and refrigerate, covered, 24 to 48 hours. Turn the pieces once or twice while marinating.

③ In a small saucepan, heat the ghee, then crush the saffron threads into it. Set aside.

④ Heat the grill until medium hot, or heat the broiler. Baste one side of the chicken pieces with the saffron butter or oil. Grill or broil according to the instructions at the beginning of this chapter, basting occasionally with the saffron mixture. Continue cooking and basting until the meat is cooked through and the skin is a roasted yellow-gold color.

Texas Barbecue Dry-Rub Chicken

SERVES 6 TO 8 This dry rub can be used on any type of meat, not just chicken. I like my chicken cooked naked, seasoned with only a spicy dry rub, but if you prefer, you can baste the rubbed chicken with a barbecue sauce during the final 10 minutes of cooking. A lemon-pepper coleslaw and some ranch-style beans make this a true Texas supper.

Texas Dry Rub

1 TABLESPOON SALT

1 TABLESPOON BLACK PEPPER

1 TABLESPOON PAPRIKA

1 TEASPOON DRY MUSTARD

1 TABLESPOON GRANULATED GARLIC

1 TEASPOON CELERY SEED

2 CHICKENS, ABOUT 3 POUNDS EACH, SPLIT IN HALF

1 LEMON, CUT IN HALF

① Mix together all dry rub ingredients. Rub the chickens on all sides with the lemon halves, squeezing out the lemon juice as you rub. Rub the spice mixture all over the chickens and inside the cavities. Let marinate in the dry rub 3 hours or up to overnight, refrigerated.

② Heat the oven to 300 degrees, or prepare the barbecue grill. If using the oven, bake the chicken for about 45 minutes, until the meat is cooked through. Finish cooking under the broiler to crisp the skin. If grilling, cook over medium to low heat, covered, for about 45 minutes to 1 hour. Start by grilling the chickens skin side up for about 40 minutes, then turn them over and finish grilling with the skin side down, checking to make sure the skin does not burn. Serve hot or at room temperature.

CHAPTER 10

Savory Stovetop Chicken

In many parts of the world, ovens are a luxury; most foods are cooked in pans directly over the flame, including these skillet dishes, stir-fries, and sautés. Take a tour de France with chicken in wine, mustard, or tarragon. Spice up your voyage with Moroccan and Indian chickens, and sweeten your day with coconut curries from the Caribbean to Malaysia.

Aussie Alfredo with Warrigal Greens

SERVES 4 A melting pot of cultures from around the world, Australia offers every type of cuisine imaginable—from Pad Thai to ravioli. But to be truly Australian, a recipe should include at least some native ingredients, known collectively as "bush tucker." Aborigines taught the early white settlers how to survive on such gifts of the land as the quandong, a tart peachlike fruit; sweet kakadu plums, excellent for jams; and the now internationally grown macadamia nut. Today, modern Aussie chefs are literally rediscovering their own backyard, plating up bush tucker specialties in posh hotels and trendy restaurants.

   Warrigal greens are from a leafy bushfood plant, also known as tetragonia and sometimes as New Zealand spinach, though the plant is not related to true spinach.

continued

129

Aussie Alfredo with Warrigal Greens *continued*

Brought to Europe by Captain James Cook, the plant is rarely sold commercially, other than in seed form. But home gardeners in France, England, and the United States cultivate it privately as a hearty, spreading green that can survive late-summer heat and drought, torturous conditions for true spinach and lettuces.

However, unlike more tender greens, warrigal greens are not at their best eaten raw, when they taste a bit like their relative, the ice plant. Selecting young leaves, blanch or boil them as you would spinach, and they do end up tasting quite a bit like true spinach, but with a texture that's pleasantly more substantial—more like Swiss chard. Dry the cooked greens well, and toss them with butter or olive oil or mix them into omelets, casseroles, or cream sauces.

12 OUNCES DRIED TAGLIATELLE OR FETTUCINE

1 PINT HEAVY CREAM

$1/2$ CUP CHICKEN STOCK OR CANNED LOW-SODIUM BROTH

$1/4$ TEASPOON FRESHLY GRATED NUTMEG, OR TO TASTE

2 CUPS COOKED SHREDDED OR DICED CHICKEN MEAT

2 CUPS COOKED WARRIGAL GREENS (SEE BELOW) OR SPINACH OR CHARD LEAVES, COARSELY CHOPPED

SALT AND FRESHLY GROUND PEPPER

$1/2$ CUP CHOPPED TOASTED HAZELNUTS

OPTIONAL: HALVED RED AND YELLOW CHERRY TOMATOES TOSSED IN BALSAMIC VINEGAR AND OLIVE OIL; GRATED PARMESAN CHEESE

① Bring a large pot of salted water to a boil. Cook the pasta according to the package directions until it's al dente. Drain.

② While the pasta cooks, heat the cream in a large, heavy skillet over medium heat. Bring to a boil, reduce heat, and simmer until reduced by half, stirring often.

③ Stir in the chicken stock, nutmeg, chicken meat, and greens. Heat until ingredients are warmed through. Mix in the pasta. Season to taste with salt and pepper. Add more broth if the mixture seems too thick.

④ Pour the pasta into a serving bowl and sprinkle with the hazelnuts. If desired, serve with the tomato, vinegar, and oilve oil sprinkled on top of the pasta to balance the richness of the sauce.

Cooked Warrigal Greens

MAKES 2 CUPS Collect 1 pound fresh warrigal greens. Use only the leaves and small buds of the greens, discarding the stems. Bring a large pot of salted water to a rolling boil. Drop in the greens, pressing down to submerge them completely. After the water returns to a boil, cook the greens for 1 to 2 minutes for a pasta sauce or salad. If serving greens as a side dish (tossed in butter or oil), cook for 4 minutes. Drain. If not using the greens immediately, rinse under cold water and drain, then refrigerate until ready to use; reheat in a microwave or skillet. (Greens may be cooked a day in advance.)

Basic Breaded Chicken Cutlets, or Scallopine

SERVES 4 Call them scallopine, Milanese, katsu, or schnitzel, but all are essentially the same dish: thin breaded cutlets, shallow-fried in butter or oil until crisp. You can make them with veal, pork, and, in this case, chicken. Use this basic recipe as a springboard to the world variations that follow.

4 BONELESS, SKINLESS CHICKEN BREAST HALVES (ABOUT 1 1/2 POUNDS)

SALT AND FRESHLY GROUND PEPPER

ALL-PURPOSE FLOUR FOR DREDGING

2 EGGS, BEATEN WITH 2 TEASPOONS WATER

1 CUP PLAIN DRY BREAD CRUMBS

2 TABLESPOONS BUTTER

4 TABLESPOONS CANOLA OIL

① *Prepare the cutlets:* Pound the chicken breast halves until about 1/4-inch thick. If the breasts are too thick to pound into very thin pieces, slice them laterally into several 1/4-inch-thick cutlets. Salt and pepper the chicken.

continued

Basic Breaded Chicken Cutlets, or Scallopine *continued*

② Dredge the chicken in flour and shake off excess. Dip each piece into the egg, draining off excess, then coat in bread crumbs.

③ Heat 1 tablespoon butter and 2 tablespoons oil in a large skillet over medium heat. When a few bread crumbs sizzle in the pan, fry two or three chicken pieces, browning on both sides, about 2 minutes per side, until cooked through. Remove from the pan and drain on paper towels. Keep warm by tenting with foil or placing in an oven on low heat.

④ Wipe the pan clean with paper towels. Repeat the process with the remaining chicken pieces, cooking in the remaining butter and oil. Serve hot and crisp.

Japanese "Chiken" Katsu

Follow the instructions for Basic Breaded Chicken Cutlets with these changes: Replace regular bread crumbs with "panko," Japanese bread crumbs that are particularly light and airy. Omit the butter and fry only in canola or other neutral oil. Slice the fried cutlets into strips. Serve over shredded cabbage or cooked rice, and drizzle with soy sauce or with Tonkatsu sauce, bottled or homemade as follows:

Tonkatsu Sosu

> $1/2$ CUP KETCHUP
>
> 2 TABLESPOONS SOY SAUCE
>
> 1 TABLESPOON MIRIN
>
> 1 TABLESPOON SUGAR
>
> 2 TEASPOONS WORCESTERSHIRE SAUCE
>
> $1/2$ TEASPOON MINCED GINGER
>
> 1 CLOVE GARLIC, MINCED

Combine all ingredients. Let stand 30 minutes to allow flavors to blend.

Quick Tip: Fast Chicken Strips

The most time-consuming task in preparing stir-fries is chopping foods into uniform sizes for even, quick cooking. To cut up boneless, skinless chicken pieces in half the time, follow this tip: Stack two pieces of boneless chicken (breast or thigh meat, for instance) on top of each other, so they're resting lengthwise from left to right on the cutting board. Use a sharp chef's knife or Chinese cleaver and cut across the chicken, slicing it into the thin strips. For smaller pieces, turn the cutting board 90 degrees and slice through the strips to get the size pieces you want.

Chicken Piccata

Follow the instructions for Basic Breaded Chicken Cutlets with these changes: Omit the egg and bread crumbs and dredge the cutlets in flour only. After frying the cutlets, deglaze the pan to make a sauce: Remove all but 1 tablespoon of fat from the pan. Over medium heat, pour in $1/2$ cup chicken broth, $1/4$ cup dry white wine, and 2 tablespoons fresh lemon juice, scraping up any browned bits from the pan bottom. Bring to a boil, then lower heat and simmer about 3 minutes to allow the flavors to blend and sauce to thicken. Stir in 2 tablespoons drained capers. Pour the sauce over the cutlets and serve.

Pollo alla Milanese

Follow the instructions for Basic Breaded Chicken Cutlets with these changes: Omit the flour dredging and go straight to the beaten egg coating, followed by dredging in fine dry bread crumbs. Fry the cutlets in butter. Sprinkle with salt and serve with lemon wedges.

Chicken Parmigiana

Follow the instructions for Basic Breaded Chicken Cutlets with these changes:
For the bread crumbs, substitute ³/₄ cup dry Italian seasoned bread crumbs and mix ¹/₄ cup grated Parmesan cheese. If desired, use half olive oil and half canola oil. Fry the cutlets as indicated. Heat the oven to 350 degrees. Lightly grease a 13 x 9-inch (or equivalent) baking dish. Spread ¹/₂ cup of your favorite tomato sauce in the bottom of the dish. Arrange the fried cutlets in the dish, overlapping them slightly. Dust with ¹/₄ cup grated Parmesan cheese, and spoon another 1 cup sauce on top. Finish with a layer of thinly sliced mozzarella cheese (about 6 ounces) and another ¹/₂ cup grated Parmesan. Cover with foil and bake 25 minutes, or until heated through. Uncover and broil a few minutes to brown the top. Serve hot.

Chicken Schnitzel

See the recipe for Chicken Schnitzel with Lemon-Mushroom Sauce in this chapter.

Caribbean Chicken in Coconut Curry

SERVES 4 Caribbean influences include Indian spices, hence the use of curry powder in many dishes, along with coconut milk. Allspice (the main spice in jerk seasonings), which hails from Jamaica, kicks up this mild curry with its own sunny island influence.

SALT AND FRESHLY GROUND PEPPER

2¹/₂ TO 3 POUNDS SKINLESS CHICKEN PIECES

1 TABLESPOON CANOLA OIL

1 RED BELL PEPPER, SLICED INTO STRIPS

3 GREEN ONIONS, GREEN AND WHITE PARTS CHOPPED

3 CLOVES GARLIC, FINELY CHOPPED

1-INCH PIECE FRESH GINGER, FINELY CHOPPED

1 TABLESPOON CURRY POWDER

1 TEASPOON GROUND ALLSPICE

1/4 CUP CHICKEN STOCK OR CANNED LOW-SODIUM BROTH

1 1/3 CUPS UNSWEETENED COCONUT MILK (TWO 5.6-OUNCE CANS)

1/4 TEASPOON SUGAR, OR TO TASTE

JUICE OF 1 LIME

GARNISH: 1/4 CUP CHOPPED GREEN ONION TOPS, RESERVED FROM ABOVE

① Salt and pepper the chicken. Heat the oil in a large, deep skillet or Dutch oven over medium-high heat. Brown the chicken on all sides. Remove the chicken from the pan and set aside.

② In the same pan, fry the bell pepper, green onions (reserving 1/4 cup chopped tops for garnish), garlic, ginger, curry powder, and allspice. Cook until the vegetables soften.

③ Over medium heat, deglaze the pan with the chicken stock, scraping up any browned bits. Return the chicken to the pot and add the coconut milk. Bring just to a boil, then reduce the heat and simmer, uncovered, until chicken cooks through, about 30 minutes, turning the pieces often to cook evenly. Taste the mixture, adding salt as needed. If the mixture needs sweetening, stir in sugar to taste. Stir in lime juice. Serve over cooked rice, garnishing with reserved green onion tops.

Chicken Adobo

SERVES 4 The most commonly served dish of the Philippines, adobo may also be made with pork. It has a delectably sharp, tart flavor and pairs well with golden annatto-flavored rice and a simple steamed green vegetable. In this recipe, the marinated chicken simmers in a tangy sauce. The pieces are then fried in a small amount of oil and returned to the sauce for serving. If you prefer not to fry the pieces, simply simmer them in the sauce until cooked through, then remove them while the sauce reduces, skipping the frying process altogether. The chicken won't be as crisp, but it will still be moist and flavorful.

continued

Chicken Adobo *continued*

> 1 CUP RED WINE VINEGAR
>
> 6 CLOVES GARLIC, MINCED
>
> ¼ LARGE ONION, SLICED THIN
>
> ½ TEASPOON FRESHLY GROUND BLACK PEPPER
>
> 2 BAY LEAVES
>
> 2 TABLESPOONS SOY SAUCE
>
> 1 LARGE CHICKEN, CUT INTO 8 PIECES (WITH OR WITHOUT SKIN)
>
> 2 TO 4 TABLESPOONS CANOLA OIL
>
> GARNISH: 2 GREEN ONIONS, GREEN AND WHITE PARTS CHOPPED; CILANTRO SPRIGS (OPTIONAL)

① Mix together the vinegar, garlic, onion, black pepper, bay leaves, and soy sauce in a large nonreactive pot. Add the chicken and marinate for 30 minutes to 1 hour, stirring occasionally.

② Bring the pot to a boil over medium-high heat. Reduce the heat to low, cover the pot, and simmer until the chicken pieces are tender, about 15 to 20 minutes, turning once.

③ Remove the chicken from the pot and dry the pieces thoroughly. Skim off any grease from the sauce. Boil the sauce until reduced to ⅔ cup.

④ Heat 2 tablespoons of the oil in a wok or large skillet until smoking hot. Carefully add the chicken pieces. Brown the pieces on all sides. If cooking more than one batch, you may need more oil.

⑤ Drain the chicken pieces briefly. Reheat the sauce, then add the chicken pieces and cook just until heated through. Serve the chicken with plenty of sauce, garnished with green onion and cilantro sprigs.

Chicken and Pork Pad Thai

SERVES 4 Other than mee krob, this is perhaps the most famous Thai noodle dish. You'll find it in every Thai restaurant, and you'll also find it made differently in every

Thai restaurant. This is a mildly hot version, with small quantities of ground meats and vegetables. Feel free to be Thai-like with this recipe and change the ingredients and amounts to suit your own taste. Rice noodles, fish sauce, and ground dried shrimp (desirable but not necessary) can be found in Asian markets.

1/2 POUND FLAT RICE NOODLES

1/2 CUP DISTILLED WHITE VINEGAR

1/3 CUP FISH SAUCE (*NAM PLA*)

3 TABLESPOONS SUGAR

2 TABLESPOONS TOMATO PASTE

3 TABLESPOONS CANOLA OIL

1 TABLESPOON GARLIC, MINCED

1/2 TEASPOON RED PEPPER FLAKES

1/2 POUND GROUND PORK

1/2 POUND GROUND CHICKEN

1/2 POUND NAPA CABBAGE, JULIENNED

1/2 POUND SNOW PEAS, TRIMMED AND SLICED IN HALF DIAGONALLY

1 LARGE CARROT, JULIENNED

2 EGGS, BEATEN

1/2 POUND BEAN SPROUTS, TRIMMED

GARNISHES:

1 TEASPOON DRIED SHRIMP, FINELY GROUND (OPTIONAL)

3 TABLESPOONS PEANUTS, TOASTED AND COARSELY GROUND

1/4 TEASPOON RED PEPPER FLAKES

1 GREEN ONION, GREEN AND WHITE PARTS DIAGONALLY SLICED

SEVERAL CILANTRO SPRIGS

1 LIME, CUT INTO WEDGES

① Pour boiling water over the noodles to cover. Soak until soft and pliable, about 10 minutes. They should be flexible but not so soft that they can be mashed with the fingers. Drain.

② In a small bowl, combine the vinegar, fish sauce, sugar, and tomato paste until all ingredients are dissolved.

continued

Chicken and Pork Pad Thai *continued*

③ Heat a wok or large skillet over high heat. Swirl 1 tablespoon of the oil in the pan until it coats the sides and bottom. Stir-fry the garlic and red pepper flakes in the oil for 20 seconds. Add the ground meats and stir-fry them until they start to crumble. Stir in the cabbage, snow peas, and carrot, and stir-fry 1 minute.

④ Pour in the vinegar sauce and bring to a boil. Stir in the noodles and toss until well coated and mixed with the meats and vegetables.

⑤ Push the ingredients to one side of the wok. Pour the remaining 2 tablespoons oil onto the empty side of the wok and immediately pour the beaten eggs onto the oiled area. Let the eggs cook undisturbed for 15 seconds, then mound the noodles on top of them. (Use more oil if the eggs or noodles start to stick to the wok.) At this point, the eggs should be almost set, but not fully cooked. Add the bean sprouts on top of the noodles. Stir and fold the noodles into the egg, until all ingredients are thoroughly mixed together and the eggs fully set, about 1 minute.

⑥ Remove the noodles to a serving platter. Sprinkle on the garnishes, starting with the dried shrimp, then the peanuts, followed by the red pepper flakes. Finally, toss on the reserved green onion and cilantro sprigs and serve with lime wedges.

Chicken Calabrese

SERVES 4 TO 6 This dish reflects the robust flavors of Calabria, the southernmost point of Italy. It practically screams to be served on a red and white checked tablecloth, by the light of a candle burning in a straw-covered flask. Serve with a hearty red wine.

1 TABLESPOON CANOLA OIL

2 TABLESPOONS EXTRA-VIRGIN OLIVE OIL

3 CLOVES GARLIC

3 SPRIGS FRESH SAGE

4 POUNDS CHICKEN PIECES

SALT AND FRESHLY GROUND PEPPER

1 CUP RED WINE VINEGAR

3/4 CUP DRY RED WINE

1 1/2 TEASPOONS FRESH THYME LEAVES, CHOPPED (OR 1/2 TEASPOON DRIED)

1 1/2 TEASPOONS FRESH ROSEMARY LEAVES, CHOPPED (OR 1/2 TEASPOON DRIED)

4 ANCHOVY FILLETS, CHOPPED

2 TABLESPOONS CAPERS, CHOPPED

① Heat both oils on medium in a large skillet or Dutch oven. With the flat of a knife, crush the garlic cloves to release their flavor; discard the peels. Add the garlic and sage to the oil. Quickly brown the chicken pieces in the oil over high heat until golden on all sides. Season the chicken with salt and pepper.

② Add the wine vinegar, wine, thyme, and rosemary to the chicken. Bring the liquid to a boil. Cover and simmer over low heat for 8 minutes. Turn the pieces over, then simmer until chicken is cooked through, about 5 minutes.

③ Remove the chicken to a serving platter and tent with foil to keep warm. Stir the anchovies and capers into the pan. Reduce the sauce over medium-high heat until thickened slightly, about the consistency of thin syrup. Remove the garlic cloves from the mixture. Return the chicken to the pot to heat through. Serve the chicken with the warm sauce.

Chicken in Wine with Balsamic-Herb Gravy

SERVES 4 My first comment after tasting this dish was, "Great! Very tasty!" I hope you agree. It's a simple dish that can be made using ingredients you likely have on hand, plus a few fresh herbs to make all the difference in the flavor.

In some dishes, a sauce is thickened by reduction after cooking, or the chicken is coated with seasoned flour before browning, which helps to thicken the sauce. In this case, the chicken is browned and removed from the pot, and flour is cooked with onions and herbs to make a roux. The chicken goes back into the pot with wine and stock, and the sauce thickens while the chicken cooks.

continued

Chicken in Wine with Balsamic-Herb Gravy *continued*

The addition of balsamic vinegar at the end of cooking brightens the flavors; because vinegars differ in acidity, add 2 teaspoons to start, then taste and add more if needed.

SALT AND FRESHLY GROUND PEPPER

1 CHICKEN, CUT INTO 8 PIECES (OR PIECES OF CHOICE)

ABOUT 1 TABLESPOON CANOLA OIL

1 SMALL TO MEDIUM ONION, DICED

3 CLOVES GARLIC, MINCED

2 SPRIGS FRESH ROSEMARY

3 SPRIGS FRESH THYME

5 BAY LEAVES

2 TABLESPOONS ALL-PURPOSE FLOUR

1 CUP DRY WHITE WINE, SUCH AS CHARDONNAY

1 CUP CHICKEN STOCK OR LOW-SODIUM CANNED BROTH

2 TO 3 TEASPOONS BALSAMIC VINEGAR

① Generously salt and pepper the chicken pieces. In a Dutch oven or other heavy pot, film the bottom with just enough oil to coat the surface. Heat on medium high. When the oil is hot, add the chicken pieces. Brown the chicken pieces on all sides, then remove them to a plate.

② Over medium heat, cook the onion in the pot with the chicken juices until the onion starts to soften. Stir in the garlic, rosemary, 2 sprigs of the thyme, and the bay leaves. Cook, stirring occasionally, until the onion starts to brown. Stir in the flour and cook 3 to 5 minutes, until the flour is cooked through and stops sizzling.

③ Pour in the wine and chicken stock, scraping the bottom of the pan to loosen the flour and browned bits. Return the chicken to the pot. Coat the pieces with the liquid. Bring just to a boil, lower the heat, and cover. Simmer until the chicken is cooked through, about 20 minutes.

④ To finish the dish, pour in 2 teaspoons vinegar. Sprinkle the thyme leaves from the remaining sprig over the chicken. Stir the chicken pieces to coat. Taste, and season with more salt, pepper, and vinegar as needed. Serve with crusty bread for sopping up every bit of the tasty gravy.

Chicken Schnitzel with Lemon-Mushroom Sauce

SERVES 4 TO 6 Almost every culture has some form of breaded, fried meat cutlets. In Austria, they're called schnitzel, and the most famous is Wiener Schnitzel, or breaded veal cutlet. With its mild flavor, chicken stands in readily for veal. In this schnitzel version, it's served with a lemon-laced mushroom sauce in lieu of the standard lemon slice. Poppyseed noodles or spaetzle makes an ideal side dish.

4 BONELESS, SKINLESS CHICKEN BREAST HALVES

SALT AND FRESHLY GROUND PEPPER

ALL-PURPOSE FLOUR FOR DREDGING (ABOUT 1/4 CUP)

2 EGGS, BEATEN WITH 2 TEASPOONS WATER

DRY BREAD CRUMBS FOR COATING (ABOUT 1 CUP)

2 TABLESPOONS BUTTER

4 TABLESPOONS CANOLA OIL

Lemon-Mushroom Sauce

1 1/2 TABLESPOONS BUTTER

1/2 CUP FINELY CHOPPED ONION

8 OUNCES SLICED BUTTON MUSHROOMS

1 TABLESPOON ALL-PURPOSE FLOUR (FROM LEFTOVER ABOVE)

1 CUP CHICKEN STOCK OR CANNED LOW-SODIUM BROTH

2 TABLESPOONS FRESH LEMON JUICE

SALT AND FRESHLY GROUND PEPPER

GARNISH: CHOPPED FRESH HERBS (SUCH AS CHIVES, PARSLEY, OR THYME)

① *Prepare the cutlets:* Pound the chicken pieces until about 1/8-inch thick, or slice thick pieces laterally into thin cutlets. Salt and pepper the chicken.

continued

Chicken Schnitzel with Lemon-Mushroom Sauce *continued*

② Dredge the chicken in flour and shake off excess. For each piece, dip into the egg, draining off excess, then coat in bread crumbs.

③ Heat 1 tablespoon butter and 2 tablespoons oil in a large skillet on medium heat. When a few bread crumbs sizzle in the pan, fry two chicken pieces, browning on both sides, about 2 minutes per side, until cooked through. Remove from the pan and drain on paper towels. Keep warm by tenting with foil or placing in an oven on low heat.

④ Wipe the pan clean with paper towels. Repeat the process with the remaining chicken pieces, using the remaining 1 tablespoon butter and 2 tablespoons oil.

⑤ *Make the sauce:* Wipe the pan clean again before making the sauce in it. For the sauce, melt $1^{1}/_{2}$ tablespoons butter over medium heat. Cook the onions until soft. Mix in the mushrooms and cook until almost soft. Stir in the flour and cook another few minutes, stirring often, so flour cooks through and the mushrooms start to brown. Stir in the stock and simmer until the sauce thickens, about 5 minutes. Stir in the lemon juice, and taste; add salt and pepper as needed. Serve the chicken pieces with the sauce spooned on top and garnished with fresh herbs.

Chicken Vindaloo

SERVES 4 Two ingredients characterize Indian vindaloo: vinegar and chiles. Every vindaloo recipe I've tasted varies in other ingredients—some add tomatoes, others omit the mustard oil—but tartness and heat unify them all. I've tamed the hotness in this recipe for typical Western palates, but fire-lovers can pump up the volume by adding more green chiles or crushed red pepper. Serve with basmati rice and a yogurt-based raita. Dairy products, by the way, are the only remedies for a chile-scalded tongue—yogurt, sour cream, ice cream, and just plain milk will douse the heat better than ice water, beer, or other nondairy beverages.

If you don't have mustard oil (sold at Indian markets), substitute canola or vegetable oil and add a teaspoon of ground mustard seeds or a half teaspoon of prepared Dijon mustard to the spice mixture.

Tip: For this recipe, measure the vinegar in a glass measuring cup, then stir in the spices; turmeric stains most porous materials. Also, the measuring cup makes pouring the mixture into the pan easier and neater.

1/2 CUP DISTILLED WHITE VINEGAR

2 TABLESPOONS GROUND CORIANDER SEED

1 TABLESPOON GROUND CUMIN

1 TEASPOON FRESHLY GROUND BLACK PEPPER

1/2 TEASPOON GROUND CLOVES

1/2 TEASPOON GROUND TURMERIC

1/4 TEASPOON GROUND CINNAMON

1/4 TEASPOON RED PEPPER FLAKES

4 CLOVES GARLIC

2-INCH PIECE FRESH GINGER

1 GREEN CHILE (SERRANO OR JALAPEÑO), SLIVERED, STEMS AND SEEDS REMOVED

2 ONIONS

2 TABLESPOONS MUSTARD OIL

1 TABLESPOON CANOLA OR OTHER NEUTRAL OIL

2 TEASPOONS SALT

1/2 CUP WATER

2 1/2 POUNDS BONELESS, SKINLESS CHICKEN THIGHS (ABOUT 10 PIECES)

GARNISH: 1 LIME, IN WEDGES

① Combine the vinegar, coriander seed, cumin, black pepper, cloves, turmeric, cinnamon, and red pepper flakes, preferably in a glass measuring cup.

② Using a food processor or by hand, finely chop the garlic, ginger, green chile, and onions. (Ingredients may all be processed together; prechunk them into smaller pieces before whizzing in the processor.) Mixture should be very moist from the onion juices.

③ Heat the mustard oil in a large skillet over medium-high heat until it reaches its smoking point. Cook a few seconds to release its pungency and mellow its harshness. Add the canola oil and turn the heat down to low.

continued

Chicken Vindaloo *continued*

④ Carefully spoon in about half of the onion mixture and immediately cover with a lid—it will splatter quite a bit at first when the liquid hits the hot oil. When the splattering stops, remove the lid and pour the rest of the mixture in. Turn the heat back up to medium-high. Stirring occasionally, cook until the onions are soft and all ingredients have cooked through, about 5 minutes. The mixture will become drier as it cooks.

⑤ Stir in the vinegar and spice mixture. Cook over medium-low, about 5 minutes.

⑥ Add and stir in the salt and water. Place the chicken pieces in the pan, coating thoroughly, and nestle them into the sauce to cook. Cover and bring to a boil on high. Turn the heat down and simmer 45 minutes, mixing the chicken pieces around halfway through for even cooking. Serve now, or for best results, let mixture rest for 15 minutes to better absorb the flavors, and reheat just before serving. The chicken pieces will be fork-tender, with plenty of flavorful sauce. Serve with lime wedges. Cooked basmati rice and warm naan (an Indian flatbread) are ideal side dishes.

Chinese Honey-Lemon Chicken

SERVES 4 Cornstarch is usually thought of as a thickener, but here it's used as a coating for frying. The batter comes out lighter and crisper than with flour. In fact, I like the texture of these chicken breasts so much that I frequently serve them without the sauce, as a variation on fried chicken. But the sauce itself is seductively light and refreshing, with a gingery sparkle. Drizzle the sauce onto the chicken, and serve with steamed rice and a cucumber salad. Shao-hsing wine is a smoky Chinese rice wine, but you can substitute dry sherry.

> 1 EGG
>
> 1 TABLESPOON SOY SAUCE
>
> $^{1}/_{4}$ TEASPOON WHITE PEPPER
>
> 4 BONELESS, SKINLESS CHICKEN BREAST HALVES
>
> 1 RECIPE HONEY-LEMON SAUCE (SEE BELOW)

CORNSTARCH FOR DREDGING

CANOLA OIL

2 GREEN ONIONS, GREEN AND WHITES PARTS DIAGONALLY SLICED

GARNISH: CILANTRO SPRIGS (OPTIONAL)

① Mix the egg, soy sauce, and white pepper together in a shallow bowl. Add the chicken breast halves, coat thoroughly, and leave to soak in the egg mixture for 30 minutes. While the chicken soaks in the egg mixture, make the Honey-Lemon Sauce (see instructions below).

② Remove the chicken from the egg mixture. Dredge it with cornstarch and shake off the excess. Pour enough oil into a skillet to come halfway up the thickest part of the chicken. Heat until very hot. Add the chicken and fry until the coating is crisp and the chicken is tender, about 3 or 4 minutes on each side. Remove the chicken and drain on paper towels.

③ Slice the chicken into long, parallel strips, about ¹/₂ inch wide. Serve the strips drizzled with the Honey-Lemon Sauce and garnished with green onions and cilantro.

Honey-Lemon Sauce

¹/₂ CUP WATER

1 (2-INCH) PIECE FRESH GINGER, QUARTERED

3 TABLESPOONS LEMON JUICE

2 TABLESPOONS HONEY

1 TABLESPOON WHITE WINE VINEGAR

2 TEASPOONS SHAO-HSING WINE OR DRY SHERRY

¹/₂ TEASPOON SALT

2 TEASPOONS CORNSTARCH

1 TABLESPOON COLD WATER

1 TEASPOON TOASTED SESAME OIL

① Combine the ¹/₂ cup water, ginger, lemon juice, honey, wine vinegar, wine, and salt in a small saucepan. Heat over low flame until all elements except the ginger are

continued

Honey-Lemon Sauce *continued*

dissolved and mixed together. Bring to a boil, turn the heat to low, and simmer, covered, for 1 minute. Discard the ginger.

② Mix the 2 teaspoons of cornstarch with 1 tablespoon of cold water, stirring until completely dissolved. Stir the cornstarch mixture into the sauce. Let the sauce come back to a boil, raising the heat slightly if necessary. Simmer for 1 minute, or until the sauce forms a thick, syrupy glaze. Turn off the heat. Cover and set aside while you cook the chicken.

③ Just before serving, uncover the sauce and warm over medium heat, stirring, until it reaches a low boil. If the sauce is too thick, add a small amount of water. Remove from the heat and stir in the sesame oil. Drizzle over the chicken, or pass the sauce on the side.

Coq au Vermouth

SERVES 4 The lovely flavor of dry vermouth comes from infusing wine with aromatic herbs, spices, barks, and peels. Then the wine is allowed to mature. Originally added for medicinal purposes, these extra flavorings make vermouth an ideal cooking wine, particularly for fish and fowl. This dish is a variation of the classic coq au vin, which simmers chicken and vegetables in hearty red wine. The dry vermouth seems to lighten the sauce while heightening the herb seasonings. To accompany the dish, mix cooked basil-flavored pasta directly into the sauce, so all the flavors are absorbed.

2 CUPS PEARL ONIONS

2 TEASPOONS OLIVE OIL

1 RIB CELERY, CHOPPED

1 CARROT, CHOPPED

1 TEASPOON SUGAR

1/2 POUND MUSHROOMS, SLICED

3/4 CUP ALL-PURPOSE FLOUR

1/2 TEASPOON SALT

1/2 TEASPOON WHITE PEPPER

1 CHICKEN, CUT INTO 8 PIECES

4 SLICES BACON, CUT INTO 1/4-INCH BITS

2 TEASPOONS CANOLA OIL

1/4 TEASPOON DRIED TARRAGON, CRUSHED

1/4 TEASPOON DRIED THYME

1 1/2 CUPS DRY VERMOUTH

2 TABLESPOONS CHOPPED FRESH CHIVES (OR PARSLEY)

① To peel the pearl onions, bring a small pan of water to a boil. Cut a small x in the bottom of each onion. Blanch the onions for 3 minutes, then drain and rinse under cool running water. Trim off the stems. The skins should slip off easily. Set the onions aside.

② In a Dutch oven or large flameproof casserole, heat the olive oil over medium heat. Add the pearl onions, celery, carrot, and sugar. Cook slowly, stirring every now and then, until the onions begin to brown and caramelize, about 4 minutes. Stir in the mushrooms and cook an additional minute. Remove the vegetables from the pan.

③ While the vegetables cook, mix the flour with the salt and white pepper. Dredge the chicken in the flour, shaking off excess.

④ Brown the bacon bits in the same pan. Remove the bacon from the pan and set aside with the vegetables. Add the canola oil to the bacon drippings in the pan and heat over a medium-high flame. When the oil is hot, brown the chicken on all sides, about 6 to 10 minutes.

⑤ Return the vegetables and bacon bits to the pan with the chicken. Crumble in the tarragon and thyme and pour in the vermouth. Bring the liquid to a boil over medium-high heat. Cover and simmer on low for 30 minutes.

⑥ Remove the chicken and vegetables to a serving platter. Pour the sauce over the chicken and serve sprinkled with the chives.

Corinthian Chicken and Olives

SERVES 4 The port of Corinth must have been founded on human determination. Twice, in 1858 and 1928, this city has been destroyed by earthquakes, and twice it has recovered. Ancient Corinth fared no better. A powerful city-state, it was a major player in the devastating Peloponnesian War, and a few centuries later it was destroyed by the Romans. Another Roman, Julius Caesar, revived the port town, but it later fell into the hands of Byzantine Crusaders, Venetians, and Ottoman Turks. About twenty-five years before being demolished by its first earthquake, Corinth was recaptured by Greek insurgents. Today, Corinth is a busy, bustling port.

Olives and wine are key commodities in this active trading center. This recipe is typical of those served on the peninsula of Peloponnesus. It's full of robust Mediterranean ingredients, and the salty green olives, dry white wine, and pungent kasseri cheese make this dish particularly Corinthian.

3/4 CUP GREEN OLIVES, STUFFED WITH PIMIENTOS

3/4 CUP FLOUR

1/2 TEASPOON SALT

1 TEASPOON FRESHLY GROUND PEPPER

4 CHICKEN BREAST HALVES

1 TABLESPOON EXTRA-VIRGIN OLIVE OIL

1 TABLESPOON CANOLA OIL

1 ONION, CHOPPED

4 LARGE ROMA TOMATOES, CHOPPED

1 TEASPOON DRIED OREGANO, CRUSHED

3/4 CUP DRY WHITE WINE

1/2 LEMON

1/3 POUND GRATED KASSERI CHEESE OR CRUMBLED FETA

GARNISH: MINCED PARSLEY

① Slice the olives in half and set aside. Mix the flour with the salt and pepper. Dredge the chicken in the seasoned flour, shaking off excess.

② Heat the oils in a large skillet or Dutch oven over medium-high heat. Brown the chicken on all sides. When it is almost brown on the last side, add the onion and cook until translucent. Stir in the tomatoes, oregano, and $^1/_2$ cup of wine. Bring to a boil, then reduce heat to low and simmer, covered, for 20 minutes.

③ Remove the lid. Stir in the olives and the remaining $^1/_4$ cup of wine, and squeeze in the juice from the lemon half (squeeze over a small sieve to catch the seeds). Top with the cheese. Continue simmering, partially covered, for 5 to 10 minutes, until the cheese melts.

④ Remove the chicken to a serving platter. Spoon the sauce over the chicken and serve garnished with a sprinkling of parsley.

Creole Mustard Chicken Breasts

SERVES 4 "Creole mustard" is the rowdy, raucous, bad boy of mustards. Open a jar and, if you're not prepared, you might just get knocked over by the heady aromas of spice, vinegar, and mustard seed, all wrapped up in a light blanket of heat. Hooey! This is not that sissy stuff passed between Rolls Royces. Creole mustard definitely adds kick to a meal. Next time you're in New Orleans, order shrimp with remoulade sauce and you may be very surprised; for there, that old boring grandfather of a sauce is made with Creole mustard, and suddenly it finds youth again. Creole mustard is available in specialty markets and at some grocers. Look for it in the condiment aisle and at the fresh seafood counter.

4 CHICKEN BREAST HALVES, WITH SKIN OR SKINLESS

SALT

$^1/_2$ CUP CHICKEN STOCK OR CANNED LOW-SODIUM CHICKEN BROTH

$^3/_4$ CUP DRY WHITE WINE

$^1/_4$ CUP CREOLE MUSTARD

1 TEASPOON WORCESTERSHIRE SAUCE

1 TEASPOON TOMATO PASTE

$^1/_4$ CUP CORN OIL

1 LEEK, CLEANED AND SLICED INTO THIN RINGS

1 ROMA TOMATO, SEEDED AND CHOPPED

① Season the chicken with salt. In a small mixing bowl, combine the broth, wine, mustard, Worcestershire sauce, and tomato paste. Set aside.

continued

Creole Mustard Chicken Breasts *continued*

② Heat 2 tablespoons of the oil in a large skillet over high heat. When hot, add the leek, making sure to separate the slices into rings. Fry until the rings become brown on the edges, but still retain their shape. Remove them from the pan and place in a single layer on a plate.

③ In the same pan, heat the remaining 2 tablespoons of oil. Add the chicken breasts, rib side up, and cook until brown, about 4 minutes. Turn them over and brown the other side.

④ When the chicken has browned, pour the mustard mixture over the breasts and into the pan. Cover, reduce the heat to low, and simmer until the breasts are tender, about 15 minutes.

⑤ Serve the chicken with the sauce. Top with the crisp leek rings and chopped tomato before serving.

Greco-Roman Chicken Rolls

SERVES 4 It is said the ancient Greeks and Romans had much in common, not the least of which was a love of fine food. Their modern-day descendents carry on this epicurean appreciation, and this recipe features two of the finest ingredients of each culture: Greek kasseri cheese and Italian prosciutto. Here, pounded chicken breasts are rolled and stuffed with prosciutto, kasseri, and puréed sun-dried tomatoes, then simmered with earthy mushrooms in an herb-infused vermouth sauce. They make an elegant but easy dinner, served with a sautéed summer squash medley and crusty bread.

Look for Sun-Dry Tomato Spread near the produce section, where sun-dried tomato products are sold. Or make your own by puréeing oil-packed sun-dried tomatoes to a thick, spreadable paste. It's great on sandwiches, and a spoonful enriches soups, sauces, and stews.

1 TABLESPOON BUTTER

1 TABLESPOON EXTRA-VIRGIN OLIVE OIL

2 CLOVES GARLIC, MINCED

8 OUNCES SLICED MUSHROOMS

4 BONELESS, SKINLESS CHICKEN BREAST HALVES

4 TEASPOONS SUN-DRY TOMATO SPREAD

8 PAPER-THIN SLICES PROSCIUTTO (ABOUT 4 OUNCES)

1/4 POUND THINLY SLICED KASSERI CHEESE

FLOUR FOR DREDGING

1 TABLESPOON CANOLA OIL

1/2 CUP DRY VERMOUTH

SALT AND FRESHLY GROUND PEPPER

GARNISH: MINCED ITALIAN PARSLEY OR OTHER FRESH HERB

① Heat the butter and olive oil in a large skillet. Add the garlic and mushrooms. Sauté until the mushrooms begin to soften and just start to brown. Remove the mixture from the pan and set aside.

② Pound the chicken breast halves until very thin, about 1/4-inch thick. Spread 1 teaspoon Sun-Dry Tomato Spread on the inside of each chicken breast. Layer 2 slices of prosciutto on top, covering as much breast as possible. Place the kasseri slices on top of the prosciutto. Starting with the small end of the breast, roll up each piece like a jellyroll and secure with toothpicks.

③ Dredge each chicken breast lightly in flour, shaking off excess. Heat the canola oil in the skillet. Add the breasts and brown on all sides, about 6 minutes. Return the mushrooms to the pan, filling in the vacant areas between and around the breasts. Pour in the vermouth, cover, and cook on low 6 to 8 minutes, depending on the size of the breasts. Season with salt and pepper to taste. (The cheese is salty, so add salt sparingly.)

④ Serve the chicken rolls surrounded by the mushroom sauce and garnished with parsley or other fresh herb. (Remove the toothpicks before serving.)

Green Chile Chicken Breasts

SERVES 4 If you live in the sun belt from California to Louisiana, it's easy to find certain Mexican staples at all times—limes, fresh cilantro, cumin, onion, cheese, and cans of roasted green chiles. With these ingredients and a few boneless, skinless chicken beasts, a lively Southwestern fiesta is just minutes away. Warm flour tortillas and beans round this out to a full meal. Roll any leftover chicken into burritos or tacos.

4 BONELESS, SKINLESS CHICKEN BREAST HALVES

2 TABLESPOONS FRESH LIME JUICE

1 TEASPOON GROUND CUMIN

¼ CUP CHOPPED FRESH CILANTRO

2 TEASPOONS CORN OIL

½ CUP DICED ONION

1 CUP CHOPPED ROASTED, PEELED GREEN CHILES (FRESHLY MADE OR CANNED)

SALT

1 CUP SHREDDED MONTEREY JACK OR CHEDDAR CHEESE

GARNISH: GROUND RED CHILES OR PAPRIKA (OPTIONAL)

① Score the chicken breasts. Marinate the chicken breasts in the lime juice, cumin, and half of the chopped cilantro for at least 10 minutes, up to 1 hour.

② Heat the corn oil in a large nonstick skillet over high heat. When very hot, sauté the onion and cook until it starts to brown on the edges. Add the green chiles and cook another minute until the mixture is very hot.

③ Push the onion mixture to the outer edges of the pan and add the chicken breasts, presentation side down. Pour any remaining marinade on top of them and season with salt. Cook 2 to 3 minutes, until chicken browns, then flip the chicken over. Sprinkle shredded cheese over the cooked side. Reduce the heat to medium low. Cover the pan, cook another 2 to 3 minutes, until chicken is almost done, then turn off the heat. Let the chicken rest for 2 minutes or so to melt the cheese and let the chicken cook through.

④ Serve the chicken breasts on top of the onion and chile mixture, and sprinkle with the remaining chopped cilantro. Garnish with a dash of red chile powder or paprika for color.

Indonesian Chicken with Green Beans

SERVES 3 TO 4 WITH RICE OR NOODLES A bowl of rice or noodles topped with this Indonesian stir-fry makes a cozy one-dish meal. Kecap manis, a staple of Indonesian cooking, is a thick, sweetened soy sauce that I enjoy drizzled on cooked rice, chicken, or noodles. Look for it in Filipino, Indonesian, and other Asian markets. If unavailable, use the same amount of regular soy sauce, sweetened with 1 teaspoon of brown sugar.

1 POUND BONELESS, SKINLESS CHICKEN BREAST HALVES

2 TEASPOONS CORNSTARCH

1/4 CUP FRESH LIME JUICE

2 TABLESPOONS MINCED FRESH GINGER

4 CLOVES GARLIC, MINCED

3 TABLESPOONS CANOLA OIL

1/2 POUND GREEN BEANS, DIAGONALLY SLICED INTO 1-INCH PIECES

1/2 MEDIUM ONION, THINLY SLICED

1/2 RED BELL PEPPER, THINLY SLICED

1 TEASPOON TURMERIC

1/4 TEASPOON RED PEPPER FLAKES

1/2 CUP CHICKEN STOCK OR CANNED LOW-SODIUM BROTH

2 TABLESPOONS KECAP MANIS (SWEET SOY SAUCE)

SALT

① Cut the chicken into thin strips and place in a shallow bowl. Toss the chicken with the cornstarch, half the lime juice, half the ginger, and half the garlic. Marinate in the refrigerator from 30 minutes to 2 hours.

② Heat the oil in a wok or large skillet over high heat; oil should ripple but not smoke. Stir-fry the remaining ginger and garlic, green beans, onion, and red bell pepper until vegetables are almost cooked through but still crisp, about 3 minutes. Remove with a slotted spoon and set aside. *continued*

Indonesian Chicken with Green Beans *continued*

③ In the same hot wok, stir-fry the chicken, turmeric, and red pepper flakes until chicken is almost cooked through but still pink inside, about 2 minutes. Pour in the chicken stock, kecap manis, remaining lime juice, and the partially cooked vegetables. Cover and simmer over medium heat 2 minutes, just long enough to finish cooking the chicken and vegetables. Season with salt to taste. Serve over cooked rice or noodles.

Irish Hen with Bacon and Cabbage

SERVES 2 Cabbage and bacon are quintessential Irish ingredients, simmered here with rich cream and a Cornish hen. This recipe makes a cozy supper for two. To serve four, add another Cornish hen, quartered, and increase the cabbage by a half-pound or so. Increase the other ingredients by half; you won't need to double them fully, as the flavors will stretch.

1 SMALL HEAD CABBAGE, PREFERABLY SAVOY (ABOUT 1 POUND)

2 LEEKS

1 CORNISH HEN (OR ABOUT 1^1/$_2$ POUNDS CHICKEN PIECES)

1 TEASPOON GLOBAL GOURMET HERB SEASONING (CHAPTER 12)

6 OUNCES SLICED BACON

4 SPRIGS FRESH THYME

^{1}/$_4$ CUP DRY VERMOUTH

1^1/$_2$ CUPS HEAVY CREAM

^{1}/$_4$ TEASPOON GROUND NUTMEG

SALT AND FRESHLY GROUND PEPPER

1 TABLESPOON CIDER VINEGAR

① Core and thinly slice the cabbage. Rinse the leeks well, split in half lengthwise, and rinse between the layers to remove hidden dirt. Thinly slice the leeks crosswise, into half-circles. Divide the Cornish hen into quarters using a sharp knife or kitchen shears. Rub the pieces with the Global Gourmet Herb Seasoning.

② Slice the bacon into ¹/₃-inch-wide pieces. In a large skillet, fry the bacon until crisp. Drain on paper towels, leaving 2 tablespoons rendered bacon fat in the pan and reserving any poured-off fat.

③ Over medium-high heat, brown the hen pieces on all sides. Reduce the heat to low and continue to cook the pieces until almost done, just slightly pink in the center. Remove from the pan and set aside.

④ In the same pan, fry the leeks for a minute or so until they begin to soften. Add the cabbage and 2 thyme sprigs and cook just until the cabbage starts to soften, adding more bacon fat if needed. Add the vermouth, and cook 1 minute. Stir in the cream and nutmeg. Place the hen pieces on top. Bring the mixture to a boil. Cover and simmer 10 to 15 minutes, to cook the hen through and to blend the flavors.

⑤ Just before serving, season the cabbage with salt and pepper to taste, and stir in the vinegar, adding more as needed to perk up the flavors. Arrange the hen pieces on top of the cabbage. Sprinkle with bacon and the remaining 2 thyme sprigs and serve.

Israeli Couscous with Chicken and Olives

SERVES 3 TO 4 Israeli couscous is decidedly not the same thing as small-grained North African–style couscous, which would overcook into mush if used in this recipe. Also known as toasted couscous, super couscous, maftoul, and pearl couscous, Israeli couscous is about the shape and size of peppercorns or tapioca pearls. More versatile than traditional couscous, these large balls of extruded pasta are toasted, giving them a nutty flavor, and can be boiled and drained like pasta, steamed, or cooked like risotto. Retoasting them in a bit of butter or oil before cooking enhances their seductive nutlike taste and aroma.

A darling of today's trendy chefs, Israeli couscous was invented in the 1950s by Israel's Osem brand, at the request of David Ben-Gurion. As an independent state, Israel was in its infancy, and its first prime minister wanted to give the Jewish

continued

Israeli Couscous with Chicken and Olives *continued*

emigrants from Africa, Asia, and the Middle East foods they were familiar with. But rice and couscous, the main staples of these peoples, were not available in Israel. As a result, according to Jewish cooking authority Joan Nathan, the Osem company (Israel's leading pasta maker) extruded wheat pastas shaped like rice (called orez Ben-Gurion) and large couscous grains. "Ben-Gurion's pasta" is now known as Israeli couscous and is sold in Middle Eastern markets.

Tips for this recipe: Be sure to grate the zest from the lemon before you squeeze the juice. Don't substitute small-grained couscous for toasted Israeli couscous. Taste to balance the flavors—the sugar and spices create a sweet crust, contrasting with the lemony flavor of the couscous and the salty bite of the olives.

Middle Eastern Spice Rub

1/2 TEASPOON GROUND CINNAMON

1/2 TEASPOON GROUND GINGER

1/4 TEASPOON GROUND TURMERIC

1/2 TEASPOON PAPRIKA (PREFERABLY HALF-SHARP, OR IF SWEET, ADD CAYENNE)

1/2 TEASPOON SALT

1/2 TEASPOON SUGAR

6 CHICKEN THIGHS, SKINLESS, OR OTHER PIECES OF CHOICE

1 WHOLE FRESH LEMON, WASHED AND DRIED

2 TABLESPOONS OLIVE OIL

1 ONION, CHOPPED

1 (8.8-OUNCE) PACKAGE TOASTED ISRAELI COUSCOUS (ABOUT 1 3/4 CUPS)

2 CUPS CHICKEN STOCK OR CANNED LOW-SODIUM BROTH

1 CUP PITTED GREEN OLIVES (PREFERABLY PIMIENTO-STUFFED)

GARNISH: 2 TABLESPOONS CHOPPED FRESH CILANTRO OR PARSLEY

① Combine spice rub ingredients in a small bowl. Rub chicken pieces all over with the spice rub. Cover and let marinate 1 hour (or longer, refrigerated).

② Remove the zest from the lemon with a grater or zester. Squeeze the juice. Set each aside separately.

③ Heat 1 tablespoon oil in a large, deep skillet over high heat. Brown the chicken pieces on all sides, cooking until spices form a mahogany-colored crust and meat is almost cooked through (about 3 minutes per side). Remove the chicken from the pan and set aside, leaving any juices in the pan.

④ In the same pan, heat the remaining 1 tablespoon oil. Cook the onion over medium heat until translucent. Stir in the toasted Israeli couscous, reduce the heat to medium low, and cook about 5 minutes until couscous turns pale golden brown, stirring often. Stir in the chicken stock and lemon juice.

⑤ Arrange the chicken pieces on top of the couscous and scatter the olives on top. Bring the liquid to a boil on high, then cover and simmer on low until couscous is tender and chicken cooked is through, about 10 to 15 minutes. (If the couscous is too soupy but the chicken is cooked through, uncover and simmer until the liquid evaporates.)

⑥ Uncover the pan, stir the couscous gently in between the chicken pieces to lift and fluff it. Re-cover and let pan stand off the heat for 5 minutes; couscous will steam and become fluffier. Before serving, garnish the chicken with the chopped herbs and grated zest. Serve with harissa or other hot chile paste on the side, if desired.

Maille Mustard Chicken and Pasta

SERVES 4 During the eighteenth century, Monsieur Maille created truly royal mustards, many of which are still in use today. He was the official vinegar distiller to the king, and it is said that Madame de Pompadour would commission his aniseed vinegar by the barrel. He was famous throughout the continent for his flavored vinegars, which he then made into equally famous mustards.

Today, most supermarkets carry the Maille brand of mustard. It comes in a squat jar with a black label. The "old style" version is wonderfully coarse, full of whole, golden seeds bathed in a heady vinegar base. The mustard acts like a magic ingredient in this dish, infusing it with a bright sparkle. Its tartness and rough texture give the sauce robust depth and body, while the creamy base is mellow enough to bring out the sweet, subtle flavor of the chicken. If you can't find Maille mustard, then substitute a coarse-ground Dijon.

Use any pasta in this dish, but I prefer spaghetti that has a touch of whole wheat flour in it. The noodles give off just enough of their own flavor to stand up handsomely

continued

Maille Mustard Chicken and Pasta *continued*

to the sauce. Noodles infused with such flavorings as basil or black pepper also work well.

2¹/₂ TO 3 POUNDS CHICKEN PIECES

SALT AND FRESHLY GROUND PEPPER

ABOUT 12 FRESH SAGE LEAVES

3 TABLESPOONS UNSALTED BUTTER

1 TABLESPOON CANOLA OIL

1 POUND SPAGHETTI

¹/₂ CUP DRY WHITE WINE

¹/₂ CUP CHICKEN STOCK OR CANNED LOW-SODIUM BROTH

1 CUP CRÈME FRAÎCHE OR HEAVY CREAM

2 TABLESPOONS WHOLE-GRAIN MAILLE OR DIJON MUSTARD

GARNISH: FRESH SAGE LEAVES

① Season the chicken with salt and pepper. Cut the sage leaves into very thin julienne; kitchen shears are ideal for this, or use a very sharp knife.

② In a large skillet or flameproof casserole, heat 1 tablespoon butter and the oil over medium-high heat until hot. Brown the chicken pieces on all sides.

③ While the chicken cooks, bring a large pot of salted water to a boil. Add the pasta and cook until al dente. Drain, reserving some of the pasta cooking water. Using the same pot, heat the remaining 2 tablespoons butter with 2 tablespoons of the cooking water. Return the pasta to the pot and toss to coat. Cover and remove from the heat while you continue with the chicken.

④ After the chicken has browned, stir the white wine and chicken stock into the pan with the chicken, scraping up any browned bits. Cover and simmer on low for 5 minutes. Stir in the crème fraîche, mustard, and sliced sage leaves. Heat on medium until the sauce coats the back of a spoon and all flavors are blended. Taste and adjust the seasonings as needed.

⑤ To serve, place the pasta on a serving platter. Arrange the chicken pieces on top and pour the sauce over the chicken and pasta. Garnish with fresh sage leaves, if desired.

Malaysian Coconut-Chicken Curry

SERVES 6 Chicken curries appear in places as disparate as the Caribbean, Australia, Africa, India, and the Far East. While coconut milk and curry powder permeate most of the recipes, each culture's local ingredients make the curry taste distinctively different. Fish sauce, lime juice, soy sauce, and chiles put a decidedly Malaysian stamp on this chicken-and-vegetable dish. It comes together quickly and makes a satisfying meal in a bowl.

6 SHALLOTS

4 CLOVES GARLIC

1-INCH PIECE GINGER

2 TO 2$^1/_2$ POUNDS BONELESS, SKINLESS CHICKEN BREAST HALVES

SALT

2 TO 3 TABLESPOONS CANOLA OIL

2 TEASPOONS CURRY POWDER

1 (13.5- OR 14-OUNCE) CAN UNSWEETENED COCONUT MILK (ABOUT 1$^2/_3$ CUPS)

1 CUP CHICKEN STOCK OR CANNED LOW-SODIUM BROTH

1 TABLESPOON SOY SAUCE

2 TEASPOONS FISH SAUCE (*NAM PLA*)

1 TEASPOON MINCED GREEN CHILE, SUCH AS SERRANO

$^3/_4$ TEASPOON SUGAR

JUICE FROM 1 LIME, OR MORE TO TASTE

$^1/_3$ CUP COARSELY CHOPPED CILANTRO

① Finely chop the shallots, garlic, and ginger (this can be done all together in a food processor).

② Chop the chicken into bite-size pieces, about 1-inch cubes. Season with salt. Heat 2 tablespoons oil in a wok or large skillet over medium-high heat. Stir-fry the chicken pieces until almost cooked through. Remove with a slotted spoon to a plate.

③ If need be, add the remaining tablespoon of oil to the pan. Dump in the shallot mixture. Stir-fry until soft and just cooked through. Stir in the curry powder and cook another minute. Stir in the coconut milk, chicken stock, soy sauce, fish sauce, green chile, and sugar. Simmer until the mixture thickens, about 10 minutes.

continued

FLAVOR PRINTS

South Pacific: Indonesia, Malaysia, and the Philippines

Muslim traders and Chinese invaders have dominated Indonesian culture, while 350 years of Spanish rule left its mark on the Philippines. Merchants from India, China, and the Middle East made Malaysian cooking as varied as it is today. But the most important aspect of this region is that it's the home of the Spice Islands, the birthplace by trade of all other cuisines that include ginger, pepper, cinnamon, allspice, and cloves in their FlavorPrints. Curries, satés, marinated and grilled meats and poultry, and rice and noodles dominate, while peanuts garnish dishes as ground bits and in sauces.

- banana
- banana leaves
- basil
- bean sprouts
- brown sugar
- chiles
- Chinese, or napa, cabbage
- cilantro
- coconut
- cucumber
- cumin
- durian
- fish sauce (patis)
- galangal
- garlic
- ginger
- guava
- hoisin
- jackfruit
- kecap manis
- lemongrass
- lime
- lumpia wrappers
- lychee
- mango
- miso
- noodles
- onion
- palm sugar
- papaya
- peanuts
- pineapple
- rice
- sambal
- screwpine leaves
- shrimp paste
- soy sauce
- sweet potato
- tamarind
- tomato
- turmeric

Malaysian Coconut-Chicken Curry *continued*

④ Pour in the chicken and any juices accumulated on the plate. Simmer another 2 minutes to finish cooking the chicken. Add the lime juice and cilantro. Taste to see if the seasonings need to be adjusted. You may need more salt, sugar, fish sauce, or lime juice for proper balance. Serve with steamed rice.

Moroccan Chicken in Spiced Tomato Sauce

SERVES 4 In the souk, or Moroccan market, caged chickens, fragrant spices, and colorful fruits and vegetables easily inspire cooks to turn them into sensual, vibrant dishes. This stovetop chicken recipe captures the exotic tastes of North African cuisine, mingling warm spices with the tart and sweet contrasts found in dried apricots and raisins. For a complete dinner, garnish with sliced, toasted almonds and serve with couscous and a tart salad to contrast the fruity flavors of the sauce.

Moroccan Spice Mixture

2 TEASPOONS WHOLE FENNEL SEED (2¼ TEASPOONS GROUND)

1½ TEASPOONS WHOLE CORIANDER (2 TEASPOONS GROUND)

2 TEASPOONS WHOLE CUMIN SEED (2¼ TEASPOONS GROUND)

6 WHOLE CLOVES (¼ TEASPOON GROUND)

1 TEASPOON GROUND CINNAMON

¼ TEASPOON GROUND HOT RED PEPPER, SUCH AS ALEPPO PEPPER OR CAYENNE

4 CHICKEN BREASTS

1 TEASPOON SALT

2 TABLESPOONS CANOLA OIL

1 MEDIUM ONION, CHOPPED

2 CLOVES GARLIC, MINCED

1 (14.5-OUNCE) CAN DICED TOMATOES

½ CUP RAISINS

½ CUP CHOPPED DRIED APRICOTS

2 TABLESPOONS HONEY

1 TO 2 TABLESPOONS FRESH LEMON JUICE

① *Prepare Moroccan Spice Mixture:* If using whole spices, grind them finely using a spice grinder. Combine all ground spices in a small bowl. Separately set aside 1 tablespoon and 1 teaspoon, both for use later.

② Season chicken on all sides with salt and the main bowl of spice mixture. Heat the oil in a Dutch oven or large, heavy skillet over medium-high heat. Brown the

continued

Moroccan Chicken in Spiced Tomato Sauce *continued*

chicken on all sides. Push the chicken pieces to one side. In the main part of the pan, cook the onion, garlic, and the reserved 1 tablespoon of spice mixture, stirring occasionally, until the onion softens.

③ Stir in the tomatoes with their juices, the raisins, apricots, and honey. Arrange the chicken pieces on top. Cover and simmer on low until chicken is cooked through, 7 to 10 minutes, turning chicken occasionally so all sides simmer in the sauce.

④ Uncover and stir in the remaining 1 teaspoon spice mixture. Simmer 2 to 3 minutes to allow the spices to release their flavors. Just before serving, stir in 1 tablespoon lemon juice, adding more as needed for a sweet-tart balance. Serve the chicken pieces with the sauce spooned over them.

Pasta with Roasted Garlic, Chicken, and Vodka Sauce

SERVES 4 Morphed from the recipe for Lemon-Rubbed Roaster with Six Garlic Heads (chapter 4), this easy pasta is essentially a concentrated blend of reductions: lemony pan juices, chicken stock, and ripe tomatoes, mellowed by sweet roasted garlic, vodka, and cream. Vodka may sound odd, but it carries the flavors here just as it does in the classic Italian dish, Penne alla Vodka. The finely diced chicken almost melts into the sauce, adding a toothsome body. I recommend using real stock here, as canned broth doesn't thicken when reduced.

1 POUND SPAGHETTINI OR SPAGHETTI

2 HEADS ROASTED GARLIC*

1 CUP CHICKEN STOCK

2 TABLESPOONS PAN DRIPPINGS*

1 POUND RIPE TOMATOES, DICED, OR 1 (14.5-OUNCE) CAN DICED TOMATOES

1^1/$_2$ TO 2 CUPS COOKED CHICKEN MEAT, FINELY DICED*

^{1}/$_4$ CUP CREAM

2 TABLESPOONS VODKA

DASH RED PEPPER FLAKES

2 TABLESPOONS BUTTER

GARNISH: FRESH JULIENNED BASIL, GRATED PARMESAN

* Reserve chicken, drippings, and roasted garlic from the recipe for Lemon-Rubbed Roaster with Six Garlic Heads (chapter 4) for these ingredients. For the drippings, refrigerate until the fat hardens and use the layer of congealed juices below the fat in this sauce.

① Bring a large pot of salted water to a boil. Add the pasta, stirring occasionally, and cook until al dente. Drain. (To keep the pasta warm, place a pot lid over the colander as soon as you drain the pasta.)

② While the pasta cooks, make the sauce. Squeeze the roasted garlic cloves out of their papery casings, and mash with a fork. In a large skillet, bring the mashed garlic, chicken stock, and pan drippings to a boil over medium-high heat, stirring to blend. Cook at a low boil until reduced by half, about 5 to 7 minutes.

③ Stir in the tomatoes and their juices. Cook on high 5 minutes. Mix the chicken into the sauce until combined. Stir in the cream, vodka, and red pepper. Simmer 5 minutes to thicken and meld the flavors. Just before serving, stir in the butter until it melts. Pour the sauce over the hot pasta and garnish with basil and Parmesan cheese.

Pollo con Pipian Verde

SERVES 4 TO 6 Mexico is one of the world's largest producers of sesame seeds, so it's not surprising that Mexican cooks include them in their traditional thick, nut-and-seed-based sauces, known in some regions as "pipians" and in others as "moles." The classic dark, rich Oaxacan mole includes unsweetened chocolate in a dense, rich sauce, but this summery green sauce is entirely different. This Sesame Pipian Verde looks thick, but because it's made mostly of blended green vegetables and herbs, it turns out light, tangy, and refreshing. Toasted sesame butter (available in whole food markets) and toasted almonds, along with a quick frying in the end, give it body and depth.

This recipe seems complicated, but if you prepare the chicken in advance, the rest of the steps come together, quickly and easily, in about 30 minutes. This is an excellent

continued

Pollo con Pipian Verde *continued*

do-ahead party dish—make the chicken and sauce one or two days before, then just combine and heat before serving. If the sauce gets too thick, add a little of the broth from the Mexican Poached Chicken recipe.

> 1 RECIPE MEXICAN POACHED CHICKEN (CHAPTER 8; YOU CAN MAKE THIS UP TO 2 DAYS BEFORE
>   AND REFRIGERATE)

Sesame Pipian Verde

> ³/₄ CUP SLIVERED ALMONDS
>
> 4 CLOVES GARLIC, UNPEELED
>
> 1 TEASPOON WHOLE CUMIN SEEDS
>
> 1 CUP CHICKEN BROTH FROM MEXICAN POACHED CHICKEN (CHAPTER 8)
>
> 8 OUNCES TOMATILLOS (ABOUT 8), HUSKED AND RINSED
>
> 4 LEAVES ROMAINE LETTUCE, COARSELY CHOPPED
>
> 1 BUNCH FRESH CILANTRO (ABOUT 2 CUPS PACKED)
>
> ¹/₂ CUP CHOPPED ONION
>
> 3 TABLESPOONS TOASTED SESAME BUTTER
>
> 2 SERRANO CHILES, STEMMED, SEEDED, AND COARSELY CHOPPED
>
> ¹/₂ TEASPOON SALT, OR TO TASTE
>
> FRESHLY GROUND BLACK PEPPER TO TASTE
>
> 2 TABLESPOONS CANOLA OIL

① *Shred the chicken and measure the broth:* Shred the meat from the cooked chicken from the Mexican Poached Chicken recipe, discarding the skin and bones. Skim the fat from the broth, and measure 1 cup broth for the pipian sauce. (Discard any vegetables remaining in the broth, and reserve the excess broth for a soup or other use.) Set the shredded meat aside while you prepare the sauce.

② *Toast the almonds:* Heat the oven to 400 degrees. Place the almonds in a single layer on a baking sheet. Cook 4 to 6 minutes, stirring halfway through, until evenly toasted and aromatic. Measure ¹/₂ cup toasted almonds for the pipian sauce, and reserve ¹/₄ cup for garnish.

③ *Toast the garlic and cumin seeds:* Place the unpeeled garlic cloves in a small, heavy skillet. Adjust the heat to medium. Let the garlic cloves pan-roast on each side until slightly browned and soft, about 15 to 20 minutes. Remove garlic cloves from the pan. Add the cumin seeds to the hot pan and set the heat to low. Toast quickly, shaking the pan, just until the seeds give off aroma, about 10 to 20 seconds. (Be careful not to toast the seeds too long or they'll turn bitter. If the seeds smell bitter rather than aromatic, toss them out and toast a new batch.) When the garlic is cool enough to handle, slip off the skins.

④ *Blend the sauce:* Start preparing the sauce while the almonds and garlic toast. Pour the reserved 1 cup chicken broth into a blender container. Quarter the tomatillos and add them to the blender. Add the romaine lettuce, cilantro, onion, sesame butter, chiles, salt, and pepper. Add the 1/2 cup toasted almonds and the toasted garlic and cumin seeds. Blend mixture until puréed, holding top of blender securely to prevent overflow.

Note: You may need to blend the tomatillos first so they settle down in the blender beaker, then gradually add and blend the lettuce, cilantro, and remaining ingredients until all have been included.

⑤ *Cook the sauce:* In a wide saucepan or deep skillet, heat the oil over medium-high heat until just smoking. Carefully pour in the blended pipian mixture all at once— the mixture will splatter, so be careful. (If you have a mesh splatter guard, place it on top of the pan as soon as the mixture is added.) Fry 4 to 6 minutes, stirring occasionally, or until the sauce darkens slightly and is thick (not as thick as a pesto, but thicker than canned tomato sauce). At this point the flame can be turned off and the sauce covered to keep warm, or refrigerated for later use.

⑥ *To serve:* Add the shredded chicken to the sauce and heat until just warmed through. Garnish with the remaining 1/4 cup almonds. Serve the chicken as a main dish or spoon into warm flour tortillas.

Porcini and Prosciutto Fricassée

SERVES 4 Gussy up the old fricassée with earthy porcini mushrooms and smoky prosciutto. If you can find it, use a type of German prosciutto (Abraham brand) sold in gourmet and specialty markets. It's heavily smoked, whereas Italian prosciutto is cured, not smoked. The German version shouldn't really be compared to the delicate taste of

continued

Porcini and Prosciutto Fricassée *continued*

true Italian prosciutto, but it has an appealing flavor all its own and comes finely diced in packages convenient for this recipe. You can use Italian prosciutto if you like, but this is one dish where I actually prefer the smokier, meatier taste, which can come from smoked ham or smoked bacon if you can't find the German prosciutto.

1 OUNCE DRIED PORCINI MUSHROOMS

1 CUP BOILING WATER

3 POUNDS CHICKEN PIECES (PREFERABLY 4 BREAST HALVES)

SALT AND FRESHLY GROUND PEPPER

3 TABLESPOONS CANOLA OIL

1 ONION, DICED

3 CLOVES GARLIC, MINCED

2 OUNCES FINELY DICED SMOKY PROSCIUTTO (ABOUT $1/2$ CUP)

$1^1/_2$ TABLESPOONS ALL-PURPOSE FLOUR

$1/2$ CUP DRY WHITE WINE

3 SPRIGS FRESH THYME LEAVES OR $1/2$ TEASPOON DRIED

$1/2$ CUP HEAVY CREAM

2 TABLESPOONS FRESH LEMON JUICE

GARNISH: FRESH MINCED HERBS (OPTIONAL)

① Soak the mushrooms in boiling water until soft. Squeeze the water from the mushrooms, reserving the water. If the water is gritty, strain through cheesecloth.

② Season the chicken with salt and pepper. Heat the oil in a large heavy pot or Dutch oven on high heat. Brown the chicken on all sides. Remove from the pot and set aside.

③ In the same pan, sauté the onion, garlic, and prosciutto on medium-low heat. When the onions start to soften, stir in the mushrooms. Cook a minute or so to heat up the mushrooms. Stir in the flour and heat, stirring until the flour cooks through, about 2 minutes.

④ Stir in the wine, reserved mushroom water, and thyme, scraping the bottom of the pot to mix in any browned bits. Return the chicken to the pot, stirring it around in the sauce. Bring the mixture to a boil. Cover and reduce the heat. Simmer 15 minutes, stirring occasionally.

⑤ Stir in the cream and lemon juice. Heat another 2 to 3 minutes until the sauce is hot. Garnish with fresh minced herbs. Serve with cooked pasta, egg noodles, or rice, and a crisp salad.

Quick Chicken, Artichokes, and Feta

SERVES 3 TO 4 Greek flavors permeate this quick and easy skillet chicken dish. Marinated artichoke hearts and canned tomatoes add instant flavor, especially if you use tomatoes that come preseasoned with basil, garlic, and oregano. The touch of sugar balances the tartness of the sauce and brings out the tomato taste, so test before adding the cheese to see if you need more sugar. Serve with crusty bread to sop up the juices and a green or Greek salad on the side.

SALT AND FRESHLY GROUND PEPPER

2 POUNDS CHICKEN THIGHS (ABOUT 6) OR OTHER CHICKEN PIECES, SKIN REMOVED

1 TABLESPOON OLIVE OIL

2 CLOVES GARLIC, MINCED

1 (14.5-OUNCE) CAN DICED TOMATOES, PREFERABLY SEASONED WITH BASIL, GARLIC, AND
    OREGANO

1 (6-OUNCE) JAR MARINATED ARTICHOKE HEARTS

1 TEASPOON SUGAR, OR TO TASTE

4 OUNCES FETA CHEESE

GARNISH: CHOPPED FRESH MINT, OREGANO, OR BASIL

① Salt and pepper the chicken. Heat the olive oil on medium high in a large skillet. Brown the chicken on all sides. During the last minute of browning, add the garlic to the pan, between the chicken pieces, and cook just until soft.

continued

Quick Chicken, Artichokes, and Feta *continued*

② Pour in the tomatoes and artichokes, both with their juices. Stir in the sugar. Bring to a boil. Lower the heat and simmer uncovered, turning the chicken pieces occasionally to cook evenly. Chicken will take about 20 minutes to cook through.

③ Turn the chicken pieces so the presentation, or top, side faces up. Crumble the feta on top and heat just until feta starts to melt. Garnish with a generous handful of chopped fresh herbs. The pan will have lots of juicy sauce flecked with soft feta chunks. Spoon the chicken and sauce into shallow bowls and serve with crusty bread or on top of cooked orzo or other pasta.

Quick Vietnamese Chicken with Crisp-Cooked Snow Peas

SERVES 4 This mildly spicy recipe is modeled after a traditional Vietnamese dish, but I've adapted it for ease and speed. The original recipe includes lemongrass and caramelized sugar syrup, a common seasoning in Vietnamese food. In this recipe, I've substituted the more readily available lemon zest and molasses respectively. The molasses adds the same type of deep flavoring as caramelized sugar, yet without the extra step of making the syrup. But don't worry: The finished dish doesn't taste at all like molasses—instead, it has just the right balance of sweet and tart.

The spicy heat comes not from chile peppers, but from finely ground black pepper, an ingredient used commonly in Vietnamese and Chinese cooking. This recipe is fairly tame, so add more pepper if you prefer more fire. Fish sauce, known as *nuoc mam* in Vietnamese and *nam pla* in Thai, is available in Southeast Asian markets and adds the necessary salty balance.

The longest step in stir-fry dishes is not the cooking, but the chopping. Notice that this dish involves very little chopping, and using whole, small snow peas makes for even less chopping. Here's a quick-cooking tip: If you stack two chicken pieces on top of each other, you can slice them in half the time using a sharp chef's knife or cleaver.

As for the snow peas in this dish, I prefer to cook them briefly in the microwave, then add them to the finished chicken dish. The microwave cooks vegetables beautifully, keeping them crisp and bright, and it's actually quicker, because the vegetables can be cooked at the same time as the stir-fry. You may substitute asparagus, carrots, celery, and other vegetables for the snow peas, but you'll need to cut them into pieces of even size.

1 WHOLE LEMON, WASHED AND DRIED

3 CLOVES GARLIC, MINCED

3 TABLESPOONS FISH SAUCE (*NUOC MAM* OR *NAM PLA*)

2 TABLESPOONS SOY SAUCE

1 TEASPOON FINELY GROUND BLACK PEPPER

DASH RED PEPPER FLAKES

2 POUNDS BONELESS, SKINLESS CHICKEN THIGHS OR BREASTS

3 TABLESPOONS DRY SHERRY

3 TABLESPOONS UNSULPHURED MOLASSES

2 TABLESPOONS CANOLA OIL

1 RECIPE CRISP-COOKED SNOW PEAS (OPTIONAL; SEE BELOW)

① Finely grate the zest from the lemon and place it in a nonreactive mixing bowl. Juice the lemon and set the juice aside (you should have about 3 tablespoons juice).

② To make the marinade, add the garlic, fish sauce, soy sauce, black pepper, and red pepper flakes to the zest. Cut the chicken into thin strips or bite-size pieces. Stir the chicken into the marinade and let rest 30 minutes or, preferably, 2 hours, covered and refrigerated.

③ While the chicken marinates, mix together the sherry, molasses, and reserved lemon juice and set aside.

④ Using a wok or large skillet over a high flame, heat the oil until almost smoking. Carefully pour the chicken into the hot oil. Stir-fry until the chicken is almost cooked through. Add the sherry-molasses mixture. Stir-fry just until the chicken cooks completely. (If desired, remove the chicken with a slotted spoon and boil the

continued

Quick Vietnamese Chicken with Crisp-Cooked Snow Peas *continued*

juices until they thicken slightly.) If using snow peas, add them now or serve them on the side. Serve hot with steamed rice or noodles.

Crisp-Cooked Snow Peas

1 TEASPOON CANOLA OIL

2 CLOVES GARLIC, MINCED

1/2 POUND SNOW PEAS, TRIMMED (PREFERABLY SMALLER-SIZE PEAS)

SALT TO TASTE

Combine the oil and garlic in a large microwave-safe bowl with lid. Cover and microwave on high 1 to 2 minutes, stirring halfway through, until garlic is soft. Rinse snow peas and drain. Leave some water clinging to the snow peas, and add the snow peas and salt to the bowl. Right before serving, cover and microwave on high 1 minute. Stir and test for doneness. Snow peas should be crisply tender; if too raw, continue to cook in short bursts until done, being careful not to overcook. Serve as a side dish or mix into a stir-fry such as Quick Vietnamese Chicken.

Quinoa con Pollo

SERVES 4 This dish combines the quinoa of the Incas with the chicken and seasonings of the Spaniards. Ironically, it was the Spaniards who forbade the Incas to grow quinoa, in an attempt to control them. For this reason, quinoa, which had been a major staple of the vegetarian Incas at the time, became less used and never appeared to transfer to European cultures, as did corn, potatoes, and other South American foods. However, after the fall of Pizarro, quinoa reestablished itself as a major crop in the mountains of Peru, Ecuador, and Colombia, and as a principal ingredient in many South American dishes. It's a healthy grain, providing all the essential amino acids, and adds a nutty, toasted flavor to this dish. Look for it in whole food stores.

1 CUP QUINOA

1 TABLESPOON EXTRA-VIRGIN OLIVE OIL

3 CLOVES GARLIC, MINCED

1 CHICKEN, CUT INTO 8 PIECES

SALT AND FRESHLY GROUND PEPPER

1 TABLESPOON CANOLA OIL

1 ONION, CHOPPED

1 GREEN BELL PEPPER, CHOPPED

4 ROMA TOMATOES, PEELED AND CHOPPED

1 BAY LEAF

1 CUP CHICKEN STOCK OR CANNED LOW-SODIUM BROTH

$1/2$ CUP DRY WHITE WINE

$1/4$ TEASPOON SAFFRON THREADS

2 TABLESPOONS CHOPPED PARSLEY

$1/2$ LEMON, CUT INTO WEDGES

① Thoroughly rinse the quinoa under cold running water and allow to drain 5 minutes.

② Heat the olive oil in a Dutch oven or large flameproof casserole over medium-high heat. Add the garlic and quinoa. Toast the quinoa until it loses all its moisture and turns golden brown, about 4 or 5 minutes, stirring often. Remove from the pan and set aside. Wipe any remaining beads of quinoa from the pot.

③ Season the chicken pieces with salt and pepper. Pour the canola oil into the pot and heat on medium high. When hot, add the chicken and brown on all sides. Remove the chicken from the pan and set aside.

④ Over medium-high heat, add the onion and bell pepper to the pan drippings and cook until tender. Stir in the tomatoes, bay leaf, chicken stock, and wine. Bring the liquid to a boil. Crumble in the saffron. Return the chicken pieces to the pan. Cover and simmer on low for 5 minutes.

continued

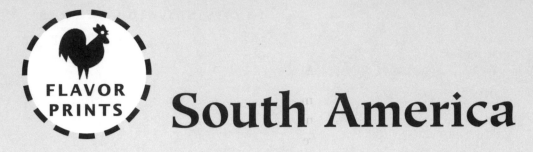

South America

As in Mexico, the FlavorPrint of South America consists largely of the collision of native Indian cooking and that of the Spanish and Portuguese invaders. One difference, though, was the influence of slaves from Africa. More recently, Italians have made "Milanese" (breaded veal cutlets) an Argentine specialty, while the Japanese brought sushi and tempura to Peru.

In so large and varied a continent, dozens of cuisines exist, but the big three come from Brazil, Peru, and Argentina, with Chile running a close fourth. Brazilian food is Creole, a mix of African, Portuguese, and Quechua Indian, with a bit of West Indies spices and cheeses thrown in by the Dutch. The staples of pre-European America continue to dominate Peruvian cooking: potatoes, corn, and chiles. Argentina is known for its charcoal-grilled and spit-roasted beef and other meats, simply seasoned. Chilean cuisine specializes in seafood.

almonds	chiles	okra	potato
annatto	cilantro	orange	pumpkin
banana	coconut	palm oil	rice
black beans	corn	papaya	shrimp
Brazil nuts	ginger	parsley	sugarcane
cashews	hearts of palm	peanuts	sweet potato
cassava	lima beans	pineapple	tomato
chickpeas	mango	plantain	

Quinoa con Pollo *continued*

⑤ Stir the quinoa into the chicken and liquid. Cover and simmer on low 20 to 30 minutes, or until the liquid is absorbed and the chicken fully cooked. Serve garnished with chopped parsley and lemon wedges on the side.

Shredded Pueblo Chicken

SERVES 4 Shredded, cooked chicken meat is a staple of Mexican cooking. It's eaten plain, stuffed into flour tortillas, nestled in crisp tacos, rolled into enchiladas, scrambled with eggs, as garnish in soup—its uses are endless. This method produces moist chicken, in a mild, herby sauce, with very little fat. As a bonus, it's incredibly simple to make.

If you live in the Southwest, look for "Menudo Mix" or "Menudo Spices" in cellophane packages in the Mexican food aisle of most supermarkets. If not available, substitute mixed dried herbs such as oregano, marjoram, thyme, and a dash of crushed red chile pepper.

2 LARGE OR 3 MEDIUM CHICKEN BREAST HALVES

1/2 ONION, COARSELY CHOPPED

3 CLOVES GARLIC, CRUSHED

1 TEASPOON MENUDO SPICES, CRUMBLED

2 BAY LEAVES

1 TABLESPOON CANOLA OIL

4 GREEN ONIONS, GREEN AND WHITE PARTS CHOPPED

1/2 TEASPOON GROUND CUMIN

2 FRESH JALAPEÑO CHILES, SEEDED AND MINCED

1 TEASPOON SALT

1 CUP PEELED, SEEDED, AND CHOPPED TOMATOES (FRESH OR CANNED)

WARM FLOUR TORTILLAS

① Nestle the chicken breasts snugly into a pot just large enough to hold them. Add enough water to cover the breasts by 1/2 inch. Remove the breasts. Add the onion, 1 clove of crushed garlic, the menudo spices, and bay leaves to the water. Slowly bring the mixture to a boil. Cover and let simmer 10 minutes.

② Return the chicken breasts to the pot, making sure the water still just barely covers them. Bring to a boil, then simmer 2 minutes, skimming off any foam that rises to the surface. Cover the pot and remove it from the heat. Let the chicken rest in the liquid for 30 minutes.

continued

Shredded Pueblo Chicken *continued*

③ Carefully remove the chicken from the still-hot broth and set it aside to cool. When cool enough to handle, skin the chicken and coarsely shred the meat from the bone. Discard the skin, bay leaves, and cooked garlic clove, but keep the broth.

④ Chop the remaining 2 cloves garlic. Heat the oil in a large, heavy skillet over medium-high heat. Add the green onions and cook until slightly browned on the edges. Add the chopped garlic and cumin to the skillet, along with the chiles, salt, tomatoes, and shredded chicken. Using a slotted spoon, scoop out the onions from the stock and spoon them into the skillet. Add ½ cup of the cooking broth. Simmer until most of the liquid has evaporated, about 10 minutes. Serve the chicken with warm flour tortillas on the side.

Note: Do not discard the remaining broth. Morph the broth into a quick side dish by simmering diced potatoes in the stock until cooked through. The potatoes end up soft but chunky, and the broth becomes thick, creamy, and comforting. Or use the broth as a base for soup.

Spiced Chicken, Fennel, Raisins, and Rice

SERVES 3 TO 4 When creating this Indian- and Persian-inspired dish, I wanted the sweetness of raisins to enhance the warm spices, fennel, and nuts. I was sure I had raisins in the cupboard, so I started the preparation. When it came time to toss in the raisins, you guessed it: I couldn't find them anywhere. But I did find some trail mix, which I keep on hand for long bike trips. So, piece by piece, I extracted just enough raisins to give this dish what it needed. Of course, the next morning I discovered that the enormous container of raisins I had been searching for was indeed in the cupboard. Right in front of my eyes. In plain sight. Next to the trail mix.

Use premixed garam masala, sold in Indian markets, or make your own using the recipe in chapter 12. Leftovers from this dish meal-morph beautifully into fried rice, tossed together with any odds and ends of vegetables and meats lurking in your fridge.

6 CHICKEN THIGHS (ABOUT 1½ POUNDS)

2 TEASPOONS GARAM MASALA

1 TABLESPOON CANOLA OIL

1 ONION

1 SMALL BULB FRESH FENNEL

1 CUP BASMATI OR LONG-GRAIN WHITE RICE

¼ CUP RAISINS

1½ CUPS CHICKEN STOCK OR CANNED LOW-SODIUM BROTH

¼ CUP ALMONDS (SLIVERED), PINE NUTS, OR CASHEW HALVES

① Rub the chicken pieces all over with 1 teaspoon garam masala. In a large, heavy skillet (or wok) with lid, heat the oil until hot but not yet smoking. Over high heat, brown the chicken pieces, skin side down first, then the back side, about 5 minutes per side. While the chicken browns, coarsely chop the onion. Slice the fennel into slender wedges or slivers, discarding the coarse inner core.

② Remove the browned chicken thighs from the pan and set aside. Pour off all but 2 tablespoons fat from the pan. Cook the onion until translucent. Dump in the rice and fennel and cook until the rice grains turn opaque (about 2 minutes), stirring frequently.

③ Stir in the raisins and the remaining 1 teaspoon garam masala. Return the chicken pieces to the pan, spacing them evenly on top of the rice, in a ring. Pour the chicken broth over the rice, bring it to a boil, then cover and reduce the heat to low. Cook for 40 minutes. Do not remove the lid.

④ Meanwhile, lightly toast the nuts in a small skillet until golden (be careful not to burn them). Set aside to cool. After 40 minutes, the chicken should be cooked through and the rice tender. Spoon some rice on each plate and top with one or two thighs. Sprinkle the nuts on top and serve.

Sweet 'n' Sour Kumquat-Kiwi Chicken

SERVES 4 A colorful variation on traditional sweet 'n' sour chicken. Fresh kumquats have a tart, citrus freshness, and once the few seeds are popped out, the entire fruit is edible, skin and all. Kiwis now come in both green and golden yellow. You may substitute fresh apricots, pineapple, mandarin oranges, or other fruits.

2 KIWIFRUITS, PEELED

10 TO 12 FRESH KUMQUATS, WASHED AND DRIED

3 GREEN ONIONS

1 POUND BONELESS, SKINLESS CHICKEN BREASTS

1 EGG

1 TABLESPOON SOY SAUCE

$1/2$ TEASPOON PEPPER

CORNSTARCH FOR DREDGING

CANOLA OIL FOR FRYING

GARNISH: CILANTRO SPRIGS (OPTIONAL)

Sweet 'n' Sour Sauce

$3/4$ CUP WATER

$1/2$ CUP DISTILLED WHITE VINEGAR

$1/2$ CUP SUGAR

$1/4$ CUP FRESH LEMON JUICE

1 TABLESPOON SOY SAUCE

$1/4$ TEASPOON WHITE PEPPER

$1/4$ TEASPOON SALT

2 TABLESPOONS CORNSTARCH

$2/3$ CUP WATER

1 TABLESPOON CANOLA OIL

4 CLOVES GARLIC, MINCED

1 TABLESPOON FRESH GINGER, MINCED

$1/4$ TEASPOON SESAME OIL

① Slice the kiwifruits in half lengthwise, then cut crosswise into $1/3$-inch slices. Slice the kumquats into $1/3$-inch-wide pieces, removing the seeds. Slice the green onions diagonally into 1-inch pieces, including green and white parts. Set aside.

② Cut the chicken into 1-inch pieces. In a medium mixing bowl, beat together the egg, soy sauce, and pepper. Stir in the chicken and let marinate 15 minutes.

③ While the chicken marinates, make the sauce: In a small bowl, combine $3/4$ cup water and the vinegar, sugar, lemon juice, soy sauce, white pepper, and salt. In another small bowl, mix together the 2 tablespoons cornstarch and $2/3$ cup water. Heat 1 tablespoon oil in a saucepan on high heat. Stir-fry the garlic and ginger until softened, about 30 seconds. Stir the vinegar mixture into the pan, cooking until the sugar dissolves into a smooth sauce. Stir the cornstarch mixture to blend it again, then add it to the sauce. Stir in the sesame oil. Heat the sauce until it bubbles and thickens, then cover and turn off the heat. Set aside.

④ Remove the chicken from the egg mixture and dredge in cornstarch, shaking off excess.

⑤ Into a wok or deep skillet pour enough oil to fill the pan $1/2$ inch. Heat the oil until hot. Fry the chicken, turning as necessary, until crisp and cooked through, about 3 minutes. Drain on paper towels.

⑥ Reheat the sauce just before serving. Stir in the kiwifruits, kumquats, and green onions. Continue heating just until everything is warmed through and the kumquats soften slightly. To serve, pour the fruit and sauce over the chicken and garnish with cilantro sprigs. Serve with cooked rice or noodles.

Tarragon Chicken and Artichoke Hearts

SERVES 4 In this southern French recipe, chicken breasts simmer with marinated artichoke hearts (a handy pantry staple), fresh mushrooms, and garlic in a tangy

continued

Tarragon Chicken and Artichoke Hearts *continued*

tarragon wine sauce. This dish comes together in a very short time, using a single skillet, with minimum fuss and maximum taste. Buttered egg noodles and a simple, steamed green vegetable complete the meal perfectly.

> 2 TEASPOONS EXTRA-VIRGIN OLIVE OIL
>
> 4 CHICKEN BREAST HALVES
>
> 1 TABLESPOON BUTTER
>
> 2 CLOVES GARLIC, MINCED
>
> 8 OUNCES SLICED MUSHROOMS
>
> 1 (14-OUNCE) JAR MARINATED ARTICHOKE HEARTS
>
> 1 TABLESPOON LEMON JUICE
>
> 1/2 TEASPOON DRIED TARRAGON, CRUMBLED
>
> 2 TEASPOONS SOY SAUCE (OPTIONAL)
>
> 1/2 CUP DRY WHITE WINE
>
> SALT AND FRESHLY GROUND PEPPER
>
> GARNISH: MINCED PARSLEY

① In a large skillet, heat the olive oil over medium-high heat. Brown the chicken skin side down, then flip and brown the other side. Remove from the pan and set aside.

② Melt the butter in the same pan over medium heat. Add the garlic and mushrooms and cook until they begin to soften. Stir in the artichoke hearts and their liquid, lemon juice, tarragon, soy sauce, and wine, scraping up any browned bits.

③ Return the chicken pieces to the skillet, and spoon some sauce over them. Season with salt and pepper. Bring to a boil, then cover and simmer over low heat 15 to 20 minutes, or until the chicken is cooked through. Use a slotted spoon to remove the breasts and vegetables to a serving platter and tent with foil to keep warm. Spoon off the grease from the sauce, if necessary, and reduce to desired consistency. Serve the chicken breasts with the warm artichoke sauce and garnish with parsley.

Three Pepper Chicken Stir-Fry

SERVES 4 WITH NOODLES OR RICE Garden-fresh bell peppers, mixed with colorful red and yellow cherry and teardrop tomatoes, cook quickly with plenty of chicken in a Chinese sauce spiked with perky ginger, garlic, and black pepper. Mushroom soy sauce is not essential to this recipe, but if you have it, it adds another layer of flavor.

Tip: Prepare the chopped veggies first, before slicing the chicken, to keep your cutting board clean and help prevent cross-contamination.

1 GREEN BELL PEPPER

1 RED OR YELLOW BELL PEPPER

12 OUNCES TEARDROP AND/OR CHERRY TOMATOES (RED AND YELLOW MIXED)

4 CLOVES GARLIC

1 (2-INCH) PIECE FRESH GINGER

2 POUNDS BONELESS, SKINLESS CHICKEN BREAST HALVES

Marinade

2 TABLESPOONS OYSTER SAUCE

1 TABLESPOON MUSHROOM SOY SAUCE OR REGULAR SOY SAUCE

1 TABLESPOON SHAO-HSING WINE OR DRY SHERRY

1 TABLESPOON CORNSTARCH

1 TEASPOON FINELY GROUND BLACK PEPPER

Sauce

$1/2$ CUP CHICKEN STOCK OR CANNED LOW-SODIUM BROTH

2 TABLESPOONS SHAO-HSING WINE OR DRY SHERRY

2 TABLESPOONS MUSHROOM SOY SAUCE OR REGULAR SOY SAUCE

1 TEASPOON CORNSTARCH

1 TEASPOON SUGAR

$1/2$ TEASPOON FINELY GROUND BLACK PEPPER

3 TABLESPOONS CANOLA OIL

① Cut the bell peppers into thin, bite-size slices. Leave the tomatoes whole, or if large, slice in half. Peel and mince the garlic and ginger. Slice the chicken into pieces

continued

Three Pepper Chicken Stir-Fry *continued*

about the same size as the peppers and tomatoes. Set each ingredient aside separately.

② *Marinade:* Combine all marinade ingredients. Toss the chicken in the marinade and let stand 15 minutes.

③ *Sauce:* Combine all ingredients and set aside.

④ *To cook:* Heat 1 tablespoon oil in a wok or large skillet on high until very hot. Stir in the peppers and tomatoes. Stir-fry until the peppers are crisp but tender and slightly brown on the edges. Remove from the pan. Pour the remaining 2 table-spoons oil into the same pan. Heat on high until hot. Dump in the garlic and ginger. Stir-fry a few seconds, until aromatic and soft. Stir in the chicken and marinade. Stir-fry until almost cooked through, just pink in the center. Pour in the sauce. Cook until the sauce boils and thickens. Return the peppers and tomatoes to the pan and stir to mix. Serve hot, with cooked rice or pan-fried noodles.

CHAPTER 11

Chicken Bakes, Casseroles, and Braises

The world knows that casseroles, baked chicken, and long-cooked braises make cozy meals for everyday dining and casual entertaining. Warm up with a Spanish paella, a Greek pot pie, or California-style chicken pieces roasted with goat cheese and fresh cherry tomatoes.

These hearty recipes use the oven, stovetop, or broiler—to bake, braise, simmer, or brown. If you enjoy a chicken dish that needs nothing more to complete the meal (except maybe salad or bread), consider these recipes:

Chapter 4
    Barcelona Brown-Bag Chicken and Vegetables
Chapter 6
    One-Pot Chicken, Mushrooms, and Saffron Rice
    Roasted Thighs with Apples, Normandy Style
Chapter 7
    Summer Chicken and Eggplant Parmigiana
Chapter 8
    African Chicken and Peanut Stew
    Belgian Chicken Braised in Beer
    Gumbo Ya-Ya
    Hungarian Chicken Paprikás

continued

Chapter 10
    Israeli Couscous with Chicken and Olives
    Spiced Chicken, Fennel, Raisins, and Rice

Bangkok Chicken

SERVES 4 Compared to many Thai dishes, this chicken is subtly seasoned and not spicy-hot at all. It has a slightly sweet flavor, which is tempered by a squeeze of lime at table. The creaminess of the coconut milk and the warmth of the ginger produce an almost calming effect. As with many foods, this chicken is even tastier the day after cooking. For a meal morph, shred the leftover meat over lettuce and top with a ginger-vinaigrette for an unusual Thai chicken salad.

> 1 LEEK
>
> 1 (2-INCH) PIECE FRESH GINGER, PEELED AND QUARTERED
>
> 4 LARGE CLOVES GARLIC, PEELED
>
> $2/3$ CUP UNSWEETENED COCONUT MILK (ONE $5^3/_4$-OUNCE CAN)
>
> $1/3$ CUP PACKED DARK BROWN SUGAR
>
> 3 TABLESPOONS SOY SAUCE
>
> $1^1/_2$ TABLESPOONS TOASTED SESAME OIL
>
> $1/8$ TEASPOON CAYENNE
>
> 2 POUNDS CHICKEN THIGHS OR PIECES OF CHOICE
>
> 1 LIME, CUT INTO WEDGES
>
> GARNISH: CILANTRO SPRIGS

① Wash and trim the leek, leaving the white part and about 2 or 3 inches of the pale green leaves. Cut in half lengthwise, rinse again in between the leaves to remove hidden dirt, then cut into 2-inch lengths. In a food processor or blender, purée the leek together with the ginger, garlic, coconut milk, brown sugar, soy sauce, sesame oil, and cayenne. Pour the mixture over the chicken, coating well. Cover and refrigerate overnight.

② Heat the oven to 375 degrees. Remove the chicken from the marinade and place it on a rack in a baking dish. Bake for 45 minutes to 1 hour, until cooked through. The chicken should have a golden crust, but if the outside is pale and the meat cooked, then broil until crisp and brown, about 1 or 2 minutes. Serve hot or at room temperature garnished with lime wedges and cilantro sprigs.

Southeast Asia: Vietnam, Thailand, Cambodia, and Burma

Hot, sour, salty, sweet—balanced in harmony—these are the underlying flavor principles of Southeast Asia. Chiles and black pepper provide the heat. Sour may be citrus (lime and sometimes lemon), lemongrass, vinegar, or tamarind. Salty is fish sauce (*nam pla* in Thailand and *nuoc mam* in Vietnam), a complex liquid made from fermented fish and anchovies. Sweet is sugar or coconut milk. Southeast Asians love to charcoal grill their meats and chicken in slightly sweet sauces balanced by lime. Almost every dish is served with fresh herbs, crisp and raw. Noodles abound in salads, soups, and alongside grilled foods. Vietnamese cuisine bears the influences of the colonial French in sauces, breads, and pâtés.

banana	dried shrimp	lettuces	rice paper
basil (European	duck	lime	wrappers
and Thai)	fish sauce (*nam pla*	mint	rice vinegar
bean curd	or *nuoc mam*)	mushrooms	rice-flour
bean sprouts	fresh leafy herbs	noodles (rice	baguettes
black bean sauce	galangal	sticks, bean	sesame seeds
black pepper	garlic	thread, wheat)	and oil
carrot	ginger	oyster sauce	shallot
chiles	green mango	palm sugar	shrimp paste
cilantro	green onion	papaya	sriracha hot
coconut	kaffir limes and	pâtés	sauce
cucumber	leaves	peanuts	tamarind
cumin	lemon	radishes	
curry pastes	lemongrass	rice	

Greek Pot Pie

SERVES 4 It's an old American custom to serve roast chicken for Sunday dinner and turn the leftovers into savory, deep-dish chicken pot pies. I love starting the week (or ending the weekend) with a simple roast bird. I also adore homemade pot pies, with their tender, buttery crusts enclosing the steamy, creamy vegetables and chicken bits.

The Greeks have their own version of pot pies, which are rich in the flavors of their magnificent culinary culture. In this recipe, buttery, paper-thin phyllo dough is filled with the savory herbs of Mt. Olympus—luscious green spinach, tender chicken pieces, and the classic Greek cheeses, feta and kasseri. Plan this meal in advance; frozen phyllo dough needs to thaw in the refrigerator for several hours or overnight (follow the package instructions).

8 SHEETS FROZEN PHYLLO DOUGH

1/3 CUP UNSALTED BUTTER, MELTED

1/2 POUND FRESH SPINACH, TOUGH STEMS REMOVED

2 LARGE EGGS

2 BONELESS, SKINLESS CHICKEN BREAST HALVES

1 TABLESPOON OUZO (OPTIONAL)

1 RIB CELERY WITH LEAVES, CHOPPED

3 GREEN ONIONS, GREEN AND WHITE PARTS CHOPPED

1 TABLESPOON MINCED FRESH MINT

1/2 TEASPOON DRIED BASIL, CRUSHED

1/2 TEASPOON DRIED MARJORAM, CRUSHED

1/2 TEASPOON DRIED TARRAGON, CRUSHED

1/2 TEASPOON FRESHLY GROUND PEPPER

1/2 POUND FETA CHEESE, CRUMBLED

1/4 CUP KASSERI CHEESE, GRATED

① Thaw the phyllo dough according to manufacturer's instructions. In some cases this may be overnight. When ready to cook, heat the oven to 350 degrees. Brush the bottom and sides of a deep 10-inch pie dish with some of the butter.

② Rinse the spinach well and place in a microwave-safe bowl. Microwave on high 1 to 2 minutes, stirring once, until wilted and cooked through. (Or cook the spinach in a dry skillet until wilted.) When cool enough to handle, squeeze the moisture from the spinach. Finely chop the spinach and place in a medium-size mixing bowl.

③ Separate 1 egg into 2 small bowls, one for the yolk, the other for the white. Break the remaining egg into the bowl with the egg white and beat lightly. Set both bowls aside.

④ Dice the chicken breasts and place them in the bowl with the spinach. Pour in the ouzo. Add the celery, green onions, mint, basil, marjoram, tarragon, pepper, feta and kasseri. Pour in the beaten egg white mixture and combine thoroughly.

⑤ Place the phyllo dough on a clean counter or work surface, and keep covered with plastic wrap throughout the assembly process, to keep it from drying out. As you assemble the phyllo sheets, lightly brush each sheet with butter before placing it in the pie dish. Place half of the first sheet of phyllo into the dish and extend half beyond the edge. Place a second sheet on top, this time extending over the opposite edge. Place two more sheets in a strip at right angles to the first two sheets, effectively forming a cross. Repeat this process with the remaining 4 sheets, brushing with butter as you go.

⑥ Spread the chicken mixture evenly in the pan. Fold the overhanging layers of phyllo up and across the chicken, sheet by sheet, brushing with butter after each sheet is in place. Finish smoothing out the top with a final brushing of butter. Beat the egg yolk lightly, then brush the top of the pie with the beaten yolk. Pierce the top in several places with a fork to allow steam to escape.

⑦ Bake 50 minutes, until the crust is crisp and golden. Let cool on a rack 10 minutes before cutting. Serve hot or at room temperature.

Paella de la Casa

SERVES 5 I call this my "paella of the house" because it was first made with ingredients on hand, inspired from a classic recipe for Paella Valenciana by Penelope Casas. If I have them around, I might also combine ingredients like smoked sausage, chorizo, rabbit, pork, green beans, red bell pepper, green onions, mushrooms, artichoke hearts, white beans, lima beans, chickpeas, parsley, thyme, marjoram, or a hearty mix of shellfish and seafood.

2^1/$_2$ POUNDS CHICKEN THIGHS (ABOUT 5 PIECES)

SALT

3^1/$_2$ CUPS CHICKEN STOCK OR CANNED LOW-SODIUM BROTH

^{1}/$_2$ CUP DRY WHITE WINE

^{1}/$_4$ TEASPOON SAFFRON THREADS

3 TABLESPOONS OLIVE OIL

1 CUP DICED GREEN BELL PEPPER (SMALL DICE)

^{1}/$_2$ RED ONION, DICED

5 CLOVES MINCED GARLIC

1^1/$_2$ OUNCES FINELY DICED PROSCIUTTO

2 TEASPOONS PAPRIKA (SWEET OR MILDLY HOT)

1^1/$_2$ POUNDS RIPE TOMATOES, CHOPPED

2 CUPS FROZEN PEAS

2^1/$_2$ CUPS ITALIAN ARBORIO RICE OR SPANISH BOMBA OR CALASPARRA RICE

2 SPRIGS FRESH ROSEMARY (OR ^{1}/$_4$ TEASPOON DRIED)

① Heat the oven to 375 degrees. Rinse and pat the chicken dry and sprinkle with salt.

② Heat the chicken broth and wine in a small saucepan until boiling. Crumble in the saffron, turn off the heat, and cover until ready to use.

③ While the broth warms, heat the olive oil in a pan—use a paella pan if you have it; a Dutch oven or a large heatproof frying or large gratin pan will also do. Brown the chicken on all sides. Remove the chicken and set aside.

④ Add the green bell pepper, onion, garlic, and prosciutto to the pan. Sauté on medium heat for about 5 minutes. Stir in the paprika, tomatoes, and peas. (The paella may be made in advance up to this point.) Stir in the rice, coating thoroughly.

⑤ Reheat the chicken broth to boiling. Stir in the rice mixture. Cook at a low boil until the mixture stops being soupy, but leave enough liquid to cook the rice through while it bakes. Nestle the chicken pieces into the rice, submerging them completely. Arrange the rosemary on top.

⑥ Bake the paella uncovered about 10 minutes, until the rice is almost done and just moist. Remove the pan from the oven, cover, and let rest 10 minutes. Remove the rosemary and serve.

Roasted Fesenjan Hens

SERVES 4 Traditionally, duck or chicken pieces are stewed in this Persian sauce, but I prefer this roasting method, suggested by author Claudia Roden. The roasted skin stays crisp because the sauce is served separately. You may substitute chicken pieces for the Cornish hens. You may also roast the birds whole, unstuffed, or with a rice and fruit stuffing, as is common in Middle Eastern cooking. Pomegranate molasses, also known as pomegranate syrup, is thick, very tart, and concentrated, so you need only a small amount. Look for it in Middle Eastern markets.

2 CORNISH HENS (ABOUT 1½ POUNDS EACH), HALVED

SALT AND FRESHLY GROUND PEPPER

1 TABLESPOON SOFTENED BUTTER OR CANOLA OIL

continued

Roasted Fesenjan Hens *continued*

Fesenjan Sauce

2 TABLESPOONS BUTTER

1 MEDIUM ONION, CHOPPED

2 CUPS GROUND WALNUTS

1 CUP CHICKEN STOCK OR CANNED LOW-SODIUM BROTH

1/4 CUP POMEGRANATE MOLASSES

2 TABLESPOONS TOMATO SAUCE

2 TABLESPOONS FRESH LEMON JUICE

1 TABLESPOON SUGAR

1/4 TEASPOON GROUND CINNAMON

SALT

GARNISH: MINCED PARSLEY OR CILANTRO

① Heat the oven to 400 degrees. Season the hens with salt and pepper, then rub the skin with butter or oil. Place hens on a roasting rack, skin side up, in a large shallow pan. Roast until done, about 20 to 25 minutes. For extra brown, crisp skin, broil for 3 to 5 minutes. If the hens are done before the sauce, tent them with foil to keep warm.

② While the hens roast, make the Fesenjan Sauce: Melt 2 tablespoons butter in a large skillet over medium heat. Brown the onion, stirring occasionally. Stir in the walnuts and cook until lightly browned, about 1 to 2 minutes (be careful not to burn them). Stir in the stock, pomegranate molasses, tomato sauce, lemon juice, sugar, and cinnamon. Stir to combine. Bring just to a boil. Reduce the heat and simmer uncovered about 15 to 20 minutes to thicken. Taste and add salt as needed. (Sauce may be made earlier in the day, refrigerated and reheated.)

③ Serve the hens with the sauce, preferably on a bed of cooked rice. Garnish with minced green herbs.

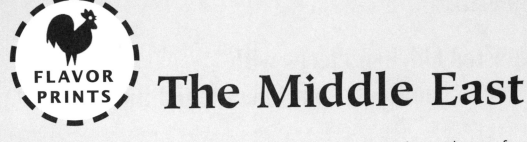

The Middle East

What has the Middle East given us? Here, some 12,000 years ago, hunters became farmers. Wheat was cultivated first, followed by barley, pistachios, figs, pomegranates, and dates. Fermentation was discovered and used to make beer and leavened bread. Sumerians created the barter system. Commercial trade proliferated, and with it the Middle East FlavorPrint evolved.

As early as 700 A.D, Arab invaders spread their diet to other lands. These Muslims carried goat's milk, dates, nuts, and foods that could be transported easily. When the Persians evolved their own cuisine using fresh fruits, rice, duck, and other meats, the predominant Middle Eastern cuisines we know today began to emerge, a synthesis of these influences and the new exotic spices the Arab traders were bringing from the Orient. As time went on, Turkey's Ottoman Empire injected its own foods, such as sweet pastries of paper-thin phyllo dough and thick, sweet coffee. Other cultures left their mark as well: yogurt from the Russians; dumplings from Mongol invaders; turmeric, cumin, garlic, and other spices from India; cloves, peppercorns, and allspice from the Spice Islands; okra from Africa; and tomatoes from the New World, via the Moors of Spain.

Religions also affect cuisine. Lamb is the main red meat, as both the Jewish and Muslim faiths forbid pork. Chicken is favored, but it must be consumed in accordance with religious customs. Jewish kosher chickens must first be brined to remove impurities, and halal chickens must be slaughtered according to Muslim practices. The Koran forbids alcohol, so regional dishes exclude it, too.

A meal might lack meat, but it would never exclude bread, which can be leavened or unleavened. A typical meal starts with the appetizer, known as mezze. Depending on what country you are in, the main course may include falafel, deep-fried chickpea balls; kebabs of grilled lamb or chicken; khoresh, a stew in a sweet-sour sauce; or any number of rice dishes mixed with meats, fruits, and nuts. Salads like tabbouleh, a tart parsley, bulgur, and tomato salad; sautéed eggplant and tomatoes with yogurt; and spinach are popular.

Aleppo pepper	duck	onion	rosemary
allspice	eggplant	orange-flower water	sesame
almonds	fennel	parsley	sumac
bulgur wheat	figs	pine nuts	tahini
chickpeas	garlic	pistachios	tomato
cilantro	honey	pita bread	yogurt
cinnamon	lemon	pomegranate	walnuts
couscous	mint	raisins	zaatar
cucumber	olives and olive oil	rose water	zhug

Roasted Chicken Pieces with Cherry Tomatoes, Goat Cheese, and Basil

SERVES 4 In this dish, cherry tomatoes roast on high heat with garlic cloves and chicken pieces. At the end of the cooking period, goat cheese and fresh basil are stirred into the pan juices released by both the chicken and the tomatoes, to create an instant tangy sauce. Don't worry about the quantity of garlic—roasting makes it mellow and soft enough to mash into the sauce. Silver Goat brand goat cheese, in 4.5-ounce pyramid-shaped containers, is commonly sold in supermarkets. It's the perfect size for this recipe.

2 TEASPOONS OLIVE OIL

12 OUNCES CHERRY TOMATOES

6 CLOVES GARLIC, PEELED AND SMASHED

$1/4$ TEASPOON DRIED OREGANO

8 CHICKEN THIGHS OR 4 BREAST HALVES, WITH BONE AND SKIN ($3^1/2$ TO 4 POUNDS)

SALT AND FRESHLY GROUND PEPPER

4 TO 5 OUNCES SOFT GOAT CHEESE

$1/4$ CUP PACKED FRESH BASIL LEAVES, JULIENNED

① Heat oven, with rack placed in center shelf, to 500 degrees. In a large baking dish (13 x 9 x 2-inch or equivalent), mix olive oil, tomatoes, garlic, and oregano, coating the tomatoes and bottom of the pan thoroughly with the oil.

② Nestle the chicken pieces skin side up between and on top of the tomatoes. Sprinkle the skin and tomatoes generously with salt and pepper. Roast 10 minutes.

③ Flip the chicken, stirring the tomatoes and garlic around. Salt and pepper the non-skin side. Roast 5 minutes. Flip the chicken again so it's skin side up and roast another 5 to 10 minutes, or until cooked through.

④ Place the chicken on a serving platter. Remove the garlic and finely chop or mash it. While the juices in the pan are still hot, stir in the goat cheese, basil, and garlic until the cheese melts evenly into the sauce. Spoon the sauce and tomatoes over the chicken and serve. Garnish with additional basil if desired.

CHAPTER 12

Salads, Sauces, and Little Bits

Cool, crunchy, and crisp—these salads feature chicken as the key ingredient. Got odds 'n' ends of cooked chicken meat from previous recipes? Toss them into salads or mix them with sauces and spices. Ground chicken plumps and crumbles in wontons or salads. Livers get lively in pâtés and bacon-wrapped cocktail nibbles, and crunchy fried chicken bites are luscious enough to make a meal in themselves.

Marinades, sauces, and spice rubs are featured in recipes throughout this book. Here's a few more to stimulate your creative juices:

Chapter 4
    Char Shu Marinade (from Char Shu Cornish Hens)
    Citrus Brine (from Citrus-Brined Chicken, Roasted with
        Near East Rub)

Chapter 5
    Teriyaki Sauce (from Sesame-Seeded Teriyaki Wings)

Chapter 9
    Anise Rub (from Aromatic Anise Chicken)
    Chimichurri Sauce (from Chicken Churrasco with Chimichurri Sauce)
    Moorish Marinade (from Chicken of the Moors)

continued

Cuban Sour Orange Marinade (from Cuban Sour Orange Chicken)
Filipino Coconut Marinade (from Filipino Coconut Barbecued Chicken)
Jerk Marinade (from Jamaican Jerk Chicken)
Grapefruit Marinade (from Juicy Grilled Grapefruit Chicken)
La Tunisia Marinade (From La Tunisia chicken and Grilled Onions)
Texas Dry Rub (from Texas Barbecue Dry-Rub Chicken)

Chapter 10
Tonkatsu Sauce (from Japanese "Chiken" Katsu)
Lemon-Mushroom Sauce (from Chicken Schnitzel with
   Lemon-Mushroom Sauce)
Honey-Lemon Sauce (from Chinese Honey-Lemon Chicken)
Middle Eastern Spice Rub (from Israeli Couscous with
   Chicken and Olives)
Moroccan Spice Mixture (from Moroccan Chicken in
   Spiced Tomato Sauce)
Sesame Pipian Verde (from Pollo con Pipian Verde)
Sweet 'n' Sour Sauce (from Sweet 'n' Sour Kumquat-Kiwi Chicken)

Chapter 11
Fesenjan Sauce (from Roasted Fesenjan Hens)

APPETIZERS and LITTLE BITS

Chicken Liver and Shiitake Powder Pâté

MAKES ABOUT 2 CUPS Dried shiitake mushrooms, ground to a powder in a food processor, flavor this faintly Asian-spiced pâté. A touch of cream cheese lightens the pâté, in both color and in richness.

1³/₄ CUPS DRIED SHIITAKE MUSHROOM PIECES (.5 OUNCE)

1 TABLESPOON UNSALTED BUTTER

2 GREEN ONIONS, GREEN AND WHITE PARTS CHOPPED

2 LARGE CLOVES GARLIC, CHOPPED

¹/₂ POUND CHICKEN LIVERS

2 TABLESPOONS HEAVY CREAM

¹/₄ CUP PLUS 1 TEASPOON DRY SHERRY

2 TEASPOONS SOY SAUCE

¹/₄ TEASPOON DRIED THYME

¹/₄ TEASPOON POWDERED GINGER

¹/₄ TEASPOON SALT, OR TO TASTE

4 OUNCES CREAM CHEESE

1 TEASPOON COARSELY GROUND PEPPER, OR TO TASTE

GARNISH: TOASTED SESAME SEEDS (OPTIONAL)

① Grind the dried shiitake mushrooms to a powder in a food processor, blender, or spice grinder. It's okay if some small flakes or bits remain in the mixture.

② Melt the butter in a skillet over medium heat. Stir in the green onions and garlic. Sauté until the onions soften. Fry the livers in the buttery mixture until cooked

continued

Chicken Liver and Shiitake Powder Pâté *continued*

through and just barely pale pink in the center, stirring and breaking up the livers as they cook. About halfway through cooking, stir in the mushroom powder. Add the cream, ¼ cup sherry, soy sauce, thyme, ginger, and salt. Simmer until the mixture is reduced to a thick liquid, easier to scrape than to pour. Turn off the heat and let the livers cool a minute or so. Scrape every luscious bit of the liver mixture into the work bowl of a mini or standard food processor.

③ Add the cream cheese to the work bowl. Purée until the mixture is smooth. Taste for salt. Drop in the pepper and the remaining 1 teaspoon sherry and pulse lightly, just enough to combine.

④ Pack the mixture into two 1-cup ramekins (or one 2-cup container). Garnish with a layer of toasted sesame seeds. Serve now, or cover and refrigerate up to 2 days and serve at room temperature. (I think the flavors blend and mellow better if left overnight.) Accompany with small slices of baguette or crackers, or slices of Asian pear or apple.

Chinese, Napa, or Nappa Cabbage

Most supermarkets now stock napa cabbage, also known as nappa or Chinese cabbage. It comes in tight barrel-shaped heads or loose-headed varieties, both with crinkly, pale green leaves and thick white ribs. Raw or cooked, napa cabbage can be a versatile ingredient; it's milder than regular cabbage and lacks any strong odor when heated. It can last two weeks in the crisper, and a small head is so compact it may weigh as much as three pounds. Napa cabbage is an excellent source of vitamins C and A, fiber, potassium, and folic acid and contains small amounts of calcium and iron as well. While much of it is indeed grown in Napa, California, the name is thought to derive from the Japanese word *nappa,* meaning "greens." Slice it thinly for salads, soups, and stir-fries. One large leaf shredded makes 1 cup, tightly packed.

Chicken Liver and Truffle Oil Pâté

MAKES ABOUT 1 CUP A small amount of truffle oil adds a lovely perfume. If you don't have truffle oil, don't worry. This pâté is perfectly rich and sinful without it.

2 TABLESPOONS UNSALTED BUTTER

2 LARGE SHALLOTS, CHOPPED (ABOUT 1/4 CUP)

1 LARGE CLOVE GARLIC, CHOPPED

1/2 POUND CHICKEN LIVERS

1/2 TEASPOON POULTRY SEASONING OR DRIED SAGE

1/4 TEASPOON SALT, OR TO TASTE

2 TABLESPOONS BRANDY

2 TABLESPOONS HEAVY CREAM

1/2 TEASPOON TRUFFLE OIL (OPTIONAL)

1 TEASPOON COARSELY GROUND PEPPERCORNS (MIXED BLACK, GREEN, AND PINK IF AVAILABLE)

GARNISH (OPTIONAL): CHOPPED TOASTED HAZELNUTS; CHOPPED FRESH HERBS; THYME SPRIGS

① Melt the butter in a skillet over medium heat. Stir in the shallots and garlic. Sauté until shallots are soft and cooked through. Fry the livers in the buttery shallot mixture until cooked through and just barely pale pink in the center, stirring and breaking up the livers as they cook. About halfway through cooking, stir in the poultry seasoning or sage and salt. When the livers are done, turn off the heat and let them cool a minute or so. Dump the liver mixture into the work bowl of a food processor, or preferably, a mini food processor.

② Heat the brandy and cream in the skillet, scraping up any little bits. Reduce to about half. Pour the brandy mixture into the work bowl with the livers. Purée until the mixture is smooth. Drizzle in the truffle oil and pulse again to combine. Drop in the peppercorns and pulse lightly to combine, or stir in with a fork. (For a stronger brandy flavor, stir a few extra drops of brandy into the pâté.)

③ Pack the mixture into a 1-cup container (or 2 smaller containers). Serve warm, or cover and refrigerate up to 2 days and serve at room temperature. If desired, garnish with chopped toasted hazelnuts, chopped fresh herbs, or thyme sprigs. Accompany with small slices of baguette, crackers, or slices of apple.

Chicken Wontons

MAKES 20 WONTONS; SERVES 4 IN SOUP Serve these tasty Chinese dumplings in Ginger-Wonton Soup with Spring Onion Oil (chapter 8), or serve by themselves drizzled with a bit of soy sauce and vinegar.

CORNSTARCH

1 CUP (ABOUT $1/2$ POUND) GROUND CHICKEN

1 GREEN ONION, GREEN AND WHITE PARTS FINELY CHOPPED

1 TEASPOON SOY SAUCE

1 TEASPOON SHAO-HSING WINE OR DRY SHERRY

$1/8$ TEASPOON WHITE PEPPER

20 WONTON SKINS

A SMALL DISH OF WATER

① While you fill the wontons, bring a large pot of water to a boil. Lightly dust a baking sheet or plate with cornstarch, to hold the wontons once they've been filled and sealed.

② Mix the chicken, green onion, soy sauce, wine, and pepper together to form a smooth paste. Separate and place several wonton skins on a sheet of waxed paper. Using 2 teaspoons or a teaspoon and a melon baller, scoop about 1 teaspoon of filling onto the center of each skin. Dab your finger in the water, then run it around 2 adjoining edges of each wonton skin to dampen. Do this to all the skins you've set out.

③ Fold the wonton skins over to form triangles. Press the edges together firmly all the way around to seal in the filling. Set the filled wontons aside on the cornstarch-dusted surface (don't let them touch or they'll stick together). Repeat with the remaining wonton skins until all are folded.

④ Gently lower the wontons with a slotted spoon into the boiling water, dropping them in successively one by one, so they don't stick together. Boil until the wontons float; about 4 to 5 minutes. Remove with a slotted spoon and distribute equally into four soup bowls (5 wontons per bowl), and ladle in the soup. Or carefully drain the wontons in a colander, making sure they don't fall apart, then use as desired.

Fried Chicken Drummettes with Hot Pomegranate Honey

SERVES 4 AS AN APPETIZER OR SNACK This is quintessential Southern fried chicken—with a kick. Southern cooks know that a spoonful of baking powder increases the lightness of the batter and the crispness of the chicken, while buttermilk makes the chicken tender and tangy. You can serve these bites with a drizzle of Hot Pomegranate Honey, or just fry 'em and eat 'em as they are. If you don't make the honey sauce, be sure to season the drummettes with a good blast of black pepper.

1 CUP BUTTERMILK

1 TEASPOON SALT

$^1/_2$ TEASPOON GRANULATED GARLIC

14 CHICKEN DRUMMETTES (ABOUT 1$^1/_2$ POUNDS)

1 CUP ALL-PURPOSE FLOUR

1 TABLESPOON BAKING POWDER

CANOLA OIL FOR FRYING

HOT POMEGRANATE HONEY (SEE BELOW)

① Combine the buttermilk, salt, and garlic in a shallow dish or zippered plastic bag. Marinate the drummettes in the mixture 1 hour to overnight, refrigerated, turning occasionally.

② Dump the flour and baking powder into a small paper or plastic bag, and shake to mix. Batter the chicken 2 to 3 pieces at a time: Lift the chicken pieces out of the marinade and let excess liquid drain off. Then drop them into the bag and shake to coat. Place battered pieces on a clean plate.

③ Heat the oil to 375 degrees in a deep-fat fryer or a large heavy skillet. Oil should be deep enough to come at least halfway up the chicken pieces if using a skillet, or enough to cover them completely in a deep fryer.

④ Fry until coating is crispy and chicken is no longer pink when cut into, about 5 minutes, turning halfway through. Drain on paper towels. Serve with Hot Pomegranate Honey drizzled on top, or as a dunk on the side.

continued

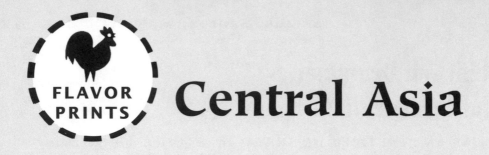

Central Asia

Afghanistan, Iran, Iraq, Armenia, Georgia, inland Turkey, and the entire Caucasus region may be politically diverse, but their peoples share many of the same foods and dishes. For centuries, wheat and barley, spit-roasted sheep and goat kebabs, dried fruits, and yogurt have sustained the locals. They also fed the Huns, Mongols, and Tatars who crossed their lands, bringing with them their own foods. Cinnamon appears in savory dishes with sweet and tart fruits. Nuts add protein and crunch. Dill and cilantro are the preferred green herbs, though the two are not usually combined in the same dish, and yogurt is the primary dairy product.

almonds	cucumber	plum	sheep and goat
apricot	dill	pomegranate	walnuts
barley	lemon	quince	yogurt
bulgur wheat	onion	raisins	
cilantro	pine nuts	rice	
cinnamon	pistachios	rose water	

Fried Chicken Drummettes with Hot Pomegranate Honey *continued*

Hot Pomegranate Honey

MAKES ABOUT ¹/₃ CUP Use a flavorful honey here, such as sage honey or buckwheat honey. The Triple Sec liqueur brightens the taste with a hint of orange, and the pomegranate molasses adds tang. The mixture should have a sweet-tart balance with a hint of chile heat, so check and adjust the flavors as needed before serving.

¹/₄ CUP HONEY

¹/₄ TEASPOON GROUND RED CHILE (SUCH AS CALIFORNIA OR NEW MEXICO)

2 TEASPOONS DISTILLED WHITE VINEGAR

1 TEASPOON POMEGRANATE MOLASSES

$1/2$ TO 1 TEASPOON TRIPLE SEC LIQUEUR

Measure the honey into a 1-cup microwave-safe measuring cup. Stir in the chile and vinegar. Microwave on high about 30 seconds, just until the mixture starts to bubble up (watch closely and stop immediately if the mixture starts to boil over). Remove the honey from the microwave. (Careful! Honey will be very hot. You may also heat the mixture in a small saucepan on medium heat.) Stir in the pomegranate molasses and $1/2$ teaspoon Triple Sec. Set aside to cool. If the mixture seems too thick, thin with more Triple Sec. Drizzle on fried chicken pieces or use as a dunking sauce. If desired, microwave the mixture for a few seconds to warm slightly before serving.

Golden Chicken Mandu (Korean Dumplings)

MAKES ABOUT 50 MANDU Mandu, Korean dumplings, can be boiled in water, then served in soups. Or, as in this recipe, you can cook them like potstickers by frying them on one side then steaming them until done. Serve fried mandu with chojang, a soy-vinegar dipping sauce (see below). If you prefer, you can make the stuffing without tofu (*tubu* in Korean), substituting ground beef, pork, or more ground chicken instead.

Tips: Koreans traditionally curve the mandu into a ring shape, so the ends meet and are sealed with water. This type of shape is ideal for soups, but for fried mandu, I prefer the flatter, half-moon shapes described below. If you have one of the potsticker gadgets that folds and seals the dumplings in one motion, you'll find the process goes much more quickly. You can also freeze

continued

Korea

Korean food is highly seasoned, more so at the peninsula's southern tip than in the north. Winters in the north are harsh and severe, while the southern climate is hot and tropical. The national dish of kimchi—spicy pickled cabbage, radish, cucumber, or other vegetable—is not for the faint of heart. Walk into a Korean market, and you may think you're in Mexico: Huge bags of ground red chiles fill the shelves and almost sizzle in the air—clearly this spice is used in great quantity, including kochujang, a seasoning paste of red chiles and fermented soybeans.

Garlic and chiles lead the list of favorite ingredients, followed by soy sauce, sesame, green onions, ginger, vinegar, and sweetness (sugar or honey). Koreans use garlic in such quantities that the Japanese call them "garlic eaters." (From a culinary standpoint, I don't consider this a derogatory statement in the least.) Korean meals consist of many small dishes—dozens of them. Namuls (cooked or raw salads), soup, noodles, and rice join kimchi at almost every meal. Beef dishes are the most prized recipes. Pulkogi (barbecued beef) and kalbi-jim (braised spare ribs) survived even beyond the Chinese introduction of vegetarian-mandated Buddhism. The ancestral love of beef does not permeate the average Korean's daily diet, though. Beef is desired at every meal, but in reality, fish, poultry, and vegetables (including spinach and eggplant) are more commonly consumed.

adzuki beans	green onion	rice
barley	kimchi	rice vinegar
chestnuts	kochujang	rice wine
chiles	mung beans and bean	seaweed
Chinese, or napa, cabbage	sprouts	sesame, seeds
cilantro	mushrooms	and oil
cucumber	noodles (yam, bean	soy sauce
eggplant	thread, wheat)	soybean paste
garlic	onion	sweet potato
ginger	pickles	tubu (tofu)
ginkgo	radish	watercress

Golden Chicken Mandu (Korean Dumplings) *continued*

the stuffed mandu on a cornstarch-dusted baking sheet to keep them from sticking together, then transfer to an airtight container and freeze until ready to use.

Chicken Mandu Filling

10 OUNCES FIRM TOFU

8 OUNCES KIMCHI, MINCED

12 OUNCES GROUND CHICKEN

2 GREEN ONIONS, GREEN AND WHITE PARTS MINCED

2 CLOVES GARLIC, MINCED

1 TABLESPOON CORNSTARCH

1 TABLESPOON TOASTED SESAME SEEDS

2 TEASPOONS TOASTED SESAME OIL

1 EGG WHITE, LIGHTLY BEATEN

1 TEASPOON SALT

1/2 TEASPOON FRESHLY GROUND BLACK PEPPER

For Mandu Wrappers and Cooking

1 PACKAGE ROUND EGG ROLL WRAPPERS (GYOZA)

CANOLA OIL

Chojang Dipping Sauce

3 TABLESPOONS SOY SAUCE

2 TABLESPOONS RICE VINEGAR

1/2 TEASPOON TOASTED SESAME OIL

1 TEASPOON MINCED GARLIC

1/4 TO 1/2 TEASPOON RED PEPPER FLAKES (OPTIONAL)

① *Make the mandu filling:* Wrap the tofu in cheesecloth or a clean kitchen towel and squeeze out the excess water. Crumble the tofu into a mixing bowl. Place the kimchi in a fine-mesh sieve or cheesecloth and press or squeeze to remove excess moisture. Add the kimchi to the tofu. Add the remaining mandu filling ingredients to the

continued

Golden Chicken Mandu (Korean Dumplings) *continued*

bowl and mix thoroughly. At this point, the mandu mixture may be covered and refrigerated up to 1 day, until you're ready to fill the dumplings.

② *Stuff the mandu:* For best results, line 2 baking sheets with waxed paper, then dust a layer of cornstarch on the waxed paper to keep the mandu from sticking. Set out a small dish of water. Place several eggroll wrappers on a cutting board. Fill each with about 1 teaspoon of filling. Dip your finger into the water and run it over the edge of the wrapper. Fold the top over and press to seal, removing as much air as possible. Set the mandu on the prepared baking sheets while you stuff the remaining wrappers.

③ *Cook the mandu:* Heat a skillet with just enough canola oil to coat the bottom surface. (To speed up the cooking process, use two skillets.) When the oil is very hot, gently place a layer of stuffed mandu in the skillet, being careful not to overlap them. When the mandu are golden brown on the bottom, flip them over. Quickly add 2 tablespoons water to the pan, cover, and steam the mandu until cooked through, about 2 minutes. Uncover the pan and place the mandu on a serving dish. (You can keep them warm in a low oven while you cook the remaining mandu.) Serve the mandu with dipping sauce.

④ To make the dipping sauce, combine all ingredients. Serve the dipping sauce in one communal bowl, or set out one small bowl and plate per person. (Sauce may be made earlier in the day and stored at room temperature.)

Mozzarella Chicken "Bruschetta"

MAKES 8 LARGE TOASTS Bruschetta is toasted peasant bread rubbed with fresh garlic and drizzled with olive oil. Italians serve it alone, as an appetizer or nibble, or with ripe tomatoes, chopped olives, cheese, or any number of other toppings. This recipe transforms bruschetta into an open-faced chicken sandwich, brimming with summer's ripest tomatoes, basil, fresh mozzarella, and a splash of balsamic vinegar. Serve the bruschetta on a bed of mixed baby greens or fresh arugula, allowing one toast per person as an appetizer, or two for a meal.

Chicken

4 LARGE BONELESS, SKINLESS CHICKEN BREAST HALVES

SALT AND FRESHLY GROUND PEPPER

2 TABLESPOONS EXTRA-VIRGIN OLIVE OIL

Bruschetta

1 LOAF ITALIAN OR FRENCH RUSTIC COUNTRY BREAD

2 LARGE CLOVES GARLIC, PEELED AND LIGHTLY CRUSHED

3 TABLESPOONS EXTRA-VIRGIN OLIVE OIL

12 OUNCES FRESH MOZZARELLA, IN $1/4$-INCH SLICES (3 [4-OUNCE] BALLS)

1 RECIPE SUMMER FRESH TOMATO SAUCE (ALSO IN THIS CHAPTER)

1 TABLESPOON BALSAMIC VINEGAR

SALAD GREENS (OPTIONAL)

① Slice each chicken breast half horizontally into 2 thin cutlets: Press your palm flat on top of each breast half, and with a gentle sawing motion, carefully slide a sharp knife through the meat, parallel to your palm and the cutting board. Place the chicken pieces on a plate, season with salt and pepper, and coat with 2 tablespoons olive oil. (This may be done several hours in advance. Refrigerate until ready to cook.)

② Diagonally slice the loaf into $3/4$-inch-wide pieces about 4 to 6 inches long. You should have at least 8 slices, depending on the size of the loaf.

③ Heat the grill. Toast the bread slices until golden brown on both sides. Rub the garlic over the top of each toast. Drizzle or brush the 3 tablespoons olive oil over the toasts. At the same time, grill the chicken cutlets until browned on both sides and just cooked inside. (The cutlets are thin, so cook them quickly on high heat.) Set the mozzarella slices on top of the warm chicken cutlets.

④ To serve, place one or two slices of toast on each plate. Top each toast with a spoonful of Summer Tomato Sauce and a chicken cutlet with mozzarella. Drizzle a splash of balsamic vinegar over the mozzarella and season with freshly ground pepper. Serve immediately. If desired, place the toast on a bed of mixed greens and spoon more Summer Tomato Sauce over the greens.

Rumaki

SERVES 6 TO 8 AS AN APPETIZER Rumaki sounds Japanese, and indeed these tasty tidbits are skewered like yakitori, but the dish's origins are a bit more murky. Legend has it that Trader Vic Bergeron introduced rumaki to the U.S. mainland in the 1950s at his outrageously popular restaurant, Trader Vic's, serving it as part of a flaming Hawaiian or Polynesian "pupu" platter. Bacon and pork are more common to Chinese cooking than Japanese, and both cultures have left their mark in Hawaii, so who's to say? However, the actual person who invented the first rumaki remains unclear. Nonetheless, it's still a fun and enjoyable appetizer that requires little effort from the cook. For a variation in flavor, toss 1/4 teaspoon granulated garlic or curry powder into the marinade.

1/4 CUP SOY SAUCE

1 TABLESPOON BROWN SUGAR

1/2 TEASPOON GROUND GINGER

12 CHICKEN LIVERS, HALVED AT NATURAL SEPARATION

12 SLICES BACON, CUT IN HALF CROSSWISE

24 CANNED WATER CHESTNUTS, RINSED AND DRAINED, OR FRESH IF AVAILABLE

① Combine soy sauce, brown sugar, and ginger. Marinate chicken livers and bacon in mixture at least 15 minutes, preferably 2 hours, refrigerated.

② Heat the oven to 400 degrees. Drain the chicken livers and bacon. Wrap a chicken liver half and water chestnut in a piece of bacon, and secure with a toothpick. Arrange rumaki on a wire rack on a rimmed baking sheet. Bake about 30 minutes, turning the rumaki over halfway through. Rumaki are done when the bacon is crisp and chicken livers are cooked through and slightly pink inside (cut one to test). (You may also broil or grill the rumaki on metal skewers or bamboo skewers soaked first in water.) Serve hot.

SALADS and SALAD DRESSINGS

Chicken "Salad" in Rice Paper Rolls

MAKES 8; SERVES 2 AS MAIN COURSE, OR 4 AS APPETIZER Rice paper wrappers—brittle, round, translucent sheets—are typically softened and rolled into Southeast Asian-style spring rolls, but that doesn't mean you have to stuff them solely with Asian ingredients. In this recipe, the wrappers are soaked in mild seasoned rice vinegar, then stuffed with grilled or cooked chicken, fresh thyme, lettuce, and assorted raw, crunchy vegetables.

Soaking the wrappers in seasoned vinegar gives them a mildly tangy flavor, enhanced by a lemony mayonnaise-caper sauce. You can make the rolls up to four hours in advance; just cover with plastic wrap and refrigerate. Pack them for a picnic or brown bag lunch. Or use smaller, 6-inch wrappers and pass them as cocktail finger food.

Note: Seasoned rice vinegar, plain rice vinegar to which some sugar has been added, is available in supermarkets in the vinegar aisle.

Lemon-Caper Mayonnaise

    3 TABLESPOONS MAYONNAISE

    2 TEASPOONS FRESH LEMON JUICE

    2 TEASPOONS CHOPPED CAPERS

Wrappers

    3/4 CUP SEASONED RICE VINEGAR PLUS 2 TABLESPOONS WATER

    8 (8 1/2-INCH) RICE PAPER WRAPPERS

continued

Chicken "Salad" in Rice Paper Rolls *continued*

Filling

    8 SMALL LETTUCE LEAVES, OR 4 LARGE ONES HALVED

    1 POUND GRILLED OR COOKED BONELESS CHICKEN, CUT INTO THIN STRIPS

    1 CARROT, JULIENNED

    2 GREEN ONIONS, JULIENNED

    1/2 BELL PEPPER (ANY COLOR), JULIENNED

    1 RIB CELERY, JULIENNED, WITH LEAVES CUT OFF AND SET ASIDE

    2 SPRIGS FRESH THYME, LEAVES PULLED OFF

① *Make the Lemon-Caper Mayonnaise:* Mix together all ingredients and set aside.

② *Prepare the wrappers:* Fill a shallow plate with the seasoned rice vinegar and water. Soak one wrapper at a time until pliable. Lift the wrapper and let excess liquid drain back into the plate. Smooth out the wrapper on your work surface. (As you remove one wrapper, replace it with another one to soak.)

③ *To assemble one roll:* In the lower third of the wrapper, place a lettuce leaf so it partially extends over the edge. Set a few strips of chicken on top. Add a few strips of carrot, green onion, bell pepper and celery, and some thyme and celery leaves. Drizzle on a small amount of Lemon-Caper Mayonnaise. Gently lift the wrapper's bottom edge up and over the filling and tighten by pulling back slightly. Give the roll a forward turn. Fold the end without the lettuce inward, and continue rolling the wrapper into a cone shape. Place seam side down, and continue making the remaining rolls. Cover with plastic and refrigerate until ready to use. Rolls will stay fresh at least 4 hours. Serve plain or with more Lemon-Caper Mayonnaise on the side.

Chicken Salad Siam

SERVES 4 Chinese Chicken Salad was arguably the most popular Asian salad a few decades ago. Then diners started discovering Southeast Asian cuisine, and a new trend was born. This Asian chicken salad features typical Thai ingredients in a refreshingly airy mix. The crisp rice stick noodles, which puff up like crunchy clouds when fried, are coated with light, sweet syrup, then topped with raw, crisp vegetables, shredded chicken, and toasted peanuts. Finally, a sharp lime dressing is drizzled on top, resulting in a tapestry of sweet and tart flavors. If you've ever enjoyed Mee Krob in a Thai restaurant, you'll love this salad variation.

Siam Dressing

1 TABLESPOON FISH SAUCE

3 TABLESPOONS LIME JUICE

1 CLOVE GARLIC, MINCED

1 TABLESPOON PEANUT OIL

1 TEASPOON SESAME OIL

1 TABLESPOON PICKLED GINGER, SLIVERED OR CUT INTO SMALL PIECES

1/4 TO 1/2 TEASPOON RED PEPPER FLAKES

Noodles

CANOLA OIL FOR FRYING

1/2 POUND THIN RICE STICK NOODLES

6 TABLESPOONS SOY SAUCE

1/2 CUP WHITE VINEGAR

1/2 CUP BROWN SUGAR

Salad Toppings

3/4 CUP NAPA CABBAGE LEAVES, FINELY JULIENNED

1 LARGE CARROT, CUT INTO MATCHSTICK JULIENNE

2 CHICKEN BREAST HALVES, COOKED AND SHREDDED

1/4 POUND FRESH BEAN SPROUTS, TRIMMED

2 GREEN ONIONS, JULIENNED INTO 2-INCH LENGTHS

3 TABLESPOONS CHOPPED TOASTED PEANUTS

3 TABLESPOONS CHOPPED FRESH MINT LEAVES

GARNISH: CILANTRO SPRIGS

① *Make the dressing:* Combine all ingredients in a small bowl.

② *Cook the rice stick noodles:* Heat about 2 inches oil in a wok or large frying pan. When the oil reaches 350 degrees, test a piece of rice stick. It should puff up immediately without turning dark brown. Drop in a handful of the rice sticks and cook until puffy, then drain on paper towels. Repeat until all noodles are fried.

continued

Chicken Salad Siam *continued*

③ Drain the oil from the wok or pan. Pour in the soy sauce, vinegar, and brown sugar. Bring the mixture a boil and boil gently on medium heat about 8 minutes, until a thin syrup is formed. Gradually mix in the cooked rice noodles until all are coated with the syrup. Remove the noodles to a serving platter.

④ *Assemble the salad:* Sprinkle a thin layer of cabbage over the noodles, followed in order by the carrot, chicken, bean sprouts, and green onion. Drizzle the dressing over these ingredients. Sprinkle on the peanuts, mint, and cilantro sprigs. Present the platter and let guests serve themselves.

Chicken Salad on Soba

SERVES 4 AS LIGHT SALAD OR APPETIZER, OR 2 AS MAIN COURSE
Japanese soba, or buckwheat noodles (available in Asian markets), are light and packed with flavor. If you can't find the dense, smoky Chinese black vinegar used here, known as Zhejiang or Chinkiang vinegar, then substitute balsamic vinegar. Shichimi togarashi (red pepper seasoning) and furikake (sesame and seaweed seasoning) are Japanese condiments for sprinkling on noodles and soups. They're not essential, but they add a spicy kick to this dish if you have them.

12 OUNCES JAPANESE ZARU SOBA (BUCKWHEAT NOODLES)

$1/4$ CUP WALNUT OIL

2 TABLESPOONS CHINKIANG BLACK VINEGAR, PLUS EXTRA

FRESHLY GROUND BLACK PEPPER

2 CUPS SHREDDED COOKED CHICKEN

1 TABLESPOON TOASTED SESAME SEEDS

2 GREEN ONIONS, GREEN AND WHITE PARTS CHOPPED

GARNISH: SHICHIMI TOGARASHI OR FURIKAKE (OPTIONAL)

① Bring 4 quarts of water to a boil. Add the noodles, stirring to separate. Cook until noodles are just al dente, stirring occasionally, about 4 to 6 minutes. Do not over-cook or the noodles will lose their texture and become mushy. Drain but do not rinse.

② In a large bowl, gently toss the warm noodles with the walnut oil. Add the black vinegar and the pepper, and toss again to mix. Noodles should rest 5 to 10 minutes before serving, to absorb the dressing. Just before serving, splash the noodles with another light sprinkling of vinegar, just enough to refresh the flavor.

③ To serve, arrange the noodles on plates. Pile shredded chicken on top and sprinkle on the sesame seeds and green onions. Grind on more black pepper to taste, and garnish with a few shakes of shichimi togarashi or furikake. Serve at room temperature.

Dilled Cucumber-Chicken Pasta Salad

SERVES 4 TO 6 Morph grilled chicken into a cooling, cucumber-dill pasta salad. Any cooked chicken breast meat will do, but in this recipe, Grilled Lemon-Dill Chicken (chapter 9) is ideal—it uses the same Sour Cream, Dill, and Cucumber Dressing as a marinade base. If the chicken breasts are large and meaty, one will suffice. Two smaller breasts will plump up the salad. Keep in mind that after their initial preparation, chilled pasta and potato salads always need doctoring, as chilling mutes the flavors and the moisture is absorbed. Be prepared to refresh this salad just before serving, pumping up the seasonings and vinegar and, if necessary, increasing the moisture with more dressing, sour cream, or mayonnaise.

1/2 POUND DRY PASTA (SUCH AS ELBOWS, SMALL SHELLS, OR ROTINI)

1/2 CUP SOUR CREAM

1/4 CUP MAYONNAISE

1/4 TO 1/2 CUP SOUR CREAM, DILL, AND CUCUMBER DRESSING (ALSO IN THIS CHAPTER)

1 TABLESPOON DISTILLED WHITE VINEGAR

1 GREEN ONION, GREEN AND WHITE PARTS FINELY CHOPPED

1 TABLESPOON FRESH DILL LEAVES, CHOPPED

1/2 TEASPOON SALT

1/4 TEASPOON GROUND WHITE PEPPER

1 CUP FROZEN PEAS, COOKED AND COOLED

DICED MEAT FROM 1 TO 2 COOKED CHICKEN BREAST HALVES (PREFERABLY FROM GRILLED LEMON-DILL CHICKEN, CHAPTER 9)

GARNISH: FRESH DILL

continued

Dilled Cucumber-Chicken Pasta Salad *continued*

① Bring a large pot of salted water to a boil. Cook the pasta until al dente. Drain, but do not rinse.

② While the pasta is still warm, combine it with the sour cream and mayonnaise in a large bowl. Mix in ¼ cup of the Sour Cream, Dill, and Cucumber Dressing (reserving the rest for refreshing) and all of the vinegar, green onion, dill, salt, and pepper. Stir in the peas and chicken. Chill until ready to serve. Just before serving, taste it and refresh the flavors with more salt, pepper, vinegar, and dressing as needed. Garnish with fresh dill and serve slightly chilled.

Napa-Hazelnut Chicken Salad

SERVES 4 What's a chicken salad without crunch? Traditional chicken salad—the mayonnaise kind served at ladies' luncheons and country clubs—usually gets its crunch from celery. But in this version, toasted hazelnuts and crisp napa cabbage put a refreshing upscale spin on the requisite crunch factor.

Note: For best results, make this salad using the moist, flavorful poached chicken breasts from Lemony Garlic Chicken and Broth (chapter 8).

> 3 CUPS SHREDDED COOKED CHICKEN (ABOUT 3 BREAST HALVES)
>
> 3 TABLESPOONS RICE VINEGAR
>
> 3 GREEN ONIONS, GREEN AND WHITE PARTS DIAGONALLY SLICED
>
> 3 TABLESPOONS MAYONNAISE, OR TO TASTE
>
> 3 CUPS PACKED SHREDDED NAPA CABBAGE LEAVES (ABOUT 6 MEDIUM LEAVES)
>
> ³/₄ CUP COARSELY CRUSHED TOASTED HAZELNUTS
>
> SALT AND FRESHLY GROUND PEPPER TO TASTE

Toss the chicken with the rice vinegar in a mixing bowl. Mix in the green onions, mayonnaise, napa cabbage, hazelnuts, and salt and pepper to taste. Chill or serve at room temperature. Before serving, taste to correct the seasonings. Add salt, vinegar, and mayonnaise as needed.

Serving suggestion: For an elegant presentation, reserve ⅓ of the cabbage and hazelnuts. Arrange the reserved cabbage on a platter, top with the chicken mixture, then garnish with the reserved hazelnuts.

Ras el Hanouth Chicken on Spinach, Kumquat, and Fig Salad

SERVES 4 Ras el hanouth is a Moroccan collection of warm spices; the actual ingredients can vary in number and quantity, depending on the preferences of the spice merchant. Use a commercial blend for this recipe, or mix your own using the ras el hanouth recipe following. Note that the chicken and Pomegranate Salad Dressing may be prepared separately up to two days in advance.

> 4 BONELESS, SKINLESS CHICKEN BREAST HALVES (PREFERABLY BRINED, SEE CHAPTER 3)
>
> 1 TABLESPOON RAS EL HANOUTH (RECIPE BELOW)
>
> 1 TABLESPOON EXTRA-VIRGIN OLIVE OIL

Salad

> 6 OUNCES FRESH SPINACH LEAVES, WASHED AND DRIED
>
> 2 SHALLOTS, FINELY CHOPPED
>
> 10 KUMQUATS (ABOUT 4 OUNCES), SLICED THIN, SEEDS DISCARDED
>
> 4 OUNCES DRIED FIGS, QUARTERED
>
> POMEGRANATE SALAD DRESSING, TO TASTE
>
> GARNISH: ¼ CUP TOASTED PINE NUTS (OPTIONAL)

① Score the chicken breast halves and rub them evenly with the ras el hanouth. Lightly coat with olive oil. Let stand 30 minutes to 2 hours, refrigerated, to absorb spices. Grill according to the basic grilling instructions in chapter 9. (Chicken may be cooked in advance and served at room temperature.) Slice the chicken meat into strips.

② *Make the salad:* Arrange the spinach on four plates. Top evenly with the shallots, kumquats, figs, and chicken strips. Drizzle with salad dressing to taste. Sprinkle with pine nuts and serve.

continued

Ras el Hanouth Chicken on Spinach, Kumquat, and Fig Salad *continued*

Ras el Hanouth Spice Blend

MAKES ABOUT 1/4 CUP Ras el hanouth means "top of the shop," a reference to the finest spices a skilled Moroccan merchant might blend together. The number of spices included can range from two dozen to a hundred, but the most common ones are cinnamon, cloves, cardamom, nutmeg, and black pepper. Specialty spice catalogs and Middle Eastern markets carry premixed blends of ras el hanouth. Here's an all-purpose recipe to blend at home using a few of the predominant spices. For best results, start with whole spices, toast them lightly, then grind them. Combine all ingredients below, and store in an airtight container.

> 2 TEASPOONS SALT
>
> 2 TEASPOONS GROUND GINGER
>
> 2 TEASPOONS GROUND NUTMEG
>
> 1 TEASPOON GROUND CINNAMON
>
> 1 TEASPOON GROUND ALLSPICE
>
> 1¹/₂ TEASPOONS GROUND CARDAMOM
>
> 1¹/₂ TEASPOONS GROUND BLACK PEPPER
>
> ¹/₂ TEASPOON GROUND TURMERIC
>
> ¹/₂ TEASPOON GROUND CLOVES
>
> LARGE PINCH SAFFRON

Pomegranate Salad Dressing

MAKES ABOUT ¹/₂ CUP

> 4 TEASPOONS WATER
>
> ¹/₄ TEASPOON SALT
>
> ¹/₄ CUP EXTRA-VIRGIN OLIVE OIL
>
> 2 TABLESPOONS POMEGRANATE MOLASSES
>
> 2 TEASPOONS HONEY

Mix together the water and salt until the salt dissolves. Combine with the remaining ingredients (whisk or shake in a sealed jar until a thick emulsion is formed). Taste.

If the dressing is too strong, add more water. If it's too sour, add more honey. Drizzle the dressing, to taste, over spinach or other greens. Refrigerate unused dressing, tightly sealed, up to 1 week.

Sour Cream, Dill, and Cucumber Dressing

MAKES 1 1/2 CUPS With its dill, vinegar, and sour cream, this Scandinavian-style dressing pairs well with chicken, fish, pasta, potatoes, and even tomatoes. It's essential to Dilled Cucumber-Chicken Pasta Salad (in this chapter), and for marinating Grilled Lemon-Dill Chicken (chapter 9).

1/2 POUND CUCUMBER (ABOUT 1/2 LARGE CUCUMBER)

3/4 TEASPOON SALT, PLUS MORE TO TASTE

2 GREEN ONIONS

1/4 CUP SOUR CREAM (REGULAR OR REDUCED FAT, BUT NOT NONFAT)

3 TABLESPOONS CREAM CHEESE (REGULAR OR REDUCED FAT, BUT NOT NONFAT)

3 TABLESPOONS DISTILLED WHITE VINEGAR

2 TEASPOONS HONEY

1/4 CUP LOOSELY PACKED FRESH DILL LEAVES

1/8 TEASPOON WHITE PEPPER, OR TO TASTE

① Peel and seed the cucumber, and chop into fine dice (corn-kernel-size). Place the cucumber in a strainer in the sink. Pour the salt on top; toss the cucumbers with your fingers to distribute the salt. Drain 30 minutes, and squeeze dry in a clean dish towel.

② Coarsely chop the green onions into 1-inch lengths, using both green and white parts. In a blender or food processor, process the cucumber, green onions, sour cream, cream cheese, vinegar, and honey until puréed. Add the dill and pulse just enough to combine. Add white pepper and more salt to taste. Refrigerate, tightly sealed, up to 4 days. Stir or shake before using.

Southeast Asian Chicken Salad with Spring Onion Oil

SERVES 2; CAN BE DOUBLED OR TRIPLED The measurements for these ingredients are merely guidelines, as the intensity of fish sauce, acidity of lime juice, and spiciness of red pepper flakes can vary. So taste and adjust the amounts as needed to reach the perfect hot-sour-salty-sweet balance that marks Southeast Asian cuisines.

Southeast Asian Dressing

1 TABLESPOON FISH SAUCE (*NAM PLA* OR *NUOC MAM*)

1 TEASPOON TOASTED SESAME OIL

3/4 TEASPOON SUGAR

1/4 TEASPOON RED PEPPER FLAKES

1 CLOVE GARLIC, MINCED

1/2-INCH PIECE GINGER, PEELED AND MINCED

JUICE OF 1 LIME

Salad

1/2 CUCUMBER

1 CARROT

2 CUPS TORN LEAFY GREENS

SHREDDED MEAT FROM 2 COOKED CHICKEN BREAST HALVES

ABOUT 3 TABLESPOONS SPRING ONION OIL (ALSO IN THIS CHAPTER)

GARNISH: CILANTRO SPRIGS, CRUSHED TOASTED PEANUTS (ABOUT 3 TO 4 TABLESPOONS)

① *Make the dressing:* Combine all ingredients. Taste to correct the seasonings, and keep in mind that the greens will be dressed with Spring Onion Oil before the dressing is poured on top.

② Peel the cucumber if it's waxed; unwaxed Asian cucumbers do not need peeling. Slice in half lengthwise, remove the seeds, and slice thinly. Slice the carrot thinly on the diagonal.

③ Divide the greens into two shallow bowls or place on plates. Toss each set of greens with 1 tablespoon Spring Onion Oil. Arrange the cucumber, carrot, and chicken on top. Spoon the dressing over the salads. Top each salad with another 1/2 to 1 tablespoon of Spring Onion Oil, making sure to include bits of the cooked spring onion. Garnish with cilantro sprigs and peanuts.

Thai Minced Chicken Salad (Larb)

SERVES 4 AS AN APPETIZER As beautiful as it is, Thailand can be excruciatingly hot in the summer. No wonder the Thais created this refreshingly light dish, for it contains such cooling ingredients as mint leaves, cilantro, lemongrass, and lime—all staples of Thai cooking. Traditionally made with beef, but in this case with chicken, this dish is known as larb or lahp or laab. It's usually served as an appetizer with cold Thai beer, but I serve it as a light meal, often with rice or spring rolls. I recently enjoyed this dish in a Thai restaurant, served with a large block of watermelon on the same plate. The sweet, juicy melon was more than just colorful; it added a harmonious complement to the salty, lime, and spice flavors of the larb, as well as a cooling, crunchy texture.

1 TEASPOON CANOLA OIL

1 POUND GROUND CHICKEN

4 GREEN ONIONS, GREEN AND WHITE PARTS MINCED

4 CLOVES GARLIC, MINCED

1/3 CUP MINT LEAVES, MINCED

1/4 CUP CILANTRO LEAVES, MINCED

2 TABLESPOONS MINCED LEMONGRASS OR LEMON ZEST

3 TABLESPOONS FISH SAUCE (*NAM PLA* OR *NUOC MAM*)

3 TABLESPOONS FRESH LIME JUICE

1 TEASPOON SUGAR

1/2 TEASPOON RED PEPPER FLAKES

GARNISH: LETTUCE LEAVES, MINT OR CILANTRO SPRIGS

① Heat the oil in a skillet. Fry the ground chicken until crumbly. Remove the chicken with a slotted spoon and place it in a mixing bowl.

② Mash the chicken with a fork to break it up into small pieces. Add the remaining

continued

Thai Minced Chicken Salad (Larb) *continued*

ingredients except the garnishes. Mix well. If not serving immediately, refrigerate. (This dish can be prepared 1 day in advance.) Bring to room temperature before serving. Taste to correct the seasonings. You may want to add more lime juice or fish sauce. Serve the salad with whole crisp lettuce leaves and garnish with mint or cilantro sprigs.

Warm Chicken-Mushroom Medley on Mixed Greens

SERVES 4 AS A FIRST COURSE, OR 2 AS A MAIN COURSE

Wild mushrooms, chicken, and mixed greens make a good enough salad by themselves, but they take on added elegance when laced with a warm dressing of balsamic vinegar, Cognac, and deep green olive oil. Serve this salad with cornbread, cheese bread, or garlic bread.

8 OUNCES MIXED GREENS (SUCH AS RADICCHIO, ARUGULA, OR LEAF LETTUCE), TORN INTO PIECES

2 BONELESS, SKINLESS CHICKEN BREASTS, COOKED AND SHREDDED

1/2 CUP EXTRA-VIRGIN OLIVE OIL

1/4 CUP BALSAMIC VINEGAR

1 TABLESPOON COGNAC

1/4 TEASPOON SALT

6 OUNCES SLICED MUSHROOMS (MIXED WILD MUSHROOMS OR WHITE BUTTON)

1 TABLESPOON MINCED FRESH PARSLEY, OR 1 TEASPOON FRESH THYME LEAVES

FRESHLY GROUND PEPPER

① Divide the greens and chicken evenly among 4 plates for appetizers, or 2 for main course.

② In a medium-size skillet over high heat, warm the olive oil, vinegar, Cognac, and salt until very hot, about 1 minute. Stir in the mushrooms. Cook until soft, stirring, about 2 minutes. Stir in the herbs. Spoon the sauce over the greens and chicken, and add pepper to taste. Let salad stand 3 minutes before serving.

SPICES, SEASONINGS, and SAUCES

Concentrated Red Chile Sauce
A Pressure Cooker Recipe

MAKES ABOUT 3¹/₂ CUPS This is a speedy way to make a traditional chile sauce. A food processor swiftly purées the ingredients, then a pressure cooker cooks the sauce in minutes to produce a rich, thick chile base for other recipes, like Pollo Rojo, enchiladas, simmered pork, or Mexican stews.

This sauce is strong in fruity, chile flavor and not overly hot—but it is quite concentrated, so thin it with some stock before using or add it to a liquid base. If making Pollo Rojo (also made in a pressure cooker; see chapter 7), the vegetables and chicken give off enough juices to thin 1 cup of this sauce naturally, without the addition of extra stock. This recipe yields about 3¹/₂ cups of concentrated sauce, which may be frozen in 1-cup batches until ready to use.

4 OUNCES DRIED RED CHILES (ABOUT 12, PREFERABLY ANCHO AND NEW MEXICO MIX)

4 CLOVES GARLIC, PEELED

1 LARGE ONION, CUT INTO LARGE CHUNKS

2 TEASPOONS CANOLA OIL

ABOUT 2 CUPS BEEF STOCK OR CANNED LOW-SODIUM BROTH

2 TEASPOONS WHOLE CUMIN SEEDS

¹/₂ TEASPOON DRIED OREGANO

¹/₂ TEASPOON SALT

① Heat the oven to 300 degrees. While the oven heats, tear up the chiles into large pieces, removing the stems and seeds. Place them on a baking sheet and toast in the oven for 4 to 5 minutes, being careful not to burn them.

continued

Concentrated Red Chile Sauce *continued*

② While the chiles toast, finely chop the garlic and onion in the food processor. Heat the oil in the pressure cooker, and sauté the onion-garlic mixture over medium-high heat, stirring occasionally.

③ When the chiles have toasted, remove them from the oven (leave the oven on). Drop them into the food processor with 1½ cups of beef stock. Process until the chiles are puréed, scraping down the sides as needed.

④ Pour the cumin seeds onto the baking sheet and toast for 1 to 1½ minutes, again being careful not to burn them or they will taste bitter. Place the cumin seeds in a spice grinder or mortar and grind to a powder.

⑤ Stir the chile purée, ground cumin, oregano, salt, and the rest of the beef stock into the pressure cooker with the cooked onion mixture. Cover with the pressure cooker lid and bring to high pressure. Maintain at this pressure for 10 minutes. Use the natural release method. The sauce will be concentrated. For every cup of sauce, thin with ½ to 1 cup chicken, beef, or vegetable stock before use.

Global Gourmet Herb Seasoning

MAKES ¼ CUP The beauty of this versatile mix is that it creates a solid flavor base, without overpowering the flavor of the food itself or added seasonings. You can rub it on a whole chicken or turkey before roasting, or season chicken pieces before sautéing or grilling. This seasoning also perks up simple pork roasts and chops, stir-fried vegetables, and even steamed rice and cornbread. For a quick but tasty chicken dish, check out the recipe for Herbed Bistro Chicken Breasts (chapter 7).

3 TABLESPOONS FREEZE-DRIED CHIVES

3 TABLESPOONS DRIED PARSLEY FLAKES

1 TABLESPOON FINELY GROUND BLACK PEPPER

1 TABLESPOON GRANULATED GARLIC

½ TEASPOON SALT

Grind all ingredients in the work bowl of a hand blender, mini-chopper, or food
processor until powdery. Store tightly sealed. The fresher the dried herbs, the longer
the mix will keep its full flavor, but plan on at least 3 months. The flavors will begin
to fade as they age, so use more mix if the aroma seems weak.

Homemade Garam Masala

There's no such thing as bottled curry powder in the true Indian household. What the
Indian cook does have are masalas—spice blends made from scratch to season traditional dishes, including curries. The process is complex: Whole spices are toasted and
ground, then mixed in varied and specific proportions to create these masalas. Indian
cooks add masalas to meat, rice, legumes, or vegetables, along with such flavorings as
ginger, onion, chiles, cilantro, garlic, and other "wet" ingredients. The whole foundation of Indian cooking is based on the use of spices—whole and ground, toasted or raw,
added together or separately—and mastering their use is a true culinary art.

Certain classic masalas are cooked with so frequently they're often made in batches and added as needed. But spices lose their flavor quickly, so even if prepared in
advance, these masalas will still be fixed in small enough quantities to be used up
before their flavors fade. Masalas vary from region to region, based on local spices,
climate and the predominant cooking methods.

Garam masala means "hot spice" and is exactly the opposite of what it sounds
like. It's a favorite of the colder northern areas and has no chiles in it, as these cause
perspiration, which in effect chills the body. Instead, it contains sweet and warming
spices like cinnamon, cumin, cardamom, cloves, and black pepper—spices that would
be at home in any good winter stew. Goda masala, made in the tropical area near
Bombay, uses coconut, sesame seeds, and white poppy seeds in its blend, among other
ingredients. And in South India, sambar masala features red chiles and mustard seeds
in a spicy, perspiration-causing mix.

Use the following version of garam masala to prepare Tandoori Chicken (chapter
9) and Spiced Chicken, Fennel, Raisins, and Rice (chapter 10). Or look for premixed
garam masala wherever Indian products are sold; the Indo-European brand is often
stocked in major supermarkets.

continued

Homemade Garam Masala *continued*

The Global Gourmet's Garam Masala

MAKES ABOUT ³/₄ CUP

3 TABLESPOONS CORIANDER SEEDS

1 TABLESPOON CARAWAY SEEDS

1 TABLESPOON CARDAMOM SEEDS

1 TABLESPOON CUMIN SEEDS

2 TABLESPOONS GROUND BLACK PEPPER

2 TABLESPOONS GROUND CLOVES

1¹/₂ TABLESPOONS GROUND CINNAMON

¹/₂ TEASPOON GROUND NUTMEG

In a heavy, dry skillet, toast the coriander, caraway, cardamom, and cumin seeds separately, each for only a few seconds, until aromatic. It's best to toast each ingredient separately, because they release their oils after different cooking times. Mix these and all other ingredients together and grind with a mortar and pestle or spice grinder. Strain through a fine sieve to remove large pieces and store in an airtight container.

Near Eastern "Sesame and Sumac" Rub

MAKES ¹/₃ CUP Look for sumac in Middle Eastern markets; it's a dark red berry with a tartness that replaces lemon juice in many recipes. Use a spice grinder to grind whole spices for the most potent and aromatic mix. Rub the mix on chicken before roasting or grilling. It makes a good pork rub, too.

8 TURKISH BAY LEAVES, GROUND

2 TEASPOONS GROUND CUMIN

2 TEASPOONS GROUND ALEPPO PEPPER, RED CHILE, OR HOT PAPRIKA

2 TEASPOONS GRANULATED GARLIC

2 TEASPOONS GROUND SUMAC

1¹/₂ TEASPOONS GROUND CORIANDER SEED

1¹/₂ TEASPOONS SUGAR

1 TEASPOON DRIED GROUND GINGER

1 TEASPOON CINNAMON

³/₄ TEASPOON SALT

¹/₄ TEASPOON ALLSPICE

³/₄ TEASPOON GROUND ANISEED

2 TEASPOONS COARSELY GROUND TOASTED SESAME SEED (DON'T GRIND TOO LONG OR IT WILL BECOME PASTE)

Combine all ingredients. Rub on all chicken surfaces, inside and out (whole, split, or pieces). Cover and refrigerate at least 1 hour, or up to overnight, before cooking. For best results, brine the chicken; rinse and dry before adding the spice rub. This recipe makes enough rub for 2 whole chickens or up to 6 pounds of chicken pieces.

Pico de Gallo

MAKES ABOUT 1¹/₂ CUPS Pico de gallo means "beak of the chicken." It supposedly earns its name because the ingredients are coarsely chopped into little bits, as if they were snipped by a chicken's beak, so they resemble chicken feed. As a condiment, pico de gallo perks up everything from eggs to tacos, and it's essential for true Tex-Mex fajitas. Pico de gallo is a rustic salsa that relies on fresh ingredients, so follow your tastebuds rather than adhering strictly to each measurement. This recipe uses green onions, but any type of onion will do.

1 LARGE RIPE TOMATO, CHOPPED

2 TO 3 GREEN ONIONS, GREEN AND WHITE PARTS CHOPPED

SMALL FISTFUL OF FRESH CILANTRO, CHOPPED (ABOUT ¹/₂ CUP CHOPPED)

1¹/₂ TABLESPOONS RED WINE VINEGAR, OR TO TASTE

1 SMALL GREEN CHILE (SERRANO OR JALAPEÑO), SEEDED AND MINCED

SALT TO TASTE

Mix all ingredients and chill for about 15 to 30 minutes before serving (any longer and the flavors weaken). Stir the mixture just before serving.

Pudine Ki Chutney

MAKES 1 CUP This refreshing lemony-mint chutney zips up everything from simple grilled chicken to flatbreads and vegetables. You'll find it used as part of the marinade for Grilled Chicken in Minty Chutney (chapter 9).

> 1 TABLESPOON GROUND CUMIN
>
> 3 GREEN ONIONS, GREEN AND WHITE PARTS CUT INTO 1-INCH PIECES
>
> 2 TO 3 SERRANO CHILES, SEEDS REMOVED IF DESIRED, COARSELY CHOPPED
>
> 1/4 CUP FRESH LEMON JUICE
>
> 1/2 TEASPOON SUGAR
>
> 1/2 TEASPOON SALT
>
> 2 CLOVES GARLIC, COARSELY CHOPPED
>
> 1 CUP PACKED FRESH CILANTRO LEAVES
>
> 2 CUPS PACKED FRESH MINT LEAVES

In the work bowl of a food processor, add the ingredients in the order listed. Process all at once until smooth. If the mixture seems thick, add more lemon juice or a few drops of water. Cover and refrigerate until ready to use.

Spring Onion Oil

MAKES 1 CUP This Vietnamese condiment is drizzled on everything from soups to salads to grilled meats. Traditionally, the green onions are cooked in hot oil for just a short time, keeping their green color. I prefer a toasted variation, which produces nutty-tasting, crisp bits of green onion. I also mix the green onion with salt before frying to add flavor. Instructions for making both the traditional "light" version and my "toasted" variation are included below.

> 3/4 CUP CANOLA OIL OR OTHER NEUTRAL OIL
>
> 6 LARGE GREEN ONIONS
>
> 1 TEASPOON SALT (TOASTED VERSION ONLY)

Wash and dry the green onions. Make sure they are completely dry before frying, to avoid splattering. Trim the roots and the tough tops away, but keep most of the green part. Cut the green onions into thin slices.

Light, traditional version: Heat the oil in a small saucepan over medium heat. Add the onions. Cook about 2 minutes, just until the green onions soften, swirling the pan or stirring occasionally. Remove from the heat and let mixture cool. Pour into a glass jar and seal. Oil will keep 2 weeks, refrigerated.

Toasted version: Heat the oil in a small saucepan on medium heat. Toss the green onion bits with the salt. Carefully pour the green onions into the oil, then raise the heat to high. Fry the onions until the edges just begin to brown, 3 to 5 minutes, swirling the pan or stirring occasionally. Turn off the heat and let the green onions continue to cook in the hot oil; they will crisp up and darken as the oil cools. When the mixture has cooled completely, pour into a glass jar and seal. Oil will keep 2 weeks, refrigerated.

Summer Fresh Tomato Sauce

MAKES ABOUT 2 CUPS

12 OUNCES (2 LARGE) FRESH, RIPE TOMATOES, CORED AND DICED

2 TABLESPOONS EXTRA-VIRGIN OLIVE OIL

3 GREEN ONIONS, GREEN AND WHITE PARTS CHOPPED (OR 3 SHALLOTS, CHOPPED)

3 CLOVES GARLIC, MINCED

1/2 CUP LOOSELY PACKED CHOPPED FRESH BASIL LEAVES

2 TABLESPOONS CHOPPED FRESH MINT OR OREGANO LEAVES

1/4 TEASPOON SALT OR TO TASTE

FRESHLY GROUND PEPPER

3 TABLESPOONS GRATED PARMESAN

In a mixing bowl, toss the tomatoes with 1 tablespoon oil, the green onions, garlic, basil, and mint or oregano. Let flavors mingle at least 30 minutes, or cover and refrigerate up to 4 hours. Just before serving, stir in salt and pepper to taste, the remaining 1 tablespoon olive oil, and the Parmesan. Serve with bruschetta, pasta, grilled chicken, fish, or vegetables.

Toasted Sesame Seeds

As it does nuts and other seeds, toasting heightens the flavor of sesame seeds. I always toast sesame seeds before storing and using them. Even if the label says "toasted sesame seeds," I find that the toasted flavor is still too mild, so I toast them at home in a large batch, where I can control the degree of doneness. After the sesame seeds are toasted, crush them slightly to release their flavor. Use a traditional mortar and pestle or an Asian sesame grinding bowl. Store the toasted seeds in an airtight container. For longer-lasting seeds, refrigerate.

Skillet method: Pour 1 cup sesame seeds into a small, heavy skillet. Cook the seeds over medium-low heat, stirring frequently to brown the seeds evenly. You'll notice that as the seeds toast they release some of their oils, making them shine. When the seeds have a pale bronze color and pleasant aroma, remove the skillet from the heat. One cup or so of seeds takes 5 to 8 minutes to cook. Lightly grind or crush the seeds to release their flavor.

Oven method: Heat the oven to 350 degrees. Spread up to 2 cups sesame seeds on a baking sheet. Toast the seeds in the oven 10 to 12 minutes, stirring every 3 to 5 minutes. The seeds are done when pale bronze and aromatic. Remove the pan from the oven. Lightly grind or crush the seeds to release their flavor.

Index

African Chicken and Peanut Stew, 81
Almonds
Barcelona Brown-Bag Chicken and
Vegetables, 27
Nutty Pounded Paillards, 56
Pollo con Pipian Verde, 163
Spiced Chicken, Fennel, Raisins and Rice, 174
Anise, Aniseed
Aromatic Anise Chicken, 109
Appetizers, 193–204
Apples
Roasted Thighs with Apples, Normandy Style, 61
Apricots
Moroccan Chicken in Spiced Tomato Sauce, 161
Sweet 'n' Sour Kumquat-Kiwi Chicken, 176
Aromatic Anise Chicken, 109
Artichoke hearts
Quick Chicken, Artichokes, and Feta, 167
Tarragon Chicken and Artichoke Hearts, 177
Aussie Alfredo with Warrigal Greens, 129

Bacon
Belgian Chicken Braised in Beer, 84
Chunky Chicken, Corn, and Potato Chowder, 88
Coq au Vermouth, 146
Irish Hen with Bacon and Cabbage, 154
Rumaki, 204
Bangkok Chicken, 182
Bangladesh Drums, 42
Barbecue, Barbecued. See also Grilling; Broiling
Barbecued Korean Drums, 110
Filipino Coconut Barbecued Chicken, 116
Texas Barbecue Dry-Rub Chicken, 128
Barcelona Brown-Bag Chicken and Vegetables, 27
Barley
Cock-A-Leekie, 90
Basic Breaded Chicken Cutlets, or Scallopine, 131
Basic Chicken Stock, 83
Basil
Roasted Chicken Pieces with Cherry Tomatoes,
Goat Cheese, and Basil, 190

Bean sprouts
Chicken and Pork Pad Thai, 136
Chicken Salad Siam, 206
Beer
Belgian Chicken Braised in Beer, 84
Belgian Chicken Braised in Beer, 84
Bell peppers. See Peppers
Boneless Breasts for a Crowd, 43
Breaded Chicken Cutlets, or Scallopine, 131
Breasts. See Chicken, breasts, bone-in; Chicken,
breasts, boneless
Brines, Brining, 22–25
Basic Recipes for Brined Chicken, 24
Halal and kosher, 13, 189
Citrus-Brined Chicken, Roasted with Near East
Rub, 30
Broiling
Basics of, 105–108
Recipes, 109–128
Broths. See soups
Bruschetta, Mozzarella Chicken, 202
Buckets of Oven-Fried Chicken, 44

Cabbage. See also Napa Cabbage
Irish Hen with Bacon and Cabbage, 154
Caribbean Chicken in Coconut Curry, 134
Char Shu Cornish Hens, 29
Cheese
Aussie Alfredo with Warrigal Greens, 129
Caribbean Chicken in Coconut Curry, 134
Chicken Liver and Shiitake Powder Pâté, 193
Chicken Parmigiana, 134
Corinthian Chicken and Olives, 148
Greco-Roman Chicken Rolls, 150
Greek Pot Pie, 184
Green Chile Chicken Breasts, 152
Mozzarella Chicken "Bruschetta," 202
Parmesan-Crusted Chicken, 73
Pasta with Roasted Garlic, Chicken, and Vodka
Sauce, 162
Quick Chicken, Artichokes, and Feta, 167

Cheese *(continued)*
> Roasted Chicken Pieces with Cherry Tomatoes, Goat Cheese, and Basil, 190
>
> Rustic Tortilla Soup, 99
>
> Sour Cream, Dill, and Cucumber Dressing, 213
>
> Summer Chicken and Eggplant Parmigiana, 76
>
> Tipsy Chicken Paillards, 78

Chicken, about. *See also* Chicken, whole; and individual parts
> Breasts, about:
> > Boning and skinning, 16, 20–21
> >
> > Cut into strips, 133
> >
> > Cutlets, 19, 131–134
> >
> > Defined, 12
> >
> > Paillard, 11
> >
> > Scoring, 13
>
> Brining, 22–25
>
> Broiling, 105–108
>
> Butterflying, 19
>
> Classifications by weight, size, age, 10, 12–13
>
> Cornish game hens, 8, 10
>
> Cutlets, 19, 131–134
>
> Cutting a chicken into pieces, 16–19
>
> Grilling, 105–108
>
> Ground chicken, 26
>
> Paillards, 11
>
> Safe handling and storage, 13–15
>
> Scallopine, *See* Cutlets above
>
> Serving sizes, amount to buy, 10
>
> Spatchcocking, 19
>
> Split birds, 19
>
> Testing for doneness, 15, 23, 106
>
> Whole, jointing into pieces, 16–19

Chicken, breasts, bone-in, recipes calling for. *See also* Chicken, pieces
> Corinthian Chicken and Olives, 148
>
> Creole Mustard Chicken Breasts, 149
>
> Cuban Sour Orange Chicken, 114
>
> Juicy Grilled Grapefruit Chicken, 123
>
> Lemony Garlic Chicken and Broth, 96
>
> Mexican Poached Chicken, 97
>
> Moroccan Chicken in Spiced Tomato Sauce, 161
>
> Porcini and Prosciutto Fricasée, 165
>
> Portuguese Grilled Chicken Oporto, 126
>
> Roasted Chicken Breasts for Sandwiches and Salads, 45
>
> Roasted Chicken Pieces with Cherry Tomatoes, Goat Cheese, and Basil, 190

Saffron Poached Chicken, 64

Pollo Rojo, 74

Shredded Pueblo Chicken, 173

Tarragon Chicken and Artichoke Hearts, 177

Chicken, breasts, boneless, recipes calling for. *See also* Chicken, pieces
> Boneless Breasts for a Crowd, 43
>
> Breaded Chicken Cutlets, or Scallopine, 131
>
> Chicken in 5-Minutes' "Thyme," 70
>
> Chicken Parmigiana, 134
>
> Chicken Piccata, 133
>
> Chicken Schnitzel with Lemon-Mushroom Sauce, 141
>
> Chinese Honey-Lemon Chicken, 144
>
> Chunky Chicken, Corn, and Potato Chowder, 88
>
> Greco-Roman Chicken Rolls, 150
>
> Greek Pot Pie, 184
>
> Green Chile Chicken Breasts, 152
>
> Grilled Chicken Fajitas, 117
>
> Grilled Lemon-Dill Chicken, 120
>
> Herbed Bistro Chicken Breasts, 72
>
> Indonesian Chicken with Green Beans, 153
>
> Japanese "Chiken" Katsu, 132
>
> Juicy Grilled Grapefruit Chicken, 123
>
> Malaysian Coconut-Chicken Curry, 159
>
> Miso-Chicken Yakitori, 54
>
> Mozzarella Chicken "Bruschetta," 202
>
> Nutty Pounded Paillards, 56
>
> Parmesan-Crusted Chicken, 73
>
> Pollo alla Milanese, 133
>
> Quick Vietnamese Chicken with Crisp-Cooked Snow Peas, 168
>
> Ras el Hanouth Chicken on Spinach, Kumquat, and Fig Salad, 211
>
> Spicy Eggplant and Chicken with Sesame, 74
>
> Summer Chicken and Eggplant Parmigiana, 76
>
> Sweet 'n' Sour Kumquat-Kiwi Chicken, 176
>
> Thai Hot 'n' Sour Chicken Soup, 100
>
> Three Pepper Chicken Stir-Fry, 179
>
> Tipsy Chicken Paillards, 78

Chicken, cooked, recipes calling for
> Chicken "Salad" in Rice Paper Rolls, 205
>
> Chicken in Saffron Cream Sauce, 50
>
> Chicken Salad Siam, 206
>
> Chicken Salad on Soba, 208
>
> Chilled Fire-Roasted Tomatillo and Grilled Chicken Soup, 86

Dilled Cucumber-Chicken Pasta Salad, 209

Fingerling and Rosemary-Smoked Chicken Hash, 53

Ginger-Wonton Soup with Spring Onion Oil, 91

Gumbo Ya-Ya, 92

Moo-shu Chicken Wraps, 55

Napa-Hazelnut Chicken Salad, 210

Pasta with Roasted Garlic, Chicken, and Vodka Sauce, 162

Rustic Tortilla Soup, 99

Southeast Asian Chicken Salad with Spring Onion Oil, 214

Vietnamese Glass Noodles Soup with Lemongrass Roast Chicken, 102

Warm Chicken-Mushroom Medley on Mixed Greens, 216

Chicken, cutlets, about 19

Basic Breaded Chicken Cutlets, or Scallopine, 131

Japanese "Chiken" Katsu, 132

Chicken Piccata, 133

Pollo alla Milanese, 133

Chicken Parmigiana, 134

Chicken Schnitzel with Lemon-Mushroom Sauce, 141

Chicken, cut-up. *See* Chicken, pieces

Chicken, drumsticks, recipes calling for. *See also* Chicken, pieces

Bangladesh Drums, 42

Barbecued Korean Drums, 110

Chicken, ground, recipes calling for

Chicken and Pork Pad Thai, 136

Chicken Wontons, 196

Golden Chicken Mandu (Korean Dumplings), 199

Ground Chicken Kebabs, 121

Thai Minced Chicken Salad (Larb), 215

Chicken, legs. *See* Chicken, drumsticks

Chicken, livers, recipes calling for

Chicken Liver and Shiitake Powder Pâté, 193

Chicken Liver and Truffle Oil Pâté, 195

Rumaki, 204

Ukrainian Portobellos and Garlic-Laced Livers, 65

Chicken, pieces, recipes calling for. *See also* specific parts

African Chicken and Peanut Stew, 81

Bangkok Chicken, 182

Bangladesh Drums, 42

Barbecued Korean Drums, 110

Belgian Chicken Braised in Beer, 84

Buckets of Oven-Fried Chicken, 44

Caribbean Chicken in Coconut Curry, 134

Char Shu Cornish Hens, 29

Chicken Adobo, 135

Chicken Calabrese, 138

Chicken Churrasco with Chimichurri Sauce, 111

Chicken in Wine with Balsamic-Herb Gravy, 139

Chicken of the Moors, 112

Chicken Stock variation, made with, 84

Cock-A-Leekie, 90

Coq au Vermouth, 146

Cuban Sour Orange Chicken, 114

Filipino Coconut Barbecued Chicken, 116

Grilled Chicken Fajitas, 117

Hungarian Chicken Paprikás, 94

Irish Hen with Bacon and Cabbage, 154

Israeli Couscous with Chicken and Olives, 155

Jamaican Jerk Chicken, 122

La Tunisia Chicken and Grilled Onions, 124

Maille Mustard Chicken and Pasta, 157

Pollo alla Diavola, 59

Porcini and Prosciutto Fricasée, 165

Portuguese Grilled Chicken Oporto, 126

Quick Chicken, Artichokes, and Feta, 167

Quinoa con Pollo, 170

Tandoori Chicken, 127

Chicken, quartered, recipes calling for

Portuguese Grilled Chicken Oporto, 126

Irish Hen with Bacon and Cabbage, 154

Chicken, Scampi-Style, 70

Chicken, split, recipes calling for

Char Shu Cornish Hens, 29

Roasted Fesenjan Hens, 187

Rosemary-Smoked Chicken Halves, 62

Texas Barbecue Dry-Rub Chicken, 128

Chicken, thighs, bone-in, recipes calling for. *See also* Chicken, pieces

African Chicken and Peanut Stew, 81

Bangkok Chicken, 182

Chicken in 5-Minutes' "Thyme," 70

Chicken, Scampi-Style, 70

Grilled Chicken in Minty Chutney, 118

Israeli Couscous with Chicken and Olives, 155

La Tunisia Chicken and Grilled Onions, 124

Chicken, thighs, bone-in, recipes calling for (*continued*)
  Paella de la Casa, 186
  Quick Chicken, Artichokes, and Feta, 167
  Roasted Chicken Pieces with Cherry Tomatoes,
    Goat Cheese, and Basil, 190
  Roasted Thighs with Apples, Normandy Style, 61
  Spiced Chicken, Fennel, Raisins and Rice, 174
  Tandoori Chicken, 127
Chicken, thighs, boneless, recipes calling for. *See also*
  Chicken, pieces
    Chicken of the Moors, 112
    Chicken Vindaloo, 142
    Grilled Chicken Fajitas, 117
    One-Pot Chicken, Mushrooms, and Saffron
      Rice, 57
    Quick Vietnamese Chicken with Crisp-Cooked
      Snow Peas, 168
Chicken, whole, recipes calling for
  Aromatic Anise Chicken, 109
  Barcelona Brown-Bag Chicken and
    Vegetables, 27
  Basic Chicken Stock, 83
  Char Shu Cornish Hens, 29
  Citrus-Brined Chicken, Roasted with Near East
    Rub, 30
  Ginger-Poached Chicken and Broth, 33
  Lemongrass Roast Chicken, 36
  Lemon-Rubbed Roaster with Six Garlic
    Heads, 35
  Southwest Skinny Chicken, 37
  Whole Chinese Red-Cooked Chicken, 39
Chicken, wings, recipes calling for. *See also* Chicken,
  pieces
    Crispy Comino Chicken Wings, 50
    Fried Chicken Drummettes with Hot
      Pomegranate Honey, 197
    Sesame-Seeded Teriyaki Wings, 46
Chicken Adobo, 135
Chicken Calabrese, 138
Chicken Churrasco with Chimichurri Sauce, 111
Chicken in 5-Minutes' "Thyme," 70
Chicken Liver and Shiitake Powder Pâté, 193
Chicken Liver and Truffle Oil Pâté, 195
Chicken Mandu Filling, 201
Chicken of the Moors, 112
Chicken Parmigiana, 134
Chicken Piccata, 133
Chicken and Pork Pad Thai, 136

Chicken in Saffron Cream Sauce, 50
Chicken "Salad" in Rice Paper Rolls, 205
Chicken Salad Siam, 206
Chicken Salad on Soba, 208
Chicken, Scampi-Style, 70
Chicken Schnitzel with Lemon-Mushroom
  Sauce, 141
Chicken Vindaloo, 142
Chicken in Wine with Balsamic-Herb Gravy, 139
Chicken Wontons, 196
Chiles. *See also* Peppers
  Chicken Vindaloo, 142
  Concentrated Red Chile Sauce, 217
  Green Chile Chicken Breasts, 152
  Grilled Chicken Fajitas, 117
  Hot Pomegranate Honey, 198
  Jamaican Jerk Chicken, 122
  Malaysian Coconut-Chicken Curry, 159
  Pico de Gallo, 221
  Pollo con Pipian Verde, 163
  Pudine Ki Chutney, 222
  Shredded Pueblo Chicken, 173
  Thai Hot 'n' Sour Chicken Soup, 100
  Vietnamese Glass Noodles Soup with Lemongrass
    Roast Chicken, 102
Chilled Fire-Roasted Tomatillo and Grilled Chicken
  Soup, 86
Chimichurri Sauce, Chicken Churrasco with, 111
Chinese Honey-Lemon Chicken, 144
Chojang Dipping Sauce, 201
Chunky Chicken, Corn, and Potato Chowder, 88
Citrus Brine, 31
Citrus-Brined Chicken, Roasted with Near East
  Rub, 30
Cock-A-Leekie, 90
Coconut
  Ground Chicken Kebabs, 121
Coconut milk
  Bangkok Chicken, 182
  Caribbean Chicken in Coconut Curry, 134
  Filipino Coconut Barbecued Chicken, 116
  Malaysian Coconut-Chicken Curry, 159
Concentrated Red Chile Sauce, 217
Coq au Vermouth, 146
Corinthian Chicken and Olives, 148
Corn
  Chunky Chicken, Corn, and Potato Chowder, 88

Cornish game hens, recipes calling for. *See also* Chicken, about.

Char Shu Cornish Hens, 29

Irish Hen with Bacon and Cabbage, 154

Roasted Fesenjan Hens, 187

Couscous

Israeli Couscous with Chicken and Olives, 155

Creole Mustard Chicken Breasts, 149

Crispy Comino Chicken Wings, 50

Cuban Sour Orange Chicken, 114

Cucumber

Dilled Cucumber-Chicken Pasta Salad, 209

Sour Cream, Dill, and Cucumber Dressing, 213

Southeast Asian Chicken Salad with Spring Onion Oil, 214

Dilled Cucumber-Chicken Pasta Salad, 209

Drumsticks. *See* Chicken, drumsticks

Doneness, testing for, 15, 23, 106

Eggplant

Spicy Eggplant and Chicken with Sesame, 74

Summer Chicken and Eggplant Parmigiana, 76

Fajitas, Grilled Chicken, 117

Fennel

Spiced Chicken, Fennel, Raisins and Rice, 174

Fesenjan Sauce, 188

Figs

Ras el Hanouth Chicken on Spinach, Kumquat, and Fig Salad, 211

Filipino Coconut Barbecued Chicken, 116

Fingerling and Rosemary-Smoked Chicken Hash, 53

Fish sauce (Nam pla, Nuoc mam)

Chicken and Pork Pad Thai, 136

Chicken Salad Siam, 206

Filipino Coconut Barbecued Chicken, 116

Lemongrass Roast Chicken, 36

Malaysian Coconut-Chicken Curry, 159

Quick Vietnamese Chicken with Crisp-Cooked Snow Peas, 168

Southeast Asian Chicken Salad with Spring Onion Oil, 214

Thai Hot 'n' Sour Chicken Soup, 100

Thai Minced Chicken Salad (Larb), 215

Vietnamese Glass Noodles Soup with Lemongrass Roast Chicken, 102

FlavorPrints, about, 3–4

Africa, 80

Caribbean, 115

Central Asia, 198

China, 32

Eastern Europe, Poland, and Russia, 65

Greece and Western Turkey, 34

India, Pakistan, and Sri Lanka, 119

Italy, More on, 68

Japan, 48

Korea, 200

Mediterranean and Iberian Europe, 52

Mexico, Central America, and Southwestern United States, 98

Middle East, 189

North Africa: Morocco, Algeria, Tunisia, and Libya, 125

Northern Europe. 60

South America, 172

South Pacific: Indonesia, Malaysia, and the Philippines, 160

Southeast Asia: Vietnam, Thailand, Cambodia, and Burma, 183

Fried Chicken Drummettes with Hot Pomegranate Honey, 197

Game hens. *See* Cornish game hens

Garam masala

Bangladesh Drums, 42

Global Gourmet's Garam Masala, 220

Grilled Chicken in Minty Chutney, 118

Homemade Garam Masala, 119

Spiced Chicken, Fennel, Raisins and Rice, 174

Tandoori Chicken, 127

Garlic

Lemon-Rubbed Roaster with Six Garlic Heads, 35

Lemony Garlic Chicken and Broth, 96

Pasta with Roasted Garlic, Chicken, and Vodka Sauce, 162

Ukrainian Portobellos and Garlic-Laced Livers, 65

Ginger-Poached Chicken and Broth, 33

Ginger-Wonton Soup with Spring Onion Oil, 91

Global Gourmet Herb Seasoning, 218

Global Gourmet's Garam Masala, 220

Golden Chicken Mandu (Korean Dumplings), 199

Grapefruit juice
  Citrus-Brined Chicken, Roasted with Near East
    Rub, 30
  Grapefruit Marinade, 123
  Juicy Grilled Grapefruit Chicken, 123
Greco-Roman Chicken Rolls, 150
Greek Pot Pie, 184
Green beans
  Indonesian Chicken with Green Beans, 153
Green Chile Chicken Breasts, 152
Grilled Chicken Fajitas, 117
Grilled Chicken in Minty Chutney, 118
Grilled Lemon-Dill Chicken, 120
Grilling, Basic, 105–108; recipes, 109–128
Ground Chicken Kebabs, 121
Gumbo Ya-Ya, 92

Hash, Fingerling and Rosemary-Smoked Chicken, 53
Hazelnuts
  Aussie Alfredo with Warrigal Greens, 129
  Chicken Liver and Truffle Oil Pâté, 195
  Napa-Hazelnut Chicken Salad, 210
  Nutty Pounded Paillards, 56
Herb Seasoning, Global Gourmet, 218
Herbed Bistro Chicken Breasts, 72
Honey
  Chinese Honey-Lemon Chicken, 144
  Fried Chicken Drummettes with Hot
    Pomegranate Honey, 197
  Honey-Lemon Sauce, 145
  Hot Pomegranate Honey, 198
Hoover, Herbert, 1, 2
Hot Pomegranate Honey, 198
Hungarian Chicken Paprikás, 94

Indonesian Chicken with Green Beans, 153
Irish Hen with Bacon and Cabbage, 154
Israeli Couscous with Chicken and Olives, 155

Jamaican Jerk Chicken, 122
Japanese "Chiken" Katsu, 132
Jewish Matzo Ball Soup, 95
Juicy Grilled Grapefruit Chicken, 123

Kebabs, Ground Chicken, 121
Kecap manis (sweet soy sauce)
  Filipino Coconut Barbecued Chicken, 116

Indonesian Chicken with Green Beans, 153
Kiwifruit
  Sweet 'n' Sour Kumquat-Kiwi Chicken, 176
Korean Dumplings, Golden Chicken Mandu, 199
Kumquat
  Cuban Sour Orange Chicken, 114
  Ras el Hanouth Chicken on Spinach, Kumquat,
    and Fig Salad, 211
  Sweet 'n' Sour Kumquat-Kiwi Chicken, 176

La Tunisia Chicken and Grilled Onions, 124
Larb (Thai Minced Chicken Salad), 215
Leek
  Bangkok Chicken, 182
  Cock-A-Leekie, 90
  Creole Mustard Chicken Breasts, 149
Lemon
  Chicken Schnitzel with Lemon-Mushroom
    Sauce, 141
  Grilled Lemon-Dill Chicken, 120
  Lemon-Caper Mayonnaise, 205
  Lemon-Rubbed Roaster with Six Garlic
    Heads, 35
  Lemony Garlic Chicken and Broth, 96
Lemongrass
  Lemongrass Roast Chicken, 36
  Thai Hot 'n' Sour Chicken Soup, 100
  Thai Minced Chicken Salad (Larb), 215
  Vietnamese Glass Noodles Soup with Lemongrass
    Roast Chicken, 102
Lemony Garlic Chicken and Broth, 96
Livers. *See* Chicken, livers

Maille Mustard Chicken and Pasta, 157
Malaysian Coconut-Chicken Curry, 159
Mandu (Korean Dumplings), 199
Mandu Filling, 201
Marinades, about
  Scoring to penetrate, 13
  Safe handling and, 15
Marinades, recipes for. *See also* Brines, Brining; Rubs
  Broiling and grilling recipes, 109–128
  Char Shu Marinade, 29
  Cuban Sour Orange Marinade, 114
  Filipino Coconut Marinade, 116
  Grapefruit Marinade, 123
  Jerk Marinade, 122

La Tunisia Marinade, 124

Moorish Marinade, 113

Matzo Ball Soup, 95

Meal morphing, 25

Menudo mix

Shredded Pueblo Chicken, 173

Mexican Poached Chicken, 97

Middle Eastern Spice Rub, 156

Mien Ga (Vietnamese Glass Noodles Soup with Lemongrass Roast Chicken), 102

Mint

Chicken Salad Siam, 206

Greek Pot Pie, 184

Grilled Chicken in Minty Chutney, 118

Pudine Ki Chutney, 222

Quick Chicken, Artichokes, and Feta, 167

Summer Fresh Tomato Sauce, 223

Thai Minced Chicken Salad (Larb), 215

Miso-Chicken Yakitori, 54

Moroccan Chicken in Spiced Tomato Sauce, 161

Moroccan Spice Mixture, 161

Moorish Marinade, 113

Moo-shu Chicken Wraps, 55

Mozzarella Chicken "Bruschetta," 202

Mushrooms

Chicken Liver and Shiitake Powder Pâté, 193

Chicken Schnitzel with Lemon-Mushroom Sauce, 141

Coq au Vermouth, 146

Greco-Roman Chicken Rolls, 150

One-Pot Chicken, Mushrooms, and Saffron Rice, 57

Porcini and Prosciutto Fricasée, 165

Tarragon Chicken and Artichoke Hearts, 177

Thai Hot 'n' Sour Chicken Soup, 100

Tipsy Chicken Paillards, 78

Ukrainian Portobellos and Garlic-Laced Livers, 65

Vietnamese Glass Noodles Soup with Lemongrass Roast Chicken, 102

Warm Chicken-Mushroom Medley on Mixed Greens, 216

Mustard

Creole Mustard Chicken Breasts, 149

Maille Mustard Chicken and Pasta, 157

Mustard oil

Chicken Vindaloo, 142

Nam pla. *See* Fish sauce

Napa cabbage, about, 194

Chicken and Pork Pad Thai, 136

Chicken Salad Siam, 206

Ginger-Wonton Soup with Spring Onion Oil, 91

Moo-shu Chicken Wraps, 55

Napa-Hazelnut Chicken Salad, 210

Near Eastern "Sesame and Sumac" Rub, 220

Noodles. *See also* Pasta

Chicken and Pork Pad Thai, 136

Chicken Salad Siam, 206

Chicken Salad on Soba, 208

Vietnamese Glass Noodles Soup with Lemongrass Roast Chicken, 102

Nuoc mam. *See* Fish sauce

Nuts. *See* specific nuts

Nutty Pounded Paillards, 56

Olives

Barcelona Brown-Bag Chicken and Vegetables, 27

Corinthian Chicken and Olives, 148

Israeli Couscous with Chicken and Olives, 155

One-Pot Chicken, Mushrooms, and Saffron Rice, 57

Onions

La Tunisia Chicken and Grilled Onions, 124

Orange juice

Citrus-Brined Chicken, Roasted with Near East Rub, 30

Cuban Sour Orange Chicken, 114

Oven-Fried Chicken, 44

Pad Thai, Chicken and Pork , 136

Paella de la Casa, 186

Paillards, about, 11

Nutty Pounded Paillards, 56

Tipsy Chicken Paillards, 78

Parmesan-Crusted Chicken, 73

Pasta. *See also* Noodles

Aussie Alfredo with Warrigal Greens, 129

Dilled Cucumber-Chicken Pasta Salad, 209

Israeli Couscous with Chicken and Olives, 155

Maille Mustard Chicken and Pasta, 157

Pasta with Roasted Garlic, Chicken, and Vodka Sauce, 162

Pasta with Roasted Garlic, Chicken, and Vodka Sauce, 162

Pâté
>   Chicken Liver and Shiitake Powder Pâté, 193
>   Chicken Liver and Truffle Oil Pâté, 195

Peanuts
>   African Chicken and Peanut Stew, 81
>   Chicken and Pork Pad Thai, 136
>   Chicken Salad Siam, 206
>   Southeast Asian Chicken Salad with Spring Onion Oil, 214

Peas. *See also* Snow Peas
>   Paella de la Casa, 186
>   Dilled Cucumber-Chicken Pasta Salad, 209

Pecans
>   Nutty Pounded Paillards, 56

Peppers, bell or sweet
>   African Chicken and Peanut Stew, 81
>   Barcelona Brown-Bag Chicken and Vegetables, 27
>   Caribbean Chicken in Coconut Curry, 134
>   Chicken "Salad" in Rice Paper Rolls, 205
>   Chunky Chicken, Corn, and Potato Chowder, 88
>   Fingerling and Rosemary-Smoked Chicken Hash, 53
>   Gumbo Ya-Ya, 92
>   Hungarian Chicken Paprikás, 94
>   Indonesian Chicken with Green Beans, 153
>   Miso-Chicken Yakitori, 54
>   One-Pot Chicken, Mushrooms, and Saffron Rice, 57
>   Paella de la Casa, 186
>   Quinoa con Pollo, 170
>   Three Pepper Chicken Stir-Fry, 179

Phyllo dough
>   Greek Pot Pie, 184

Pico de Gallo, 221

Pieces. *See* Chicken, pieces

Pine nuts
>   Ras el Hanouth Chicken on Spinach, Kumquat, and Fig Salad, 211
>   Spiced Chicken, Fennel, Raisins and Rice, 174

Poached chicken. *See* Soups and broths

Pollo alla Diavola ("Devil-Style Chicken"), 59

Pollo alla Milanese, 133

Pollo con Pipian Verde, 163

Pollo Rojo, 74

Pomegranate molasses
>   Roasted Fesenjan Hens, 187

Fried Chicken Drummettes with Hot Pomegranate Honey, 197
>   Hot Pomegranate Honey, 198
>   Pomegranate Salad Dressing, 212

Porcini and Prosciutto Fricasée, 165

Pork
>   Chicken and Pork Pad Thai, 136

Portuguese Grilled Chicken Oporto, 126

Potatoes
>   Barcelona Brown-Bag Chicken and Vegetables, 27
>   Belgian Chicken Braised in Beer, 84
>   Chunky Chicken, Corn, and Potato Chowder, 88
>   Fingerling and Rosemary-Smoked Chicken Hash, 53

Pressure cooker recipes
>   Concentrated Red Chile Sauce, 217
>   Pollo Rojo, 74
>   Southwest Skinny Chicken, 37

Prosciutto
>   Greco-Roman Chicken Rolls, 150
>   Paella de la Casa, 186
>   Porcini and Prosciutto Fricasée, 165

Pudine Ki Chutney, 222

Quick Chicken, Artichokes, and Feta, 167

Quick Vietnamese Chicken with Crisp-Cooked Snow Peas, 168

Quinoa con Pollo, 170

Raisins
>   Moroccan Chicken in Spiced Tomato Sauce, 161
>   Spiced Chicken, Fennel, Raisins and Rice, 174

Ras el Hanouth Chicken on Spinach, Kumquat, and Fig Salad, 211

Ras el Hanouth Spice Blend, 212

Recipes
>   About these recipes, 26
>   Listed by chapter and page number, x
>   Meal morphing, 25

Rice
>   One-Pot Chicken, Mushrooms, and Saffron Rice, 57
>   Paella de la Casa, 186
>   Spiced Chicken, Fennel, Raisins and Rice, 174

Rice paper wrappers
>   Chicken "Salad" in Rice Paper Rolls, 205

Roasted Chicken Breasts for Sandwiches and Salads, 45

Roasted Chicken Pieces with Cherry Tomatoes, Goat Cheese, and Basil, 190

Roasted Fesenjan Hens, 187

Roasted Thighs with Apples, Normandy Style, 61

Rosemary-Smoked Chicken Halves, 62

Rosemary-Smoked Chicken Hash, Fingerling and, 53

Rubs, dry

    Anise Rub, 109

    Global Gourmet Herb Seasoning, 218

    Global Gourmet's Garam Masala, 220

    Middle Eastern Spice Rub, 156

    Moroccan Spice Mixture, 161

    Near Eastern "Sesame and Sumac" Rub, 220

    Ras el Hanouth Spice Blend, 212

    Texas Dry-Rub, 128

Rumaki, 204

Rustic Tortilla Soup, 99

Saffron

    Bangladesh Drums, 42

    Chicken in Saffron Cream Sauce, 50

    La Tunisia Chicken and Grilled Onions, 124

    One-Pot Chicken, Mushrooms, and Saffron Rice, 57

    Paella de la Casa, 186

    Quinoa con Pollo, 170

    Ras el Hanouth Spice Blend, 212

    Saffron Poached Chicken, 64

    Tandoori Chicken, 127

Salads, 45; 205–216

    Chicken "Salad" in Rice Paper Rolls, 205

    Chicken Salad Siam, 206

    Chicken Salad on Soba, 208

    Dilled Cucumber-Chicken Pasta Salad, 209

    Napa-Hazelnut Chicken Salad, 210

    Ras el Hanouth Chicken on Spinach, Kumquat, and Fig Salad, 211

    Roasted Chicken Breasts for Sandwiches and Salads, 45

    Southeast Asian Chicken Salad with Spring Onion Oil, 214

    Thai Minced Chicken Salad (Larb), 215

    Warm Chicken-Mushroom Medley on Mixed Greens, 216

Sauces

    Chimichurri Sauce, 112

    Chojang Dipping Sauce, 201

    Concentrated Red Chile Sauce, 217

    Fesenjan Sauce, 188

    Honey-Lemon Sauce, 145

    Hot Pomegranate Honey, 198

    Lemon-Caper Mayonnaise, 205

    Lemon-Mushroom Sauce, Chicken Schnitzel with, 141

    Pico de Gallo, 221

    Pudine Ki Chutney, (Minty Chutney) 222

    Saffron Cream Sauce, Chicken in, 50

    Sesame Pipian Verde, 164

    Siam Dressing, 207

    Sour Cream, Dill, and Cucumber Dressing, 213

    Southeast Asian Dressing, 214

    Spring Onion Oil, 222

    Summer Fresh Tomato Sauce, 223

    Sweet 'n' Sour Sauce, 176

    Teriyaki Sauce, 46

    Tonkatsu Sosu, 132

Sausage

    Gumbo Ya-Ya, 92

Scampi-Style Chicken, 70

Scallopine (or Chicken Cutlets), 131–134, 141

Sesame seeds

    Barbecued Korean Drums, 110

    Chicken Liver and Shiitake Powder Pâté, 193

    Chicken Salad on Soba, 208

    Ginger-Wonton Soup with Spring Onion Oil, 91

    Golden Chicken Mandu (Korean Dumplings), 199

    Ground Chicken Kebabs, 121

    Near Eastern "Sesame and Sumac" Rub, 220

    Sesame Pipian Verde, 164

    Sesame-Seeded Teriyaki Wings, 46

    Spicy Eggplant and Chicken with Sesame, 74

    Teriyaki Sauce, 46

    Toasted Sesame Seeds, 224

    Whole Chinese Red-Cooked Chicken, 39

Shredded Pueblo Chicken, 173

Siam Dressing, 207

Snow peas

    Chicken and Pork Pad Thai, 136

    Crisp-Cooked Snow Peas, 170

Snow peas *(continued)*
Quick Vietnamese Chicken with Crisp-Cooked Snow Peas, 168
Soups and broths
Basic Chicken Stock, 83
Chilled Fire-Roasted Tomatillo and Grilled Chicken Soup, 86
Chunky Chicken, Corn, and Potato Chowder, 88
Cock-A-Leekie, 90
Ginger-Poached Chicken and Broth, 33
Ginger-Wonton Soup with Spring Onion Oil, 91
Jewish Matzo Ball Soup, 95
Lemony Garlic Chicken and Broth, 96
Mexican Poached Chicken, 97
Rustic Tortilla Soup, 99
Saffron Poached Chicken, 64
Shredded Pueblo Chicken, 173
Thai Hot 'n' Sour Chicken Soup, 100
Vietnamese Glass Noodles Soup with Lemongrass Roast Chicken, 102
Sour Cream, Dill, and Cucumber Dressing, 213
Southeast Asian Chicken Salad with Spring Onion Oil, 214
Southeast Asian Dressing, 214
Southwest Skinny Chicken, 37
Spatchcock chicken. *See also* Chicken, about
Aromatic Anise Chicken, 109
Char Shu Cornish Hens, 29
Pollo alla Diavola, 59
Spiced Chicken, Fennel, Raisins and Rice, 174
Spicy Eggplant and Chicken with Sesame, 74
Spinach
Aussie Alfredo with Warrigal Greens, 129
Greek Pot Pie, 184
Ras el Hanouth Chicken on Spinach, Kumquat, and Fig Salad, 211
Spring Onion Oil, 222
Stews. *See also* Soups
African Chicken and Peanut Stew, 81
Gumbo Ya-Ya, 92
Hungarian Chicken Paprikás, 94
Stocks. *See* Soups
Summer Chicken and Eggplant Parmigiana, 76
Summer Fresh Tomato Sauce, 223
Sweet 'n' Sour Kumquat-Kiwi Chicken, 176
Sweet 'n' Sour Sauce, 176

Tandoori Chicken, 127
Tarragon Chicken and Artichoke Hearts, 177
Teriyaki Sauce, 46
Texas Barbecue Dry-Rub Chicken, 128
Thai Hot 'n' Sour Chicken Soup, 100
Thai Minced Chicken Salad (Larb), 215
Thighs. *See* Chicken thighs
Three Pepper Chicken Stir-Fry, 179
Thyme, Chicken in 5-Minutes', 70
Tipsy Chicken Paillards, 78
Toasted Sesame Seeds, 224
Tom Yam Kai, 100
Tomatillos
Chilled Fire-Roasted Tomatillo and Grilled Chicken Soup, 86
Pollo con Pipian Verde, 163
Tomatoes, fresh or canned
African Chicken and Peanut Stew, 81
Aussie Alfredo with Warrigal Greens, 129
Corinthian Chicken and Olives, 148
Hungarian Chicken Paprikás, 94
Moroccan Chicken in Spiced Tomato Sauce, 161
Mozzarella Chicken "Bruschetta," 202
Paella de la Casa, 186
Pasta with Roasted Garlic, Chicken, and Vodka Sauce, 162
Pico de Gallo, 221
Quick Chicken, Artichokes, and Feta, 167
Quinoa con Pollo, 170
Roasted Chicken Pieces with Cherry Tomatoes, Goat Cheese, and Basil, 190
Rustic Tortilla Soup, 99
Shredded Pueblo Chicken, 173
Summer Fresh Tomato Sauce, 223
Three Pepper Chicken Stir-Fry, 179
Tomatoes, sun-dried
Barcelona Brown-Bag Chicken and Vegetables, 27
Greco-Roman Chicken Rolls, 150
Tonkatsu Sosu, 132
Tortillas, about warming, 56
Grilled Chicken Fajitas, 117
Moo-shu Chicken Wraps, 55
Rustic Tortilla Soup, 99

Ukrainian Portobellos and Garlic-Laced Livers, 65

Vegetables. *See also* individual vegetables
  Barcelona Brown-Bag Chicken and
    Vegetables, 27
  Miso-Chicken Yakitori, 54
  Southwest Skinny Chicken, 37
Vermouth
  Coq au Vermouth, 146
  Greco-Roman Chicken Rolls, 150
  Herbed Bistro Chicken Breasts, 72
  Irish Hen with Bacon and Cabbage, 154
Vietnamese Chicken with Crisp-Cooked Snow
  Peas, 168
Vietnamese Glass Noodles Soup with Lemongrass
  Roast Chicken ("Mien Ga"), 102
Vinegar, Chinese black (Chinkiang)
  Chicken Salad on Soba, 208
Vodka
  Pasta with Roasted Garlic, Chicken, and Vodka
    Sauce, 162

Walnuts
  Roasted Fesenjan Hens, 187
  Warm Chicken-Mushroom Medley on Mixed
    Greens, 216

Warrigal Greens, 131
Water chestnuts
  Rumaki, 204
Wine
  Chicken in Wine with Balsamic-Herb Gravy, 139
Wine, Chinese (Shao hsing)
  Char Shu Cornish Hens, 29
  Chicken Wontons, 196
  Chinese Honey-Lemon Chicken, 144
  Spicy Eggplant and Chicken with Sesame, 74
  Three Pepper Chicken Stir-Fry, 179
  Whole Chinese Red-Cooked Chicken, 39
Wings. *See* Chicken, wings
Whole chicken. *See* Chicken, whole
Whole Chinese Red-Cooked Chicken, 39
Wontons
  Chicken Wontons, 196
  Ginger-Wonton Soup with Spring Onion Oil, 91

Yakitori, Miso-Chicken, 54
Yogurt
  Grilled Chicken in Minty Chutney, 118
  Tandoori Chicken, 127